THE GOSPEL ACCORDING TO ST. LUKE

NEW TESTAMENT FOR SPIRITUAL READING

VOLUME 5

Edited by

John L. McKenzie, S.J.

THE GOSPEL
ACCORDING TO ST. LUKE

Volume I

ALOIS STÖGER

CROSSROAD · NEW YORK

1981
The Crossroad Publishing Company
575 Lexington Avenue, New York, NY 10022

Originally published as *Das Evangelium nach Lukas I*
© 1964 by Patmos-Verlag
from the series *Geistliche Schriftlesung*
edited by Wolfgang Trilling
with Karl Hermann Schelke and Heinz Schürmann

English translation © 1969 by Burns & Oates, Limited, London
Translated by Benen Fahy

Library of Congress Catalog Card Number: 81-68166
ISBN: 0-8245-0114-4

PREFACE

From ancient times the three Gospels of Matthew, Mark, and Luke have been grouped as " synoptic." The term originally meant, most probably, that the resemblances between the three documents make it possible for the gospels to be formed into a synopsis. A study of the gospels demands an investigation both of the resemblances and of the differences; for it is the differences which disclose the peculiar presentation of each gospel. The gospel is a threefold presentation of a single witness. The object of the witness is a single object, Jesus Messiah and Lord. The mystery of the object and the wealth of the witness were too great to be incorporated into a single document. The wealth of the gospels, in turn, is too great to be exhausted in any single work of interpretation. The church and each of its members encounters Jesus anew each time the gospel is read, and each generation of the church and each member must make its own act of faith in the Jesus whom it encounters. The work which is offered here is intended to set forth the Gospel of Luke in such a way that the reader is aware of his encounter with Jesus.

There is an ancient tradition, not well supported by historical criticism, that Luke was an artist. There is no doubt that the great Christian artists have drawn more scenes from Luke than from the other gospels. Luke has given us most of the nativity scenes, the annunciation and the visitation, the boy Jesus in the temple, the good Samaritan, the prodigal son, the rich man and Lazarus, and other scenes which artists have found easy to portray. The interpreter of Luke must remember that he is dealing with a writer who could draw pictures with words; and he must show the imagination which produces this kind of writing. The prosy interpreter does not do justice to the artist.

The gospels are distinguished from each other by the themes which they select for emphasis. These themes were determined not by the writers alone, but also by the character of the readers and listeners for whom they wrote, as well as the period in the development of primitive Christianity in which they wrote. Father Stöger, for example, points out that Luke's version of the apocalyptic discourse of Jesus (Luke 21) is manifestly influenced by the destruction of Jerusalem and the experiences of early Christian missionaries. Luke composed this discourse as prophecy fulfilled. Other allusions to the experience of the church occur in the gospel and are pointed out in their proper place. Furthermore, Luke was a gentile who wrote for gentiles. The apostolic church never attempted to detach Jesus from the Judaism which he professed and in which he lived, just as it never presented him as any other kind of saviour than the Jewish Messiah. But Luke and his readers knew that they had been liberated from the law; there was no reason why they should be deeply concerned with the problem of reconciling law and gospel as Jewish Christians were concerned, nor even with the explanation of Jewish beliefs and practices which we find in Matthew and Mark. In Luke, as interpreters have noticed from the beginning of interpretation, Jesus is the Jewish Messiah who is the saviour of mankind.

In particular, Luke presents Jesus as the saviour of those who were most in need of saving, the poor. The sympathy of Jesus for the poor is manifest in all the gospels, but it is most emphatic in Luke. Within the same theme the Christian duty of almsgiving is also most emphatic in Luke. By almsgiving the Christian enters into the sympathy of Jesus for the poor and helpless; almsgiving is the means by which the church carries on the healing and saving works of Jesus. Luke also is most emphatic concerning the supreme act of almsgiving, the renunciation of wealth. Assisting the poor by occasional or even frequent donations is not enough; the generosity of Christians should drive them to the point where conditions are equalized. If wealth cannot be perfectly shared, poverty can.

Interpreters have also noticed from earliest times that women have a prominence in Luke which they do not have in the other gospels. This emphasis is a part of the theme of poverty; for women in the ancient world were a depressed class. Luke was a companion of Paul, who wrote that in Christ there is neither male nor female (Galatians 3:28). The theme was not created by Paul nor by Luke, but by Jesus himself. No one of the three suggests a social revolution, just as they do not suggest a revolution to improve the condition of the poor or to liberate slaves. What they present is a Christian attitude towards persons which makes it impossible for the Christian to treat the poor, slaves, or women as subhuman classes, whether social conditions change or not. The Christian response to persons cannot await political and social reforms.

It is another commonplace of interpreters that Luke emphasizes the compassion and forgiveness which Jesus exhibited towards sinners. Surely this theme again is not peculiar to Luke; his emphasis can be seen best by his inclusion among " sinners " of those who are social outcasts. In the community of Judaism such outcasts were tax collectors, Samaritans and gentiles, as well as Jews who were not faithful to the entire obligation of the law. The history of the apostolic church makes it clear that its appeal was addressed primarily to the lower classes and the social outcasts. Paul, it seems, could have said to all his churches what he said to the Corinthians, that there were not many wise or powerful or well-born among them (1 Corinthians 1:26). A human being should not have to be " forgiven " such defects, but in human society it is often forgiveness for such things which is sought and denied. To say that Jesus forgave " sinners " is not enough; he also forgave those whom the wise and powerful and well-born often condemn to be sinners by their state and condition in life. The woman of Luke 7:36–50 is an example of one who is forgiven by God but not by men. The conduct of Jesus in this episode is both encouragement and example.

A distinctive feature of each gospel is its structure and organization. If one takes the trouble to consult a synopsis of the first three gospels, he will be surprised and puzzled at the freedom with which the writers locate incidents and sayings in different contexts. He may conclude that the arrangement is simply the result of random selection. In fact the sayings and incidents had no context before the gospels were written. The writers were free to arrange the material in the order which was most suitable to their purpose. Father Stöger has been at pains to show the perspective and the emphasis which Luke achieves by his structure and by grouping incidents and sayings in the manner which he chose. The artistry of Luke can be seen to best effect in the large section called the "journey narrative" (9:51—18:14), which has very few parallels in Matthew and Mark. Luke had more freedom here than elsewhere, and the arrangement is calculated to emphasize his favorite themes.

The primary purpose of a commentary of this type is not to untangle the historical and critical problems of the gospels; it is to set forth the permanent value and meaning of the words and deeds of Jesus as they are relevant to this generation in this world. The Christian seeks an answer to the questions of his life in the gospels; that someone else in another time has found the answer to his questions may not mean much to the contemporary Christian. The task is delicate. At first glance, the situation of the gospels is so different from the modern situation that the reader may be tempted to think that the gospels have nothing to say to him. The problem of poverty does not take the form of a beggar starving at the door of a rich man. He does not encounter the neighbor in need as a wounded victim of robbers who lies by the roadside. The principle of nonresistance does not seem applicable to the citizen of a modern state at war. What Jesus does and tells him to do seem to be simply impossible in his situation. Yet he does believe that the gospel is the word of life.

It is indeed a subtle and challenging task for the interpreter to discern and to set forth the principles implicit in the concrete sayings and events of the gospels which are applicable at all times and in all places, and upon which the Christian can form a particular decision. The interpreter knows that he runs the risk of error; but if he remains silent he surrenders the problems to secular solutions. He must remember that the gospel is no more of a challenge now than it was when it was first proclaimed. Its sayings were never anything but a challenge to the world, its values, and its ethics. The situation of the gospels, upon close examination, may prove to be not so different from the modern situation as we are inclined to think. The interpreter must show that the principles of Jesus are never impractical; many believe that they are even if they are not so candid as to say it. But the principles cannot be detached from their foundation in the gospel and in the " conversion " which the gospel proclaims as the first movement of man towards God. The principles are indeed impractical for one who has not been converted. The interpreter must make clear what conversion means.

Father Stöger has accepted this part of his task with enthusiasm and dedicated himself to it with painstaking labor. He has sought to set forth the meaning of the words and deeds first in their proper context, without which no further exploration is possible, then the meaning of these words and deeds for the reader who believes that the gospel is a way of life. He has taken nothing away from the challenge of the gospel; it does not become a reed shaken by the wind. It remains what Jesus calls it, in words which Luke gives us, a denial of self and a carrying of the cross. This phrase, which has become a Christian commonplace, must be translated into the urgent tasks of life. No one can say that the emphases of Luke deal with trivia in the human community. The gospel makes these themes the points by which the Christian is judged. To make the themes relevant and practical is difficult; it has always been difficult. Father Stöger has done his work in the conviction that the gospel does not become more meaningful by depriving it of its original meaning, or by turning its emphases in another direction than the direction given by its author.

The work is presented to the public, according to the title of the German original, as " a spiritual reading of the Bible." We believe that this volume fulfills the definition, if we remember that the Spirit, when he comes upon the Twelve at Pentecost, kindles a flame.

John L. McKenzie, S.J.

INTRODUCTION

I.

St. Luke bequeathed two books to humanity: his gospel and the Acts of the Apostles. He describes his gospel and the Acts as a " word " (see Acts 1:1f.). God's word is the factor common to both books, and it is this which binds together the two eras of which the two books treat: the time of Jesus and the time of the church which follows on this. The purpose of St. Luke's " history " is to describe the history of God's word which is addressed to men through Jesus and continues to be effective in Christian missionary activity (see Acts 13:32f.).

The gospel is the point of departure and the basis for the events whose development is described in the Acts. The word sent by God is really Christ's saving activity in Judea (Acts 10:36f.). It is the story of Jesus Christ that is God's word. The " Christ-event " is a word which finds expression in the apostles' preaching. St. Luke presents the Christ-event as the fulfillment of the prophecy made to the patriarchs, and as the source of the missionary activity described in the Acts. Everything we are told about God's word in the Acts is already outlined in Jesus Christ. The key to the proper understanding of the gospel, therefore, is to be found in the Acts of the Apostles.

Jesus is portrayed in the gospel as a prophet who is " powerful in word and act " (24:19). He is more than just an ordinary prophet ; he is the prophet promised for the last stage of time, God's Holy One, the Son of God. His word, therefore, is the final revelation, the decisive and conclusive word. The Holy Spirit, the power from on high, is the eschatological gift which enables the proclamation of salvation to reach all hearts and loosen the tongues of all men (Acts 1:8 ; 2:4). It was with this Spirit that Jesus was anointed from the very beginning, and he was the gift which the apostles received from the glorified Christ. By his means, Christ's witnesses acted with great power, lending credibility to their message by the signs and wonders the Lord performed through them (Acts 4:33f.; 14:8f.), just as Jesus himself who was anointed with the Holy Spirit had power over illnesses and demons, over death and sin.

The Lord's word spread throughout the entire country (Acts 13:49). It "grows" (Acts 6:7), "grows and increases" (Acts 19:20), giving proof of its power. The whole aim of the Acts of the Apostles is to describe how the promise made by the risen Christ was fulfilled (Acts 1:8). The first stage of the long journey accomplished by God's word, of its spread to the ends of the earth, is described in the gospel; Luke tells us again and again how it was meant to spread all over the world. In this connection, St. Luke describes our Lord as constantly journeying about.

The word which God made known in Jesus Christ is the word the apostles preach. As God's servants, they proclaim his word (Acts 4:29), giving testimony of what they have seen and heard (Acts 1:8, 22). The gospel tells us that Jesus recruited these witnesses in Galilee and that they were his constant companions until he was taken up into heaven. Each of the sections devoted to Jesus' ministry in Galilee ends with the calling of some disciple (5:1ff. ; 5:27ff.) and a description of the activity the disciples engaged in (8:1ff. ; 9:1ff ; 9:49ff.). All those who welcome God's word become apostles and preachers of the word themselves ; the number of the disciples grows as God's word spreads.

II.

The Christians of the first generation were convinced that Jesus' resurrection would quickly be followed by his second coming and the general resurrection (Rom. 13:11; 1 Thess. 4:15). Their expectation was not realized. When St. Luke came to write his gospel and the Acts of the Apostles, the persecution of Nero had already taken place. Jerusalem had been taken and the temple destroyed by fire; but Christ's second coming was delayed. The Acts of the Apostles remind Christians: " It is not your business to know the time or the hour which the Father has appointed by his own authority " (1:7). Between Christ's ascension and his second coming a longer period of time must be allowed for than they had previously expected, a period which must have some significance in the course of salvation history. According to St. Luke's conception, the course of salvation history from the beginning of the world until Christ's second coming is divided into three epochs. The first of these is the " time of the promise," during which God prepared his people for the salvation to come by means of " the law and the prophets," as he states in his gospel (16:16). This era came to an end with St. John the Baptist. The second epoch is the time of fulfillment, " the welcome year of the Lord " (4:18), " the time of Christ." This lasted from the beginning of his life on earth until the ascension, and can also be referred to as " the midst of time." In this period what the time of the promise had foretold was fulfilled, at least initially, within a certain geographical area and during a short span in the history of the world, under the Roman emperors Augustus and Tiberius. The promises God made by the prophets were more than fulfilled. The demons were routed; illness and death were overcome; the gospel was preached to the poor; sins were forgiven, and God's love was there. The " midst of time " is followed by an epoch in preparation for which Jesus endowed his disciples with power and with the Holy Spirit. It is in this period that God's word spreads to the ends of the earth. This is the " time of the church," the basis of which is to be found in the midst of time, and this epoch is still in the course of realization.

These three epochs are mutually related. The midst of time is the accomplishment of the time of the promise. That is why scripture prepared for it and pointed to it (24:44–47). St. Luke rarely quotes scripture, but in the sections which are peculiar to him his presentation of his subject is often a texture into which a variety of threads from the Old Testament is woven; the events of the time of Christ are interpreted in the light of the Old Testament. The time of the promise looked forward to the midst of time; the time of the church, on the other hand, looks back to it. The midst of time contains everything by which the time of the church lives. The Holy Spirit who is the power of the church was also Jesus' power. Jesus' life is the model of the church's life; it is the gospel which explains the life and teaching of the church.

III.

It is God who acts throughout the various epochs of history, and St. Luke is anxious to describe the great things he accomplished. In this sense he is an historian who reports events. Jesus " must " accomplish God's saving design (see 24:25f.). St. Luke emphasizes this " must " more than any of the other evangelists. Jesus acts in God's name; God becomes visible in all that he does. His activity flows from his prayer, from the Son's loving converse with the Father who has entrusted everything to him, to whom he owes his power and his teaching. It is from his union with God that Jesus receives wisdom; it is this which inspires him in the choice of his disciples. The divine glory which came to him in his baptism, transfiguration, and resurrection springs from this.

God is determined to make it clear that it is he who is at work throughout the different epochs of salvation history; salvation comes from God, not from man. Man's contribution, the contribution he must make, is his poverty. The whole program of Jesus' saving activity is contained in the passage of scripture which he read in the synagogue at Nazareth, adding that it was now fulfilled (Is. 61:1f.; 58:6). So it is that St. Luke's gospel is the gospel of the poor, of those who endure physical poverty; it is the gospel of sinners, of debtors, of women, and of those who weep. Presuming on one's own strength closes one's heart to God, and God closes himself to those whose hearts are closed against him. At every stage of salvation history, God wants those who are to receive his salvation to be humble.

A man becomes lowly by repentance. Jesus was sent to bring salvation; before a man can receive this salvation, he must repent (5:32). The words " to repentance " occur only in St. Luke.

If it is true that it is God who takes the initiative in the time of salvation, it is only right that praise be offered to him. Again and again, St. Luke's accounts of Christ's powerful actions end with an expression of praise for God. The " Benedictus " and the " Magnificat " are the most elaborate praises addressed to God for his saving activity. However, St. Elizabeth (1:41ff.) and those who heard about Jesus' birth (2:20) also offered praise to God. Jesus' miracles, too, are an occasion for giving him praise (4:15; 13:31; 18:43). Jesus himself expected those who had been cured of their illnesses to praise God (17:15.18).

St. Luke's gospel begins in the temple and it is in the temple that it comes to a close. The liturgical offering of incense forms the introduction to the story of salvation; the religious celebration in the synagogue at Nazareth marks the opening of Jesus' public life and, finally, the infant church assembles in the temple at Jerusalem: "And they were always in the temple, blessing and praising God " (24:53).

OUTLINE

xix

THE EVANGELIST'S INTENTION (1:1-4)

St. Luke introduces his book with a prologue which is in keeping with the literary usage of his time. In a long and carefully constructed sentence, he speaks of the content, the sources, the method, and the purpose of his work, and of the occasion which gave rise to it. A door must be opened to the world of Greek civilization.

¹Many have undertaken to give an account of the events which occurred among us, ²as they who were eye-witnesses and servants of the word from the beginning have handed it down. ³Therefore, I too, having investigated it all carefully from the beginning, have decided to write it down for you in order, most worthy Theophilus, ⁴that you may appreciate how reliable the words concerning which you have been instructed are.

St. Luke's gospel was not the first; it had a number of predecessors. It makes use of St. Mark's gospel and is related to that of St. Matthew. " Many have undertaken "—this expression is clearly inspired by the literary form of the prologue. Anyone who writes a gospel undertakes a great work. St. Luke dares to do it only because others have done it before him.

He intends to write about the events promised by God which were now in the course of being accomplished among the Christians to whom St. Luke writes. God " sent the word to the sons of Israel and proclaimed the gospel of peace through Jesus " (Acts 10:36). This divine word which proclaims and imparts salvation takes its origin from Jesus Christ (Heb. 2:3) who is the center of all history and *the* saving act of God. The word began from Galilee and spread throughout the whole of Judea, which is Pales-

3

tine (Acts 10:37). After Jesus had been taken up into heaven, the apostles preached it in Jerusalem, in the whole of Judea and Samaria, and to the ends of the earth (Acts 1:8), in the power of the Holy Spirit. Since that time the word has continued its course uninterruptedly ; proclaiming and imparting salvation, it achieves all that God has promised.

The source for St. Luke's account and that of his predecessors is the tradition which was handed down in the church and which is based on the accounts of eye-witnesses who had lived through the great events of saving history. After the ascension, only those could be apostles who had been witnesses " all the time the Lord Jesus was with us, coming and going, beginning from John's baptism until the day he was taken from us " (see Acts 1:21f.). Those who had been witnesses " of all that Jesus did in the country of Judea and in Jerusalem " (Acts 10:39) also became servants of the word.

St. Matthew begins his gospel with the words : " The book of the genealogy of Jesus Christ," while St. Mark says : " The beginning of the gospel of Jesus Christ." Both authors remain anonymous. St. Luke, on the other hand, is quite open : " I have decided." His gospel is intended to be a literary work which will find a place in the world of literature. As its author, he gives the tradition which had been handed down a stronger personal coloring than either of his predecessors, although he preserves the original form of Jesus' preaching. St. Luke writes as an educated Hellenist, as a doctor, and as a disciple of St. Paul (Col. 4:14). By the fervor of their own faith, the evangelists wanted to kindle a fervent faith in their readers while always remaining loyal to what had been handed down.

An historian must go about his work carefully. He traces events back to their beginning and investigates everything guaranteed by eye-witnesses. Finally, he must give an orderly account of the facts he has gathered. St. Luke was careful to do all this. His gospel is

4

closer than any of the others to being an historical account of Jesus' life. He is " God's historian." However, St. Luke did not set out merely to write a life of Jesus, any more than the other evangelists did; on the contrary, he wished to proclaim the good news in the service of salvation.

The work is dedicated to the " most worthy Theophilus." Who was this Theophilus? Was this his real name? Or is it only the name St. Luke gives him because he was a " friend of God " (*Theo-philos*) ? What kind of a person was he ? He was in any case an influential man holding high office; otherwise, he would not have been addressed as " most worthy " (see Acts 23:26). He was held in esteem and was a man of means. The gospel was dedicated to him to win his patronage; someone would have to be found to bear the expense of having it copied and distributed. The incarnate Word depended upon human beings, and God's written word depends upon human collaboration in the same way.

The church's proclamation of the faith had inspired faith in Theophilus. St. Luke wishes to give this faith a reliable historical basis by means of his gospel. Our faith is not based on myths or legends invented by men ; it is based on historical events. The faith which is believed and lived in the church is founded in Jesus Christ who was active on this earth at a precise moment in history.

THE BEGINNING OF SALVATION (1:5—4:13)

The time during which salvation was only a promise comes to a close with St. John the Baptist; the time in which this promise is fulfilled begins with Jesus. St. John the Baptist is " the greatest among those born of woman, but the least in the kingdom of God is greater than he " (7:28). Jesus is greater than the Baptist.

In three different passages St. Luke begins with John the Baptist only to continue his story by talking about Jesus. Each time that the Baptist's story serves as an introduction in this way, we see that it is in the service of Jesus; this is true of the promise of their birth (1:5–56), of their birth and childhood (1:57—2:52), and of their public life (3:1—4:13). The story follows the same plan in each case, but the information we are given about Jesus surpasses that which we are given about St. John even by its very length. Jesus must increase while John decreases (Jn. 3:30).

The Baptist prepared the way for Jesus as a worthy successor of the great personages of Israelite history, Samson, Samuel, and Elijah. Old Testament terms which are used to describe these men are also used by St. Luke to describe St. John the Baptist and Jesus. Salvation history does not destroy what it has built up; on the contrary, it takes up what already exists and completes it. The light grows constantly brighter until the day breaks; God's intervention becomes increasingly marked. Christ is the fulfillment of salvation history and the goal towards which it aims.

The Promise (1:5–56)

The future birth of John (1:5–25) and Jesus (1:26–38) is announced by the same messenger from God, the archangel Gabriel. They meet when their mothers greet one another (1:39–56).

St. John the Baptist is Announced (1:5-25)

His Pious Background (1:5-7)

⁵It happened that in the days of Herod, king of Judea, there lived a priest by the name of Zechariah who belonged to the priestly class of Abijah. He had a wife who was descended from Aaron and her name was Elizabeth. ⁶Both were upright in God's eyes and they were blameless in obeying all the commandments and ordinances of the Lord. ⁷They had no child because Elizabeth was barren and both of them were well on in years.

God's saving activity takes places within human history. Like the infancy gospel in this passage, the Book of Judith also begins with the words: " In the days of Arphaxad " (1:1). This is sacred history and it demands a biblical style. " The days of Herod " fell in the period from 40 B.C. to 4 B.C. John's birth is connected with the reign of king Herod of Judea (Palestine), but Jesus' birth occurs during the reign of the emperor Augustus who held sway over the entire " inhabited world " (2:1). John remains within the narrow confines of Judea, while Jesus heralds salvation for the whole world.

The announcement of John's coming is surrounded with an aura of sanctity. As the Precursor of the salvation which was to come, he stood at the threshold of the time of salvation. By asserting his dominion in Christ, God makes his name holy (11:2; Ezek. 20:41).

St. John's parents were among those Jews who were noted for their sanctity. His father was a priest of the priestly class of Abijah and his mother's ancestor was Aaron, the first high priest. Their marriage was in keeping with the sacred obligation of the law for priests; a priest must marry the daughter of a priest. Among the Jews, the priesthood was handed on by natural descent. St. John the Baptist was a priest, holy and consecrated to God's service. But the service he offers God will be very different from that offered by his father.

7

Zechariah (" God remembered ") and Elizabeth (" God has sworn ") were holy because they were upright in God's eyes. They observed all the commandments of God's law. They lived up to their holy ancestry and their calling by obeying God's will. Holiness consists in obeying God.

Many of the great figures of salvation history were children of mothers who were barren; they were a gift from the all-holy God, the result of his intervention when nature had failed. Such, for example, were Isaac (Gen. 17:16), the judge Samson (Judg. 13:2), and Samuel (1 Sam. 1–2). The Baptist, too, was to take his place in this series of great names. The way St. Luke describes the announcement of St. John's birth is inspired by the way in which these men were announced. John was a child of God's grace; as such, he was sanctified and consecrated to God in a new way.

He Is Announced at a Sacred Moment (1:8–12)

[8]*It happened that, while he was exercising his office as a priest before God, in the order of his class,* [9]*it fell to his lot, as was customary among the priests, to offer the sacrifice of incense as soon as he entered the temple of the Lord.* [10]*And the whole people persevered in prayer outside, waiting for the hour of sacrifice.* [11]*But an angel of the Lord appeared to him, standing at the right of the altar of incense,* [12]*and Zechariah was terrified when he saw him and fear gained the upper hand over him.*

The story of the Precursor begins in the sanctuary of the temple. Only priests could enter there; the people must pray outside. Even a priest could enter only when the lot fell to him to conduct the sacred ritual in such close proximity to God. God is close to his people in his temple, but to draw near to him is reserved to those whom he calls by his own choice and by lot. The all-holy God is the remote, inaccessible God.

The Baptist's birth was announced at a time of solemn prayer.

8

The incense offering is a symbol of the prayer which ascends to God (see Ps. 141:2). The priest poured grains of perfumed incense over the glowing coals on the altar and fell down to worship. Meanwhile, the people prayed outside. The great moments of Jesus' life, too, which were charged with significance for salvation history, occurred during prayer, the theophany at his baptism, his transfiguration, the choice of the apostles, his acceptance of his passion in Gethsemane, and his death.

"An angel of the Lord appeared." The good news finds its origin in heaven. The angel was standing to the right of the altar of incense; the right side means salvation (Mt. 25:33f.). These events call for a holy silence inviting us to reflection. The phrase itself is a very old one in religious language; it is an indication of what is now about to take place.

The vision threw Zechariah into confusion and made him afraid; he felt a supernatural apprehension in the face of the divine being. God is the totally Other, the Unapproachable (see Is. 6:5). God's messenger is surrounded by God's awe-inspiring holiness and glory. The announcement of St. John's birth comes on the forbidden ground of the temple sanctuary, surrounded by all the observances of divine worship, and shrouded in the awe-inspiring might of all that is holy; it is part of the spiritual world of the Old Testament.

A HOLY CHILD (1:13-17)

[13]*But the angel said to him: " Do not be afraid, Zechariah. Your prayer has been heard and your wife Elizabeth will bear you a son, and you will give him the name John.* [14]*Joy will be yours and jubilation, and many shall rejoice at his birth."*

When someone from heaven or an apparition—whether it is God himself, or one of the angels, or Christ—addresses a human being, he always prefaces his words with an expression of encouragement :

"Do not be afraid!" God wants to raise man up, not to crush him down.

Zechariah's prayers have been answered, his prayers for a son and for the fulfillment of the promises concerning the Messiah. The last period of time brings to fulfillment all the hopes and yearnings of the human race.

God himself appoints a name for the child, and together with his name he gives him his mission and endows him with power. The name the child is to have means " God is gracious." The time of God's gracious visitation is now at hand, and John will proclaim the imminent coming of the time of salvation.

His birth will be a cause of joy such as is characteristic of the last stage of time; it will inspire a jubilant cry of salvation. His parents are not the only ones who will rejoice; many others, too, the whole multitude of those who have faith, will share their joy. John the Baptist has a role to play in salvation history; he brings the time of the promise to an end and proclaims the time of salvation which brings happiness and rejoicing with it. The first Christian church at Jerusalem celebrated the liturgy " with joy and simplicity of heart, giving praise to God " (Acts 2:46).

¹⁵" *For he will be great in the sight of the Lord; he will drink neither wine nor strong drink, and from his mother's womb he will be filled with the Holy Spirit.*"

" He will be great in God's eyes." The position the Baptist occupied in salvation history raised him above all the other great figures who had a part in it. They only looked forward to the coming of God's kingdom and his salvation ; John stood on the threshold and proclaimed its coming (see Lk. 7:28).

In his way of life, the Baptist would be in no way inferior to the great men of the past. Those who are consecrated to God never indulge in strong drink. We see this in the case of Samson (Judg. 13:2–5.7) and the prophet Samuel (1 Sam. 1:15f.).

Being filled with the Holy Spirit, John was a prophet, to make known God's word and his divine will. Others received the gift of prophecy only when they were already old ; the Baptist was a prophet from the first moment of life, from his mother's womb. The time of salvation makes its presence felt by the abundant gift of the Holy Spirit which accompanies it. There is a tendency towards progressive interiorization and deepening of religious attitudes from Samson, through Samuel, to St. John the Baptist. Samson abstained from cutting his hair, while Samuel abstained from strong drink. St. John adopted only the latter practice, but his whole life was filled by the Spirit.

[16]" He will bring back many of the children of Israel to the Lord their God. [17]And he will go before his face in the spirit and power of an Elijah, to win the fathers for their children, and make the disobedient well-disposed like the just, to prepare for the Lord a people well-qualified to receive him."

Zechariah's son was to prepare the way for the introduction of a new covenant. In him would be fulfilled the prophecy Malachi made concerning the last stage of time: "See, I am sending my messenger before me, to prepare a way for me. He will reconcile the sons with their fathers and the fathers with their sons, so that he will not be forced to come and put the land under a curse" (Mal. 3:1, 24). Men must be united with him in the unity of a single people which can then be united with God. God showed himself gracious in John ; by his means, he wanted to make his coming a time of salvation, not a severe judgment. That was why he sent the Precursor to prepare a people well-qualified to receive their Lord. Converting Israel which had fallen away, so that they became true members of God's people, and making the impious virtuous, would mean preparing a people fit to receive the Lord.

¹⁸And Zechariah said to the angel : " How can I be sure of this ?
I am an old man, and my wife is advanced in years." ¹⁹And the
angel said to him in reply : " I am Gabriel and I stand before God's
face. He sent me to speak to you and to make this good news
known to you."

Like the great men of Jewish history, Zechariah asked for a sign.
After he had been promised that he would receive Canaan as his
inheritance, Abraham said: " Lord, Lord, how can I be sure that
I will inherit it ? " (Gen. 15:7f.). Gideon, too, wanted a sign that
God would keep his word (Judg. 6:36ff.), as did king Hezekiah
when God promised to prolong his life (2 Kings 20:8). " The Jews
ask for signs" (1 Cor. 1:22). Man is afraid of being deceived.
God is prepared to provide a sign, but he wants man to wait for
the sign he chooses to give him, and to be prepared to believe even
without a sign. " It is well for those who do not see and yet
believe " (Jn. 20:29).

The envoy who brought the news guaranteed the truth of the
promise. His name was Gabriel, " God is powerful." The message
came from a source which was as close to God as possible ; Gabriel
was one of the seven angels at the throne who stand before God's
face (Tob. 12:15 ; Rev. 8:2). This was the angel who made the
revelation that there were to be seventy weeks of years before the
fulfillment of the promise (Dan. 9:24) after Daniel had prayed
fervently to God at the time of the evening sacrifice (9:4-19).
Now all this was to be accomplished ; the Baptist would usher in
the time of salvation.

²⁰" And see, you will be dumb; you will be unable to speak until
the day when this happens, because you have not believed my words
which will be fulfilled in their own time."

God's intervention became palpable in Zechariah's sudden loss of speech and hearing (1:62f.). His lack of faith in demanding a sign and putting God to the test made the announcement of salvation a sentence of condemnation. It was the demand for a sign such as this that frustrated the offer of salvation God made to his people through Jesus, so that it became a cause of judgment instead (11: 29f.). All those mentioned in the infancy gospel who welcomed the message of salvation in a spirit of faith were overjoyed; they became ambassadors of the joy salvation brings. Doubt and the demand for a sign kill this joy and silence the lips which should be jubilant in proclaiming the good news.

Zechariah's punishment, which was also a sign, came to an end when the promise was fulfilled. Neither his hesitation nor the Jews' unbelieving demand for a sign could prevent the coming of salvation. When John was born, Zechariah's guilt was wiped out. When Christ comes again at the end of time, Israel, too, will attain salvation as God's people; the tongues will be loosed to praise God which remained silent during the time of the church (Rom. 11:25f.).

²¹And the people were waiting for Zechariah, and they were amazed that he stayed so long in the sanctuary. ²²But when he came out, he was unable to speak to them, and they realized that he had seen a vision in the sanctuary. He made signs to them and remained dumb.

The Jewish priests never delayed over the sacred rites, to avoid making the people anxious. The men of the Old Testament regarded God's proximity as dangerous. Zechariah's dumbness led the people to conclude that God had appeared to him. God's revelation is at once a source of salvation and perdition; of perdition for those who doubt, and of salvation for those who have faith.

The people knew by Zechariah that God had spoken to him, but they did not understand the meaning of the revelation because he

13

could not speak. Saving events need God's word to explain them and make them clear. The God who sends us salvation also sends us his word to explain it, his word concerning Jesus' birth and death, and his sacraments.

²³And it happened that when the time for performing his sacred duty was over, Zechariah went back to his home.

Not all of the priests lived in Jerusalem; many of them had their homes in the various towns of Palestine. Zechariah's turn of a week's duty was over and he left the holy city. He took his great secret with him, the fulfillment of his dreams, the sign that he had made no mistake, that God would keep his word. Even though God had punished him he went home full of the certainty that God is gracious.

GOD'S PROMISE IS FULFILLED (1:24-25)

²⁴After these days, his wife Elizabeth conceived and remained in retirement for five months, saying to herself: ²⁵" It is the Lord who has done this for me at the time when he looked favorably on me, to take away my reproach among men."

Elizabeth was one of those historic women who were barren, but conceived in the normal way by God's providence. Such were Sarah who became the mother of Isaac (Gen. 17:17), Manoah's wife, who was Samson's mother (Judg. 13:2), and Samuel's mother, Hannah (1 Sam. 1:2.5). God opened their wombs (Gen. 29:31) which had formerly been closed (1 Sam. 1:5). Mary will conceive by the Holy Spirit without any human intervention. Elizabeth, on the other hand, still belonged to the Old Testament; God's "new creation" begins with Mary, that new creation to which man can contribute nothing except to await and accept salvation in a spirit of faith.

14

God arranges the events of history without abolishing man's freedom. Elizabeth remained in seclusion for five months. No one knew what had happened. When the sixth month came, the messenger God sent to Mary referred to Elizabeth: "This month is her sixth, and she used to be called barren ! " (1:36). She was the sign God gave Mary.

Why did Elizabeth remain in retirement ? The mother of John who is consecrated to God lives as one dedicated to God. This had been God's will for Samson's mother (Judg. 13:6f.). Such a life demands seclusion. In her great hour, St. Elizabeth had recourse to her knowledge of the Bible to learn what God's will was.

Her months of waiting and looking forward were filled with prayer. She gave thanks to God: "It is God who has done this for me." She constantly recalled all that God had done for her ; he looked favorably on her, and she never forgot her humiliation ; he had taken away the shame of her childlessness. She had experienced the history of her people in her own life: "Think how the Lord your God led you for forty years in the desert, the whole way. He let you suffer oppression to put you to the test, to see what the thoughts of your heart are like... The Lord your God is bringing you into a glorious and spacious land, a land full of streams, springs, and surface waters which spring up in the valleys and on the hills " (Deut. 8:2-7).

Jesus' Birth Is Foretold (1:26-38)

The form in which St. Luke cast the story of the annunciation of Jesus' birth made it a work of art, while its content makes it a " golden gospel." The angel speaks three times to Mary, and Mary replies three times. We are told three times what God intends to accomplish in Mary, and her reaction to the divine initiative is also described three times. The angel approaches Mary (1:26-29), announces the birth of the Messiah (1:30-34), and reveals his virginal conception (1:35-38).

²⁶In the sixth month the angel Gabriel was sent by God to a town of Galilee called Nazareth, ²⁷to a virgin who was engaged to a man whose name was Joseph, of the house of David, and the virgin's name was Mary.

The announcement of Jesus' coming looks back to the prophecy of John's birth. " In the sixth month "—John exists to serve Jesus: the fact that Elizabeth who was barren had conceived points towards Mary's virginal conception. Jesus came later than John, yet he takes precedence over him (Jn. 1:27).

Once again, the envoy who brings the news is Gabriel. When John's birth was foretold, the angel's mission ended in the temple, God's sanctuary, holy, secluded, and unapproachable. But when Jesus was announced, his mission ended in a town of Galilee, in the " Galilee of the gentiles " (Mt. 4:15), a part of the holy land which was regarded as being profane. God seemed to have forsaken it; it had " never produced a prophet " (Jn. 7:52). The name of the town is not even mentioned immediately, as if the evangelist was loath to pronounce it. Finally, it comes: " Nazareth." The town had no claim to historical fame. The Old Testament never mentioned it, and the Jewish historian Flavius Josephus has nothing to say about it. A contemporary of Jesus says: " Can any good come out of Nazareth ? " (Jn. 1:46). God chooses what is insignificant and despised by men as being of little value. The law governing the incarnation is contained in the words: " Jesus . . . emptied himself " (Phil. 2:7).

The Baptist's story begins with Zechariah who is a priest and his wife Elizabeth who comes from the family of Aaron ; Jesus' story begins with a girl of perhaps twelve or thirteen years of age. She was engaged, which was the normal thing for a girl of that age. Mary's future husband was called " Joseph." He had not taken her into his own home ; neither had they lived together as man and wife. She was a virgin. Joseph belonged to the family of David ; God had arranged everything so that Mary's son would be the son of a virgin, the legal son of Joseph, and a descendant of the royal family of David. God disposes all things wisely.

"The virgin's name was Mary." This was also the name of Aaron's sister (Ex. 15:20), but we have no idea what it means. "Lady," perhaps or, "beloved by Yahweh"?

[28]*He went in to her and said: " Rejoice, you who are full of grace. The Lord is with you; you are blessed among women."*

When he announced John, the angel simply appeared there, but he " went in " to Mary and greeted her. John's birth was announced in the temple sanctuary, while Jesus' coming was foretold in the virgin's home. In the Old Testament, God lived in the temple; in the New, he makes his home among men. " The Word was made flesh and pitched his tent among us " (Jn. 1:14).

The angel gave Zechariah no greeting, but he greets Mary. He greets the girl from Nazareth, although it was not the custom among the Jews for a man to greet a woman. This greeting occurs in two forms, each of which consists of a greeting and a form of address. " Rejoice, you who are full of grace " is the first form. Greek speakers used the formula " Rejoice," while those who spoke Aramaic used the words " Peace be with you," the greeting Jesus himself gave his disciples after his resurrection (Jn. 20:19.26; Lk. 10:5; 24:36).

St. Luke's infancy gospel (chs. 1—2) is full of reminiscences and words taken from the Old Testament. St. Matthew, too, makes use of citations from the Old Testament to illustrate his account of Christ's infancy. But he introduces his quotations with solemn formulas, whereas St. Luke tells the story with texts from the Old Testament. He invites us to understand the events he has gleaned from tradition in the light of God's word.

" Rejoice " was a stereotyped prophetical and liturgical formula which was occasionally employed when the prophet's statement produced a happy result (see Zeph. 3 : 14; Joel 2 : 21). Now the angel makes use of this messianic acclamation to greet Mary.

The angel addresses her as " you who are full of grace." John's parents were without reproach because they observed God's law; Mary enjoys God's favor because he overwhelmed her with his grace. This divine favor is explained in the prophet's acclamation, the first words of which were used by the angel in greeting Mary : " The Lord has routed your opponents and put your enemies to flight; the Lord is in your midst . . . From now on, you will see no further trouble . . . Do not be afraid . . . The Lord your God is in your midst, a warrior to help you. He rejoices over you, full of gladness. He will renew his love. With loud rejoicing, he exults because of you . . ." (Zeph. 3 : 15–17).

Mary is the city in whose midst (womb) God dwells, the divine king who is a valiant warrior. She is the faithful remnant for whom God fulfills his promises, the nucleus of the new people of God which has God dwelling in its midst (see Mt. 18 : 20; 28 : 20).

The second form of greeting used by the angel begins with the words: " The Lord is with you." Other great figures of salvation history had the same words addressed to them to sustain them and encourage them. This was the case with Moses when he was called by God in the desert to be the leader and the saviour of his people. An angel of God appeared to him in a burst of flame which came from a thorn bush (Ex. 3 : 2). He felt that he was not equal to such a calling, but God told him : " I am determined to be with you. This will be a sign for you, to show that I am with you . . ." (Ex. 3 : 12). Gideon the judge had the same experience (Judg. 6 : 12, 15–17). The greeting the angel gives her puts Mary on the same level as the great liberators of salvation history. God bestowed his special grace on her and let her share his protection.

The greeting is followed once more by a form of address : " You who are blessed among women." These words, too, are sacred and consecrated by ancient biblical usage. Jael, the heroine who annihilated the enemies of her people, is praised with the words: " Jael is blessed among all women " (Judg. 5:24). Uzziah, the leader of the people, addressed Judith who had killed the oppressor of her native city with the words: " Blessed are you, daughter, among all the women on earth, by the Lord the most high God . . . Today he has brought such glory to your name that your praise shall never vanish from the lips of men who remember the Lord's power forever " (Jdt. 13:18f.). Mary, therefore, takes her place among the heroic women of her people; she brought forth the redeemer who would deliver men from all their enemies (see Lk. 1:71).

²⁹*But she was terrified at the greeting. And she wondered what kind of a greeting it could be.*

Zechariah had been afraid of the vision of the angel ; Mary was terrified at the solemnity of the greeting addressed to her. She wondered what this unusual greeting meant. Her whole life and her prayer were steeped in the ideas contained in scripture. She must, therefore, have had some inkling of the extraordinary nature of the event which was announced in such terms.

A Promise Full of Grace (1:30–34)

³⁰*And the angel spoke to her: " Do not be afraid, Mary, because you have found grace with God. ³¹And see, you will conceive in your womb and give birth to a son, and you shall call his name Jesus."*

Moses (Ex. 3:11f.), Gideon (Judg. 6:15f.), Sion (Zeph. 3:16f.), and Israel itself all needed to be encouraged with the assurance that God was determined to come to their aid. " Do not be afraid. I am with you " (Is. 43:5). They were all afraid of the mission God gave them ; they knew their own weakness. It was the same with Mary, but God's grace will sustain her.

The power of God's grace was about to accomplish something extraordinary: " And see." The angel reveals the role for which God has chosen Mary. The words he uses are reminiscent of the prophecy in which Isaiah foretold the coming of Immanuel ("God with us "): " See, the virgin will conceive and give birth to a son and call his name Immanuel " (Is. 7:14 ; see Mt. 1:23).

The words in which the Baptist's coming was announced were addressed to Zechariah, and they concerned his wife. Now, however, the angel speaks only to Mary; she will conceive and give birth and give her son his name. There is no mention of a father or a husband. The mystery of Christ's virginal conception is about to be revealed.

" You will conceive in your womb." Why does the angel say this ? The phrase is not one used in the Old Testament. But the prophet Zephaniah had said twice: The Lord (will be) in your midst. This is now going to be fulfilled in an unheard of way. God will dwell within, in the virgin's womb ; he will be with her (Immanuel). She will be the new temple, the new holy city, the people of God in whose midst he dwells.

The child must be called Jesus. God chose the name, but it is Mary who gives it to him. No explanation of the name is given, just as no explanation was given of John's name. Everything we are told about them serves to explain their names. The mission God entrusted to them is implied in their names. In Jesus God wishes to be a saviour: " The Lord your God in your midst, a valiant warrior " (Zeph. 3:17).

32" *He will be great, and he will be called Son of the Most High, and the Lord God will give him the throne of David his father.*

³³He will rule over the house of Jacob forever, and of his kingdom there will be no end."

John is " great before God," but Jesus is great without any further qualification or limit. He shall be called, and shall be, the Son of the Most High. This name indicates his nature. It is God who is the Most High, and the power of the Most High will overshadow Mary. That is why her son will be called " the Son of God."

In the child whose coming was now announced, the prophecy God made to king David by the prophet Nathan was to be fulfilled (2 Sam. 7:12–16). Jesus is to be a ruler from the family of David and, at the same time, God's Son ; he is the Son of David and God's Son.

" He will rule over the house of Jacob forever." In him will be fulfilled what was foretold of the servant of Yahweh (Is. 49:6). Jesus will gather the people of God together, and the gentiles, too, will be taken into their company. He will found a kingdom which will encompass the whole world, with all its peoples and all its ages.

³⁴But Mary said to the angel: " How will this be, because I do not know any man ? "

Her answer to God's message is a question. Zechariah, too, had asked a question (1:18), just like Mary. He asked for a sign to prove the truth of the message ; Mary believed the message without asking for a sign. Zechariah was willing to believe only when his difficulties had been resolved; Mary believed first of all and only then did she look for a solution to the problems which arose.

Mary's question underlines the impossibility on a human level of reconciling motherhood and virginity. At the same time, Mary's question serves to introduce the explanation God is about to give of this mystery (1:35). We are not interested so much in discovering what interior or exterior circumstances prompted Mary to ask this question, or in what frame of mind she put it. Mary's question must not be taken as the starting point for a psychological analysis of the impression made on her, a betrothed virgin, by the promise that she would become a mother. St. Luke was content to put the question on record ; he offered no explanation. The question seemed important to him; it makes the reader attentive. It is a problem for us, too: How can virginity and motherhood be reconciled ?

A CONCEPTION FULL OF GRACE (1:35–38)

[35]And the angel said to her in reply: "A holy spirit will come upon you and the power of the Most High will overshadow you. That is why he who is to be born will be called holy and God's Son."

What God was about to do was something completely new. In former times, women who were barren and advanced in years had been enabled to conceive miraculously when unaided nature had failed them. Now, a virgin was to become a mother without any intervention on a man's part. Jesus' conception is God's doing and it surpasses everything that had ever happened to the great figures of salvation history: Isaac, Samson, Samuel, and John the Baptist.

"A holy spirit will come upon you." It is God's power, not man's which will give life to Mary's womb. The holy spirit in question here is a lifegiving and regulating power (Gen. 1:2; Ps. 104:30). The spirit is God's creative power which calls Jesus into existence. The miracle of Christ's conception by a virgin without the collaboration of an earthly father is the supreme revelation of God's creative freedom. It marks a new beginning which is wholly and entirely due to God's power. The patriarch of the new people of God is born by God's free creative act, but with the cooperation of the old race through Mary. Jesus is God's Son in a way unequalled by anyone else (3:38).

" The power of the Most High will overshadow you." The cloud which hides the sun casts a shadow on the earth and is at the same time a symbol of fertility because it brings rain with it. We are told of the tent of meeting in the Old Testament that: " The cloud descended on it and the Lord's glory filled the dwelling " (Ex. 40 : 34). When the temple was dedicated in Solomon's time, a cloud overshadowed it (1 Kings 8 : 11). The God who dwells in his temple does not remain inactive; he is a God who is ever at work. God's glory which is a divine power fills Mary and is the cause of Jesus' life in her. In Jesus, God's glory is revealed by means of his incarnation in Mary. She is the new temple in which God manifests himself to his people through Jesus; Mary is the ark of the covenant in which the Messiah lives continually, the symbol of God's presence among men.

His virginal conception through the Spirit and the power of the Most High implies that Jesus, the child who was to be born, is holy and God's Son. Jesus is called the " Holy One " (Acts 2 : 27); he is the Holy One of God (4 : 34). Because he was conceived and born through the Spirit, Jesus possesses the Spirit from the first moment of his conception. John possessed this Spirit from his mother's womb; the prophets and the holy people of the Old Testament were seized by the Spirit for a certain time. But Jesus surpasses all those who shared in the Spirit. It is because he possessed the Spirit in all his fullness from the beginning, that he has power to distribute the Spirit as he wishes (24 : 49; Acts 2 : 33).

Jesus is called, and is God's Son. He is the Son of the Most High (1 : 32; 8 : 28), God's Son, because he is born by the power of the Most High. He is not God's Son like Adam (3 : 38)—simply because God created him. He is God's Son because he is born of him from the beginning, from his conception, not like those who practice charity and receive the quality of sons of the Most High as a great reward (6 : 35).

23

³⁶"*And see, Elizabeth your cousin—she too has conceived a son in her old age and this month is her sixth—and they call her barren!* ³⁷*No word that comes from God remains ineffective."*

Although Mary had not demanded a sign, God assisted her readiness to believe with a sign; he did not ask for blind faith. It was a sign which was suited to her. At this moment there could have been nothing to which she was more susceptible and sympathetic than the thought of motherhood. Elizabeth, too, had conceived, she who was regarded as being barren. " This month is the sixth." It was quite clear that she was a mother, and it was a sign of God's miraculous intervention.

" No word that comes from God remains ineffective." Nothing is impossible for God. God himself said to Abraham what the angel said to Mary : " Why is Sarah laughing? Why does she say to herself : 'Am I really to be a mother, even now that I have grown old?' Is nothing whatever impossible for the Lord?" (Gen. 18:13f.). Mary's faith is confirmed by the saving event which has been realized in Elizabeth and by the testimony of scripture concerning Abraham. The whole of salvation history and the life of the church is a sign.

A bridge stretches from Abraham and Isaac, through Elizabeth and John, to Mary and Jesus. The power which sustains salvation history and God's saving activity which began in Abraham and reached its highest point under the old dispensation in John until it was consummated in Jesus is " God's word which is never ineffective." Abraham had a son by Sarah because he had found grace in God's eyes (Gen. 18:3); Mary conceived a Son, because she found grace (1:30).

Mary was Elizabeth's cousin. Therefore she, too, must have come from the tribe of Levi and been related to the high priest Aaron. By reason of his birth from Mary, Jesus belonged to the tribe of Levi, while he was legally the Son of Joseph and therefore a descendant of David (and Judah). In Jesus' time, the Jews fervently hoped that there would be two Messiahs, one from the tribe of Levi who would be a priest, and one from the tribe of Judah who would be a king. However, it was God's plan that Jesus should combine in his own person both the priestly and the royal dignity. To what extent was St. Luke influenced by this idea? Whatever the answer to this question may be, the Christ he portrays is more a priest than a king; his Christ is the saviour of the poor, of the wretched, and of sinners.

^{38a}*" Behold, the handmaid of the Lord. May it be done to me according to your word."*

God's message had been delivered; Mary's inquiry had been satisfied and the sign had been offered. Now an answer was awaited. God inspires longing; he draws and solicits; he overcomes all opposition and convinces, but he never forces anyone. Mary must give her consent by her own free decision.

Mary learned God's will from the angel's message. She obeyed this will as a " handmaid of the Lord." God's will was everything with her. The story of salvation begins with Abraham's act of obedience. God told him: " ' Go, then, out of your native land . . . into the land which I shall show you. I want to make you a great people . . .' Abraham set out, as the Lord had commanded him " (Gen. 12:1-4). According to a Jewish tradition, God called Abraham—" Abraham." And Abraham replied: " Behold, I am your servant." In the beginning, as at the end, God's offer of salvation demands obedience. Christ's entry into the world was accompanied by an act of obedience (Heb. 10:5-7), and it was by obedience that he left it (Phil. 2:8). Man can attain salvation only if he obeys (Mt. 7:21).

^{38b}*And he went away from her.*

Once Mary had signified her assent, the angel's mission was accomplished. We are not told how Jesus' conception took place. Silence is the only fitting attitude in the face of the greatest of all events. St. John sums up what St. Luke omits with the words: "And the Word was made Flesh" (Jn. 1:14).

A Meeting (1:39-56)

The meeting between Mary and Elizabeth brings the story of John's annunciation into contact with that of Jesus, while at the same time forming a bridge between the account of Jesus' birth and the account of his childhood. Her encounter with Elizabeth gave Mary a deeper insight into the message she received from God (1:39-45). Full of gratitude, she sings a hymn of praise for God's saving providence (1:46-55). A brief reference to Mary's stay with Elizabeth and her return home (1:56) closes this section which is enveloped in a wonderful atmosphere of fervor and religious warmth.

TWO MOTHERS WHO ARE FULL OF GRACE (1:39-45)

[39]*In those days, Mary rose up and journeyed hurriedly into the mountains, to a town of Judah.* [40]*She came into Zechariah's house and gave Elizabeth greeting.*

Mary's departure took place "in those days," soon after the annunciation. The way led from Nazareth to a town of Judah in the hill country bordered by the Negeb, the desert of Judah, and the Shephelah. According to an ancient tradition, the town occupied the site of the present-day Ain Karim, about four miles west of Jerusalem. The distance Mary had to travel would take from three to four days.

Mary went into the hill country "hurriedly." It was not an easy journey, and yet she went quickly. The great journeying which fills St. Luke's historical work, the gospel and the Acts, has now begun.

26

God's word journeys from heaven to earth, from Nazareth to Jerusalem, from Jerusalem to Judea and Samaria, to the ends of the earth—without regard for the difficulties involved, and always hurriedly.

At the end of her journey, Mary entered Zechariah's house and greeted Elizabeth. In this, too, she acted hurriedly; she greeted only Elizabeth to whom God had referred her; she greeted no one else on her way. She behaved like those whom Jesus would later send out with the injunction: " Greet no one on the way " (10:4). The infancy gospel gives us the basic outline of Jesus' future activity; and Jesus' activity is a model for the church's life.

⁴¹*It happened that, when Elizabeth heard Mary's greeting, the child leaped in her womb, and Elizabeth herself was filled with the Holy Spirit.*

Mary carried the Messiah in her womb. In the greeting she gave her, Elizabeth and, through her, John encountered the salvation the Messiah brings. " The child leaped in her womb." The child's natural movements became a sign of the joy which the encounter with the saviour inspired. Similarly, when the twins Esau and Jacob moved in Rebekah's womb, it had a deeper meaning: " The children pushed at one another in her womb. Then she said: ' If that is the way it is, why should I continue to live?' She went to the Lord to ask him, and the Lord answered her: ' These are two races in your womb, two opposing nations will spring from you. One will be more powerful than the other; the elder will be at the service of the younger ' " (Gen. 25:22f.).

Elizabeth was " filled with the Holy Spirit." As Mary entered the house and greeted Elizabeth, the blessings associated with the time of salvation were inaugurated. What happened at Pentecost happened also in Zechariah's house within the narrower compass of the infancy gospel: " In the last days, it will come to pass that

I will pour out my Spirit over all flesh . . . and your sons and daughters will prophesy " (Acts 2:17–21; Joel 3:1–5). The story of the infant church is a repetition of the infancy gospel.

⁴²And she cried out with a loud voice and said: " Blessed are you among women and blessed is the fruit of your womb. ⁴³How could this happen to me, that the mother of my Lord should come to me? ⁴⁴For see, when the voice of your greeting sounded in my ears, the child leaped in my womb for joy. ⁴⁵It is well for you, because you believed that what the Lord said to you would be fulfilled."

Filled with the Holy Spirit, Elizabeth speaks ecstatically. Stirred up by a divine influence, she adopts a solemn liturgical tone, like the Levites singing before the ark of the covenant (1 Chron. 16:4). She proclaims salvation as a servant of the Lord who has appeared in her house.

Speaking as a prophetess, Elizabeth takes up the words of praise the angel used and confirms them: " Blessed are you among women." Then she gives the reason for this blessing: " And blessed is the fruit of your womb." Mary is given a blessing because God had already filled her with all the blessings which are summed up in Christ (Eph. 1:3).

" How could this happen to me? " King David had used the same words when the ark of the covenant was about to be transferred to Jerusalem (2 Sam. 6:2–11). It seems that this text influenced St. Luke's account of the visitation. Mary is regarded as the New Testament ark of the covenant. In her womb she carries the Holy One, he who is God's self-revelation, the source of all blessing, the cause of all joy, and the center of the new worship. Mary's greeting found an answer when the child leaped in the womb. The joy of the messianic time of salvation was now at hand.

Elizabeth's song of praise ends with a phrase which contains a form of blessing for Mary: " It is well for you, because you believed." Mary became the mother of Jesus Christ because she gave

28

her consent in a spirit of faith and obedience. When the woman in the crowd blessed her with the words: " Blessed is the womb that bore you and the breasts you sucked," Jesus replied: " Yes, blessed are those who hear God's word and put it into practice " (11:27f.). The saving history of Israel begins with an act of faith; Abraham travels to an unknown land with his barren wife for the sole reason that God had called him and promised him a glorious posterity (Gen. 12:1–5). The saving history of the world begins in the same way with an act of faith; Mary believed God's message that she, a virgin, would give birth to the Messiah.

A Hymn of Praise (1:46–55)

As a result of the angel's message and the words of the inspired prophetess Elizabeth, and with the help of the scriptures whose term both of them had used, Mary realized what an extraordinary thing God had accomplished in her. Her " response " (a song sung in " response " to a reading from scripture) is a hymn which celebrates God's saving activity on behalf of her people which has now been brought to completion. The infant church celebrated God's marvels in similar hymns.

⁴⁶*And Mary said:*
  " My soul celebrates the Lord's greatness,
  ⁴⁷*and my spirit rejoices in God my saviour;*
  ⁴⁸*because he looked graciously upon the lowliness of his*
    handmaid.
  See, from now on all ages will bless me."

The depths of Mary's heart were penetrated with God's praise, and an eschatological messianic joy filled her soul and her spirit. God's saving actions inspired her worship which was characterized by joyful praise.

Mary counts herself among the lowly, the poor, and the insignificant to whom the prophets and the psalms repeatedly promise sal-

vation. Jesus adopts this promise as one of his beatitudes (Mt. 5:3).
" God is a God of the humble, a helper for the lowly, a support for
the weak, a protector for those who are rejected, a saviour for those
who are in despair " (Jdt. 9:11).

Mary's praises which Elizabeth inaugurated will never end. All
ages will raise their voices to bless her. The kingdom of the king
who is her child will never end; so, too, the king's mother will be
praised eternally.

> [49]" *He who is mighty has accomplished great things in me,*
> *and his name is holy;*
> [50]*his mercy lasts from age to age, for those who fear him."*

Might, holiness, and mercy are the most brilliant traits of the Old
Testament idea of God. There is a vital power in God whose force
is directed outwards in an effort aimed at making everything in the
world belong to God, and it is in this power that God shows he is
holy (Ezek. 20:41). A holy God, he is also merciful. He is a saviour
and a redeemer for the faithful remnant of Israel because he is God,
and not a human being. The great things God accomplishes in his
might are proof of his merciful love.

> [51]" *He has given proof of his might with his own arm,*
> *routing those who think proud thoughts in their hearts.*
> [52]*He has hurled those who wielded power from their thrones*
> *and raised up the lowly.*
> [53]*He has filled those who are hungry with good things*
> *and sent the rich away from him empty-handed."*

In these lines Mary expresses the experience of her own race. " The
Egyptians mistreated us; they tormented us and imposed a harsh
slavery on us. We cried out to the Lord, the God who is our Father.
The Lord listened to our cry and saw our torment, our labor, and
our distress. He brought us out of Egypt with a strong hand and an

outstretched arm, showing signs and wonders with awe-inspiring power. He brought us to this place and gave us this land, a land flowing with milk and honey " (Deut. 26:6–9).

Those who took pride in their wealth and their greatness came to a fall—Pharaoh at the exodus, the enemies of Israel in the days of the judges, and the powerful king of Babylon. Presumptuous reliance on one's own ability closes one's heart to God, and God closes himself to those whose hearts are closed.

> [54]" He espoused the cause of his servant Israel,
> in memory of his mercy,
> [55]as he told our fathers,
> Abraham and his posterity forever."

Mary's great hour is also the great hour of her people. In the opening lines of her hymn, she spoke of the blessings God had prepared for her, but now she speaks of the salvation which is dawning for her people. What was accomplished in Mary is also accomplished in God's church. Mary represents the people of God.

God's servant is the people of Israel (see Is. 41:8f.). The promise of salvation was made to Abraham and his posterity (Gen. 12:2). Abraham received the promise; Mary sees it fulfilled in herself; and the people of God will receive its benefits.

The hymn of praise chanted by Jesus' virginal mother takes up the hymn sung by a barren woman to whom God had granted a child. Samuel's mother Hannah sang: " My heart is jubilant in the Lord; my happiness in the Lord is beyond measure. Now I need no longer be silent in the presence of my detractors; I have good reason to rejoice in your aid. There is no one so exalted as the Lord. Besides you, there is no one else, no other god like our God . . . The bows of the mighty are broken, while those who are weak gird themselves with power. Those who have had enough must hire themselves out to buy bread, but the man who was hungry now has more than enough . . . He raises up the defenseless from the dust, and pulls the poor out of the mud. He gives them a seat next to the princes and shows them to a place of honor . . . He keeps a careful watch over the steps of his faithful, while the evil-doers are lost in the darkness. Man is incapable of winning victory by his own power " (1 Sam. 2:1-10). The " Magnificat " is not a reproduction of Hannah's hymn; both songs are inspired by God's actions in the history of salvation.

Mary's grateful reflections are expressed in the language of the Old Testament hymns. The sons of her people became her song, and her song becomes the song of the people of God. As the church looks back over the day in a spirit of meditation at vespers, she sings the " Magnificat."

MARY'S STAY AND HER JOURNEY HOME (1:56)

⁵⁶*Mary stayed with her about three months and then went back home.*

Mary stayed with Elizabeth about three months. She was probably no longer there when St. John the Baptist was born. He still belonged to the old era, while Jesus was part of the new era. John's birth took place during the time of the promise and it was only right that it should have been surrounded by all the signs of that time.

Mary spent the same length of time in Elizabeth's house as the ark of the covenant spent in Kiriath-jearim, but only about. St. Luke is writing about an historical event and he refuses to force the facts; he has no wish to represent something whose significance is primarily religious as the fulfillment of a prophetical event in the Old Testament. What he tells us about Mary is not invented; it is based on an historical fact which helps to explain God's word.

The fact that Mary returned to her own house shows that Joseph had not yet brought her to his home. Her secret was once more covered with a veil. The glory which shone from her had made itself felt only for a brief moment. It was in this way, too, that Jesus spent his childhood and his active life, and the same is true of the church.

Birth and Childhood (1:57—2:52)

The Child John (1:57–80)

THE JOY AT HIS BIRTH; HE IS GIVEN A NAME (1:57–66)

⁵⁷Elizabeth's time was up for her to give birth, and she bore a son. ⁵⁸And her neighbors and relatives heard that the Lord had given such great proof of his compassion for her, and they rejoiced with her.

John's birth was surrounded with joy. Elizabeth was delighted and all her relatives and neighbors with her. Their joy was prompted by the fact that a child had been born, and this of a mother who was regarded as barren and was already well on in years. As yet, such joy owed nothing to the thought that this birth marked a significant moment in salvation history.

The joy in their hearts overflowed in a song of praise to God: "The Lord had given such great proof of his compassion for her." Grateful recognition of God's compassionate dealings gives joy not only to those who have received God's mercy but also to those who recognize it and praise it.

⁵⁹And on the eighth day they came to circumcise the child, and they tried to call him by his father's name.

The rite of circumcision was performed eight days after a child's birth. This was prescribed in the law: "This is my covenant which

33

you must keep between me and you and your posterity. Every male child among you must be circumcised. This circumcision must be performed on your foreskins. This is to be the sign of the covenant between you and me. Every male child must be circumcised when it is eight days old " (Gen. 17:10ff.; see Lev. 12:3).

The imposition of a name was associated with the rite of circumcision (2:21). The right to decide on a name and give it to the child belonged to the father and mother, but the guests were also expected to help in choosing it (Ruth 4:17). It was assumed that the new-born child would be called Zechariah after his father, just as Tobit was called after his father (Tob. 1:1.9).

⁶⁰And his mother replied and said : " No. He is to be called John."
⁶¹And they said to her : " There is no one among your relatives who is called by this name." ⁶²But they made signs to his father, asking what he wanted him to be called.

Elizabeth chose the name John; her spirit of prophecy (1:41) had made God's will known to her. Her relatives, however, judged everything in the light of what had always been done. But now a new age was dawning, and Elizabeth had already perceived some hint of it. The Spirit chooses new paths which are not always easily traced. In the infant church, he would later descend even on the gentiles: " Then the faithful who practiced circumcision, who had come with Peter, were astonished that the grace of the Holy Spirit should be poured out over the gentiles too " (Acts 10:45). The Spirit does not always act according to men's plans; he often goes quite contrary to them.

⁶³And he asked for a small writing-tablet and wrote on it the words : " John is his name," and they were all amazed. ⁶⁴But immediately his lips and his tongue were loosed and he spoke, giving praise to God.

In those days, people wrote on wooden tablets covered with wax. Elizabeth and Zechariah agreed in their choice of a name. The decision seemed strange to their friends and they wondered. God's will and his command place those whom he chooses before the necessity of departing from the common norm. This was true of Abraham, Moses, and the prophets. And Christ's experience, what will that be when he preaches his new doctrine? "No one who has drunk mature wine wants young wine. He will say: 'The mature wine is better ' " (5:39).

The name given him revealed the secret of the new-born child's mission. His name meant: "God shows himself gracious." Zechariah's period of punishment was over; he had no further need of a sign. The first words which came from his lips and his tongue, when they were loosed, were a hymn of praise to God. In the Precursor's birth the time of salvation was announced—but still within a restricted radius. His birth set his father free to proclaim God's wonderful actions.

[65]*And fear came on all those who lived in the neighborhood, and all these events were discussed throughout the highlands of Judea.* [66]*All those who heard about them took them to heart and said: " What, then, will become of this child?" For God's hand was with him.*

The news of these extraordinary happenings spread from the small circle of relatives and neighbors of the priestly family all over the Judean highlands. The message of salvation is always intent on reaching a wider audience.

It is not enough in itself to experience saving events or hear about them. They must also be taken to heart. The man who hears about them must also come to terms with them interiorly. God's power and guidance were revealed in the child John. Anyone who took that to heart was bound to be amazed.

In his canticle, Zechariah interprets the period of saving history which has dawned with John. His song draws on the treasury of songs in existence in his day. God's Spirit enlightened Zechariah concerning the mission entrusted to his child and the future which dawned in him. He praises God with words which are old, but which convey a new message.

The first part of the canticle is an eschatological psalm which praises God for all that he has accomplished in salvation history (1:68–75). The second part is a nativity hymn which expresses congratulations for the child's birth and announces his mission (1:76–79).

> *67 And his father Zechariah was filled with the Holy Spirit and*
> *spoke in prophetic terms:*
> *68 " Praised be the Lord, the God of Israel.*
> *He has visited his people and brought them salvation.*
> *69 He has raised up a horn of salvation for us from the family of*
> *his servant David,*
> *70 as he promised through the mouths of his holy prophets from*
> *of old."*

Four of the five books of psalms end with the words: " Praised be the Lord, the God of Israel." All the psalms have as their theme God's actions in creation and in salvation history. The event which John's birth announced marked the completion and the crowning of all God's wonderful deeds. In a spirit of prophecy, Zechariah speaks of the future as if it was already present. The promises made by the prophets during the time of preparation which announced the coming of a messianic ruler and king from the family of David were about to be fulfilled.

> *71 " Deliverance from our enemies*
> *and from the hands of all those who hate us,*
> *72 to have mercy on our fathers*
> *and to remember his holy covenant."*

The Messiah was to deliver Israel from the power of its enemies and those who hated and oppressed it. The salvation God had accomplished on behalf of his people when he delivered them from oppression in Egypt was now about to be repeated in a far more wonderful way. The covenant God made with Abraham was now being fulfilled. The Messiah was the fulfillment of all the promises and institutions, of all the hopes and longings of the old covenant. Those who were already dead and lived in another world looked towards him, as do those who are alive now, and all those who have still to come. He is the central figure of all humanity.

> [73]" *Remember, too, the oath he swore to our father Abraham that he would enable us—*
> [74]*freed from fear and from the hands of our enemy—*
> [75]*to render service in holiness and justice before his face all our days."*

God said to Abraham: " I swear an oath by myself : ' Because you have done this and not refused me the sacrifice of your only son, I will bestow rich blessings on you. I will make your descendants as numerous as the stars of the heavens . . . And your descendants will gain control of their enemies' gates ' " (Gen. 22:16f.). Everything that binds a man to keep his word is predicated of God; he has given an assurance and a promise; he has made a covenant, and even sworn an oath.

Once Israel is rescued from the power of its enemies, it will be free to serve God. It will be able to offer service to God in his presence, so fulfilling the priestly mission it is bound to exercise among the nations. God told the people of Israel: " You are to be a kingdom of priests for me, and a holy people " (Ex. 19:6). The Messiah would provide the people of God with the opportunity and the freedom to worship God. But he also prescribed that this free opportunity was to be used to worship God in a way which is characteristic of the last stage of time (see Jn. 4:21-26).

Such service must be offered to God in holiness and justice. The essence of all religious behavior consists in surrender to God's will in a life of holiness. " Offer your thanks to God as a sacrifice; keep the vows you made to the Most High. Appeal to me when you are in distress and I will save you. This is the honor you must pay me " (Ps. 50:14f.).

> [76]"*And you, child, will be called a prophet of the Most High;*
> *you will go before the Lord's face,*
> *to prepare his way.*
> [77]*to give his people knowledge of salvation*
> *in the forgiveness of their sins,*
> [78a]*through the mercy of our God.*

John was God's prophet; he prepared the Lord's way. I am sending my messenger on ahead (Mal. 3:1). His is to be the voice of one who cries out: " Make a road through the desert " (Is. 40:3).

The Precursor prepared the way by means of the gift of the knowledge of salvation. The people of God come to know salvation because they experience its reality in practice. God makes it known to them by giving it to them (Ps. 98:2). Salvation is accomplished by the forgiveness of sins. The man whose sins are forgiven is delivered from a power which constrains him more than the hands of his enemies and those who hate him (1:71). The time of salvation for which John prepared the way was the time of God's mercy. God's activity in the revelation which marks the last stage of time is prompted by his merciful heart.

> [78b]" *By this means, the Rising Sun will visit us,*
> [79]*to give light to those who crouch in darkness and death's*
> *shadow,*
> *to direct our feet into the way of peace.*"

The Rising Sun, the Messiah, comes to us by God's mercy. He

brings redemption to man who is oppressed by the weight of sin and death. " The people who walked in darkness saw a powerful light; a brilliant light shone over those who lived in a land of darkness " (Is. 9:1).

The church recites Zechariah's hymn of praise each morning, as the darkness of the night is dispelled by the rising sun. It recites it also at the graveside; Christ, the rising sun, shines through the night of death. By his resurrection he overcame the power of sin and death, and inaugurated the restoration of all things in a new universe (Rev. 21:3f.).

JOHN'S CHILDHOOD (1:80)

80The child grew and became strong in spirit, and he lived in the desert until the day when he was manifested to Israel.

We are told of Samson: " The woman gave birth to a son and she called him Samson. The child grew up and the Lord blessed him. The Lord's spirit began to be active in him " (Judg. 13:24f.). St. Luke's picture of the Baptist as a young boy is painted with words taken from the scriptures. He does not say expressly that the Lord blessed him because all physical and spiritual growth is subject to the Lord's blessing, in Samson's case as in John's; both were men of God. They matured as their mission demanded.

St. John withdrew to the desert of Judah to prepare for the day when he would be presented before Israel and invested with his office. There, remote from all human contact, he equipped himself for his future mission in close union with God. The people of Israel expected the Messiah to appear from the desert; it was after their sojourn in the desert that they had captured the promised land. When the caves at Qumran were discovered together with the writings which describe the lives of those who lived there, it was thought that the mystery of the Baptist's stay in the desert could also be solved. However, it is doubtful whether he ever had any contact with the Qumran community, with whom, however, he shared his ardent expectation of the Messiah. It is hard to see how Zechariah who was a priest could have sent his son to a group of people who had gone into the desert in protest against the temple priesthood in Jerusalem.

St. John's whole life was determined by his mission. He was chosen from his mother's womb; he spent his life in the desert—clearly as a result of a divine inspiration—and he was invested with his office by God. All this took place in full view of the whole of Israel; the Messiah and his people filled John's life. God had chosen him to serve them.

Jesus' Birth (2:1-20)

BORN IN BETHLEHEM (2:1-7)

¹It happened in those days that an order went out from the emperor Augustus that the whole world was to be registered. ²This census was the first under Quirinius, the governor of Syria. ³And everybody went to be registered, each in his own town.

As an historian, St. Luke gives salvation history its proper place in world history. The Roman emperor Augustus (30 B.C.—14 A.D.) ruled over all the countries which made up the Roman empire all over the world. The inscription at Priene in Asia Minor (9 B.C.) extols the day of his birth, saying that he had " given the whole world a new aspect." In the year 27 B.C., the Senate conferred the honorary title " Sebastos " (" Augustus ") on the emperor. This involved a declaration that he was entitled to adoration. By God's providence, Augustus who ruled over the whole world was made to serve the true saviour of the world by his decree. This was the saviour who fulfills the hopes people expected Augustus to fulfill. The emperor had power to give people what they looked for within certain limits, but he could never fulfill all their desires.

Augustus ordered a census. This included two things: the registration of land and immovable property (land-register assessment), and a property valuation to assess taxes. The emperor's command was promulgated in Palestine by Quirinius, the governor of Syria. Herod the Great who was king of Palestine had to allow the census because he held his throne only by the emperor's favor. This was the first census made among the Jews, and it took place under Quirinius, the governor of Syria. Why does St. Luke tell us all this? Obviously because he wanted to make the date clear. At the same time, his remarks show that Palestine was no longer free, and everybody went to be registered. Records found in Egypt show that people who no longer lived in their native country had to go back to their home town. Wives were bound to appear with their husbands before the registering officer. Each one went to his own city where he owned property.

Joseph, therefore, left the town of Nazareth in Galilee and went to Judea, to the town of David which is called Bethlehem, because he was from the house and family of David, ⁵to be registered with Mary his espoused wife who was then pregnant.

Joseph went with Mary to Bethlehem. It is clear that he owned property there. In the time of the emperor Domitian, there were still farmers living at Bethlehem who were relatives of Jesus. David's descendants had owned land there. St. Luke calls the town "the town of David"; Joseph came from David's house and family. All these points have religious implications. The Messiah was to be born at Bethlehem; he was to come from the house of David, and he was to occupy his father's throne. The prophet Micah had foretold all this: "But you, Bethlehem, in the country of Ephrata, are certainly the least among the tribes of Judah. However, from you will go forth he who is to be the ruler of Israel. His origins are from the far distant past, from the days of old " (Mic. 5:1). God makes the history of the world serve salvation history. He subordinates Augustus' decree to his eternal plan of salvation.

Mary is referred to as Joseph's espoused wife. He had already taken her into his home; otherwise, by Galilean custom, she could never have traveled alone with him. She is described as his espoused wife because she was a virgin. Joseph had lived with her like a fiancé with his betrothed; they had not lived a married life. She was pregnant—at once a virgin and a mother-to-be. This expression of St. Luke's reveals the secret which was shrouded in mystery in the account of the annunciation.

⁶It happened that while they were there her time was up, so that she must give birth. ⁷And she gave birth to her son, her first-born, and wrapped him in swaddling clothes and laid him in a manger, because there was no room for them in the inn.

The account of the nativity is sober, straightforward, objective, and brief. " She gave birth to her son." Mary brought her Son into the world as a true mother. We are told of Elizabeth that she gave birth to " a " son (1:57), while Mary gave birth to " her " son. His virginal conception is implied in every syllable. He is her first-born. Does St. Luke mention this because Jesus was the first of many sons? The expression need not necessarily be explained in this way. An inscription on a fifth-century tomb in Egypt is sufficient proof of this. The text puts the following words in the mouth of a young woman, Arsinoe, who had died: " Fate brought my life to an end as I was in labor over my first-born son." Arsinoe's first-born son was also her only son. St. Luke chose this title because Jesus had all the obligations and the rights of a first-born son (2:23), and because he was the bearer of the promise.

For the first time Mary performed a mother's office for her son. She "wrapped him in swaddling clothes." New-born children were wrapped up tightly in clothes so that they could not move, in the belief that this would make their limbs grow straight. She "laid him in a manger," in a trough from which animals took their feed. The Lord whose coming was promised appears as a small, helpless child, lying in the manger in a stable.

PROCLAIMED BY THE HEAVENS (2:8–14)

⁸And there were shepherds staying in the same district in the open country keeping watch over their flocks by night.

Shepherds were a despised class. They were suspected of not being very particular about what was theirs and what belonged to others. For this reason they were excluded from giving evidence in court. Shepherds, tax collectors, and publicans, among others, were regarded as being unsuitable for the office of judge or as witnesses. It is those who are despised and of no account that God chooses. They are well qualified to receive the gift of revelation and salvation.

"Pasture" animals, in contrast to stall-fed animals, remained out on grass day and night from the feast of the Pasch until the autumn rains, that is, from March to November. In the evening they were driven into pens or sheepfolds as a protection against thieves and wild animals. The shepherds were responsible for looking after them and keeping them safe; they used erect huts of branches where they could rest at night, sheltered from bad weather. Keeping watch, as they did, shepherds were among those who observed what went on about them; they were always ready, at any hour of the day or night. This is exactly the attitude which is decisive in the last stage of time.

⁹Then an angel of the Lord came to them and the glory of the Lord

43

shone all about them, and they were very much afraid. ¹⁰And the angel said to them: " Do not be afraid. See, I make known to you a great joy which is about to come upon the whole people. ¹¹Today the saviour has been born for you, Christ the Lord, in the town of David. ¹²And this will be a sign for you; you will find a baby wrapped in swaddling clothes and lying in a manger."

The great moment in the history of the world which had dawned with the birth of Jesus was announced to the shepherds by God himself through his angel. The message the angel proclaimed to the shepherds was a message of joy and victory ("gospel "). This joy was not for the shepherds alone; it was to come upon the whole people. The shepherds were the first fruits in the harvest of joy the time of salvation brings; their joy was a spring from which flowed a stream of joy which would fill Israel and the whole world.

What was the content of this joyful message? Today the saviour has been born. It was to this " today " that all the promises looked forward. Today they were fulfilled. " Today the scripture is fulfilled " (4:21). The last stage of time, the time of fulfillment, has begun.

The child who was born was the saviour; he was the " Christ " and the " Lord ". The essence of the Christian profession of faith, " Jesus Christ [is] the Lord " (Phil. 2:11), comes from God himself through the mouth of an angel. From the very day of his birth, Jesus could claim such a profession of faith.

" In the town of David ": it is significant that Jesus' birthplace is not given its usual name Bethlehem; instead, it is given a name which underlines its exalted role in salvation history. Joseph left the town of Nazareth in Galilee and went to Judea, to the town of David which is called Bethlehem (2:4), that Jesus might be born in David's town. It was here that David had his home; and this was Joseph's home town because he came from the house and the family of David. Jesus is the " Son of David "; in him the promises were fulfilled which were mentioned at the annunciation (1:32f.).

44

The angel's announcement is so constructed that it recalls the inscription at Priene. Augustus, we are told there, was sent as a " saviour." He puts an end to all feuds; the birth of the emperor-god marked the inauguration of a message of joy for the world. The account of the declaration of the heir to the throne as being of age, and especially of the emperor's accession to the throne, is a consequence of this. A new era dawns. To the message of emperor worship, the New Testament opposes the unique gospel of the birth of Jesus. It speaks the language of its time because it is anxious to remain close to the people and in touch with reality.

The shepherds were given a sign by which they were to recognize the truth of the message; a baby wrapped in swaddling clothes, lying in a manger. These were the three signs by which they were to recognize the Lord Jesus Christ. All this was in stark contrast to what the Jews expected, and even to what the message itself told them. Could a helpless child be the saviour of the world? Could a child wrapped in swaddling clothes be the Messiah? Could the Lord be found lying in a manger? What St. Paul says of Christ crucified was true also of his birth : To the Jews he was a stumbling block, and to the gentiles, utter foolishness (1 Cor. 1 : 23). But " what seems foolishness in God is wiser than men; what appears weak in God is stronger than any human being " (1 Cor. 1 : 25).

[13]*And suddenly there was a multitude of the heavenly host with the angel, praising God and saying:* [14]*" Glory to God in the highest and on earth peace to the men who are the objects of his good pleasure."*

The angel's message was accompanied by a song of praise; a multitude of angels gathered round the one who had brought the good news. According to the ancients, the heavenly hosts were the multitude of stars, each of which describes its path and has a position assigned to it in the heavens, but the term also referred to the angels who moved the stars. The angels are God's court. God is often referred to as " Yahweh Sabaoth " (the " Lord of Hosts ").

45

The angels take an active part in the history of salvation (Heb. 1:14).

The angels' song is a messianic acclamation. It is not a wish, but a proclamation of God's saving activity; not a prayer, but a solemn and grateful act of homage. In two corresponding verses, we are told what Jesus' birth means in heaven and on earth, to God and to man. The fact that heaven and earth are affected by this birth means that its significance is universal. Jesus unites heaven and earth.

"Glory to God in the highest." God dwells in the highest heaven. In Jesus' birth God shows his own glory; he reveals his own divine being. Jesus is the perfect revelation of God, the radiance of the divine splendor (Heb. 1:3).

"Peace on earth to men who are the objects of his good pleasure." The earth is inhabited by men. For them the birth of this new-born child meant peace; Jesus is the prince of peace (Is. 9:5). Peace includes all God's saving blessings. It is an effect of the covenant God made with Israel which is renewed in Jesus (Is. 54:10). Peace means reconciliation, perfect joy; the message Jesus preaches is a " gospel of peace " (Eph. 6:15); he himself is this peace.

Peace is given to men because God has shown them his favor; they are the objects of his good pleasure. It is Jesus who assures men of God's good pleasure. It is only because of this that man is saved. The hymn the angels sing extends God's good pleasure to all men.

The angel in his solemn proclamation praised the new-born child as the Messiah-king; the song sung by the angel hosts praised him as the prince of peace, the saviour, and the priest who reconciles and unites heaven and earth. The child in the manger is the priest and the king of the time of salvation

The angels' song is related to the acclamations shouted by the people who accompanied Jesus on his entry into Jerusalem at the beginning of Holy Week. The people cried out: " Blessed be the king who is coming in the name of the Lord. Peace in heaven and glory on high " (19:38). His entry into Jerusalem where death and glorification awaited him would bring the work of salvation to an end; the peace and glory of heaven would be communicated to men. What began with Jesus' birth will be completed with his death. His entry into the world finds its full achievement in his entry into Jerusalem and in his entry into the world at his second coming. Bethlehem—Jerusalem—the world, these are the great stages of salvation history.

PROCLAIMED BY THE SHEPHERDS (2:15–20)

15And it happened that, as the angels went away from them into heaven, the shepherds spoke to one another: " Let us go to Bethlehem and see this message which has happened, which the Lord has made known to us." 16And they went quickly and found Mary and Joseph and the child lying in the manger.

The message spoken by God was not merely an abstract message; it was also an event—" the message which has happened." Once they had heard the news, the shepherds were to become eye-witnesses of the event. Like Mary, they " went quickly," to carry out God's command. The offer of salvation suffers no delay. Mankind had already begun to turn to the child in the manger. In Jesus is salvation, and he brings honor to God.

By God's guidance and with the aid of the sign given them, the shepherds found what they sought. It is God who guides men so that they find what they seek. The sight which met their eyes was " Mary and Joseph, and the child lying in the manger." Nothing else; they saw nothing concerning a virgin mother; none of the great things implied in what the angel had said about this child were visible. But, enlightened by God's revelation, they saw the child. The proof that God's revelation had become an historical reality stood before them in Mary and Joseph, and the child lying in the manger. The splendor of the Christmas gospel comes from the explanation God gives of the birth of Jesus which was an historical fact. But this splendor resides in the child who was born.

¹⁷When they had seen for themselves, they made known the message which had been given to them concerning this child. ¹⁸And all those who heard it wondered at what the shepherds told them. ¹⁹But Mary kept all these words in her heart, putting them all together.

Once they had seen, the shepherds made known. They became apostles and messengers. The content of their preaching was " the message which had been given to them concerning this child "— Jesus' birth as an event which had taken place in history, and the revelation they had received about this child. The preaching of the Christian message always takes this form. " I make known to you . . . the gospel . . . that Christ died for our sins, in keeping with the scriptures " (1 Cor. 15 : 1–5).

Not everyone was in a position to witness this event with their own eyes, but only the witnesses God had appointed beforehand. The others must hear the message from these witnesses. The result of hearing the shepherds was that people wondered. St. Luke remarks more frequently than any of the other evangelists that Jesus' words and actions made those who witnessed them wonder. The man who experiences God's revelation is forced to wonder. The man who is astonished when the divine revelation comes to him has not yet got faith; he is on the threshold of faith. He has received an impulse which can arouse faith, but can also give rise to doubts. The decision involved in faith is one which each person must make for himself.

The shepherds had news for Mary, too, concerning her child. Elizabeth had completed what the angel Gabriel told her, but now the shepherds added a new depth to this message. Not only was she astonished; she " kept all these words in her heart." She listened to the word the way God wants men to listen to it. Mary was constantly hearing new revelations concerning her child. The wealth which lies hidden in Christ's revelation can be conveyed only little by little. But these partial revelations are meant to be compared and put together. Mature faith fits the various pieces together and incorporates each new revelation into what is already known. Mary is the archetype of all those who receive the word in the right way; she is the archetype of faithful Christians and so of the church which receives Christ by faith and bears him in herself.

[20]*And the shepherds returned, glorifying God and praising him for all they had heard and seen, as had been told them.*

God chose the poorest of the poor, the shepherds who were keeping watch, and called them to hear the message of the saviour's birth. He made them eye-witnesses of the new-born Messiah, inspiring them and making them fit to make known the good news. Now he led them back once more to their everyday lives. They " returned." From that day forward, they glorified and praised God. In this passage we are reminded once more of the reason for the homage of praise and adoration which the shepherds offered to God: " All they had heard and seen, as had been told them." The saving event, together with the commentary God gives on it, is at the center of all Christian worship; it is these which lead Christians to give praise and glory to God.

The Child Is Given a Name; the Presentation (2:21–40)

All the prescriptions of the law were carefully observed regarding the child Jesus. He came "from a woman, becoming subject to the law" (Gal. 4:4). In complying with the subjection he owed to the law, his glory was revealed at the circumcision (2:21) and in the temple (2:22–39).

The road traveled by the child Jesus in his mother's womb led from

Nazareth, the small and insignificant village in Galilee where he was conceived, to Bethlehem, the town of David where he was born—in poverty and glory—and from there to Jerusalem, the city where he was "taken up" (9:51). This forms the climax of the infancy gospel. Jesus' public life will follow the same road from Galilee to Jerusalem where he died and was glorified.

John's greatness was celebrated in the prophetic words spoken by his father when his name was being chosen. Jesus, however, received still greater glory from the Holy Spirit who spoke through the prophet Simeon and the prophetess Anna. John was extolled in Zechariah's house; Jesus was extolled in the temple. Jesus is greater than John.

The Imposition of a Name (2:21)

²¹And when the eight days were up, so that he must be circumcised, he was given the name which the angel gave him before he was conceived in his mother's womb.

As a result of his birth, Jesus became a member of Joseph's family and of the people of Israel. He shared the lot of the poor and the humble and he was subject to the obligations of the law. The law of Moses governed every day, week, and year of a Jew's life. " When the eight days were up " and he had to be circumcised, the obligations of the law affected Jesus for the first time; " he became obedient " (Phil. 2:8).

St. Luke does not say explicitly that Jesus was circumcised. The law and compliance with it formed the framework within which Jesus' whole life took place. He " fulfilled " the law; in other words, its meaning was fully accomplished in him. His obedience marked the dawn of a new era.

The imposition of a name was associated with the rite of circumcision. God himself had chosen a name for this child. He was given the name the angel said he was to have. By means of the name he chose for him, God also gave Jesus his mission; God is a redeemer (saviour).

²²When the days of their purification were completed, according to the law of Moses, they brought him up to Jerusalem, to present him to the Lord, ²³as it is written in the law of the Lord: " Every male child which opens the womb must be regarded as being sacred to the Lord;" ²⁴and to bring the offering there, as it is prescribed in the law of the Lord, a pair of turtle doves or two young pigeons.

The law of purification prescribed that: " When a woman's time has come and she gives birth to a boy, she remains impure [that is, excluded from religious functions] for seven days. On the eighth day, his foreskin must be circumcised. Then she must still remain thirty-three days at home, the time during which her blood is purified. She must not touch anything sacred [that is, meat offered in sacrifice], or set foot in the sanctuary, until the days of purification are over " (Lev. 12 : 1–4).

A " purification " took place in Jesus' case, too. St. Luke says the time for their purification was completed. " Purifying " here means the same as " declaring sacred." The law prescribed for every first-born offspring: "Among the Israelites, the first offspring to come from the womb, whether of a human being or of an animal, belongs to me " (Ex. 13 : 12). This precept was intended to remind the Israelites how God had delivered them and led them out miraculously from the slavery of Egypt (Ex. 13 : 14.f).

The first-born of animals had to be offered in sacrifice, while a first-born male child had to be redeemed. The price was five shekels, which could be paid to any priest in the whole country. Mary offered the purification sacrifice. A yearling lamb was pre-scribed as a burnt offering, and a young pigeon or a turtle dove as an expiatory sacrifice. However, if a person could not afford a lamb, two turtle doves or two young pigeons had to be offered, one as a burnt offering and the other as an expiatory sacrifice. The offering Mary presented was the offering of the poor.

St. Luke does not say that, as a first-born son, Jesus was redeemed for the prescribed sum of money. He was brought to the temple to be presented there. This presentation would result in his being consecrated to God; it was a declaration that he belonged to God. Samuel's mother, Hannah, brought the child to whom she gave birth despite her apparent sterility to the temple and dedicated him to God's service (1 Sam. 1:28). Samuel was consecrated to the Lord, as was St. John the Baptist; but Jesus was consecrated to God to a greater extent than either of them. He was holy because he was born of a virgin by the power of the Holy Spirit (1:35). The presentation in the temple made known publicly what had previously been veiled in him.

THE TESTIMONY OF THE PROPHET (2:23–35)

[23]*And see, there was a man in Jerusalem by the name of Simeon, and this man was holy and God fearing; he waited for Israel to be consoled, and the Holy Spirit rested upon him;* [26]*and the Holy Spirit had told him that he would not see death before he had seen the Lord's anointed.*

At Bethlehem, the shepherds who had been instructed by an angel proclaimed the glory of the new-born child. In the temple at Jerusalem, Simeon and Anna, two prophetic figures enlightened by the Holy Spirit, bore witness to the child's significance for salvation in the same way. The piety of the Old Testament had borne a rich harvest in Simeon. The whole conduct of his life bore the impress of the law and of that wisdom which begins by fearing God. He waited for consolation to be given to Israel, that is, for the salvation the Messiah would bring; and he waited also for him who would bring it. Simeon excelled the other prophets in that he saw the Lord's anointed, the Messiah, before his death. The other prophets proclaimed his coming in the distant future; Simeon had the experience of seeing him present.

²⁷And in the Spirit he came to the temple; and while his parents were bringing in the child Jesus to do with him according to the customs of the law, ²⁸he took him in his arms and praised God.

By the impulsion and under the guidance of the Spirit, Simeon came to the temple at the very moment the child was being carried in. He recognized the Messiah as the law of the Old Testament was being fulfilled, and Jesus' parents heard the prophetic revelation he made concerning the child. Like the temple and its worship, the law and the revelation of the Old Testament pointed to the Messiah and led to him.

Simeon stood there, enlightened by the Holy Spirit and filled with faith; and as he held the child in his arms, he gave praise to God. He was a symbol of all those who have received salvation.

²⁹And he said :
" Now, Master, let your servant go,
according to your word, in peace;
³⁰for my eyes have seen your salvation,
³¹which you have prepared in the sight of the nations :
³²A light of revelation for the gentiles
and for the glory of Israel your people."

The prophet's canticle of praise reëchoes the revelation he had received concerning the child he held in his embrace. This is his life's evensong and it is filled with the words and the spirit of the book of Isaiah. Those who are enlightened by the Holy Spirit are able to interpret scripture properly and discern saving events.

God is a master, while man is his servant. Life is a hard drudgery. Simeon may have had to put up with a lot of difficulties because of his ardent longing for the Messiah. Death will now bring all this to an end. The yearning of a lifetime has been satisfied. " It is well for the eyes which see what you see " (10 : 23).

Jesus is the Messiah whom God sent to save the world. Isaiah's words were fulfilled: " The Lord has shown his holy arm before all the nations. All the ends of the earth see our God's salvation " (Is. 52 : 10).

The child Simeon holds in his arms is a light to enlighten the nations. The prophecy is now fulfilled: " I am appointing you as a light for the gentiles; the salvation I give reaches to the ends of the earth " (Is. 49 : 6; see 42 : 6). Jesus, the light, is rising in Israel, but this light shines beyond the confines of Israel on to the gentile nations. How could Jesus fail to bring glory to Israel? It is from Israel that God's splendor shines forth through Jesus, and the gentiles glorify Israel.

³³And his father and mother wondered at what was said about him.

Although they were closer to Jesus than any other human being, Mary and Joseph, too, needed God's revealing word to enable them to grasp all that God had done for man in Jesus—" The good news of the inexhaustible riches of Christ " (Eph. 3 : 8). No matter how much we may grasp of the fullness of this mystery, there is always more which escapes our understanding.

³⁴And Simeon blessed them and said to Mary his mother:
" See, this child is appointed for the fall
and the resurrection of many in Israel,
and as a sign which will be contradicted.
³⁵And as for you, your soul, too, a sword will pierce,
so that the thoughts of many hearts will be revealed."

By means of their child Mary and Joseph had brought Simeon a blessing. In return, the aging prophet gives them a blessing.

The words of the prophet are fulfilled in Jesus. " He will be an

54

occasion of sanctification for you, a stumbling block, a stone to trip you up, for both the houses of Israel; he will be a snare and a trap for the inhabitants of Jerusalem. Many of them trip and fall; many are crushed, entangled and taken prisoner " (Is. 8 : 14). But those other words of Isaiah also apply to Jesus. " I am laying down a stone in Sion, a stone which has been tested, a priceless cornerstone (keystone), which is firmly set. The man who trusts in him will not be shaken " (Is. 28 : 16). It was Jesus' destiny, appointed by God himself, that the whole of Israel should take its stand for or against him. The man who is united with him will be raised up; he will be saved. The man who opposes him is destined for a fall. It is not because Israel is God's chosen people that it receives salvation and is redeemed; it is because it has taken its stand for Jesus. It is not the fact that he belonged to Israel that will save a man at the judgment, but the fact that he chose in favor of the sign appointed by God. Only those who decide for Jesus really belong to the people of God.

Jesus is a sign because he presents mankind with a choice. He will be " contradicted." Contradiction is something which fills the whole history of revelation. St. Stephen concludes his summary of salvation history with the words : " You stubborn people, your hearts and ears are still uncircumcised. You are always striving against the Holy Spirit, just like your fathers. There is no difference between you " (Acts 7 : 51). Opposition to God culminated in opposition to Jesus.

Jesus' mother is associated with her son's fate. The opposition Jesus encounters will affect her also. " Your soul a sword will pierce." She will feel sorrow in her soul because of the hostility Jesus endures.

The opposition Jesus encountered and the agony Mary experienced were ordained by God that " the thoughts of many hearts might be revealed." The choice which must be made for or against the sign which is Jesus uncovers the hidden depths of a man's heart. In Jesus, with whom Mary is associated, judgment is passed on mankind. "Judgment consists in this: the light came into the world and men loved the darkness more than the light, because their actions were evil" (Jn. 3:19).

The Testimony of the Prophetess (2:36–38)

³⁶And there was a prophetess there, Anna the daughter of Phanuel from the tribe of Asher. She was well on in years, as she had lived seven years with her husband after her maidenhood. ³⁷By this time, she had been eighty-four years a widow. She never left the temple and she served [God] with fasting and prayers day and night.

A prophetess adds her testimony to that of the prophet. Israel had always had women who were gifted with the Spirit; rabbinical theology put their number at seven. It had been foretold for the last stage of time that Israel's sons and daughters would then prophesy (Joel 3:2; Acts 2:18). After the grave warning of judgment, contradiction, and the sword, comes a message of comfort and consolation which raises the hearts of those who hear it. The names of the prophetess and her ancestors symbolize salvation and a blessing. Anna means "God is gracious," while Phanuel means "God is light"; Asher in its turn signifies "happiness." Names such as these are not without significance.

Like Simeon, Anna had been formed by the piety of the Old Testament. Her advanced age was an indication of the divine favor which rested on her. At the time of her encounter with Jesus she was more than one hundred years old. She led a well-ordered and chaste life. She was still a virgin when she contracted a marriage which lasted seven years. Her chaste widowhood had by this time lasted twelves times as long (eighty-four years). Her life was taken up with praying, visiting the temple, and fasting—day and night. She lived for God alone, "in God's sight."

³⁸She came on the scene at that very moment and she gave praise to God and she spoke about him to all those who waited for the deliverance of Jerusalem.

Anna is a witness of the temple's great moment of grace. In the child whom Mary had brought to the temple, she recognized the Messiah by the light of the Holy Spirit. She praised God in a way which was really a " response " (an answering acclamation of praise) to what Simeon had said. Again and again, she spoke about him to all those who waited for the redeemer, but the message she proclaimed was limited in its efficacy by their readiness to welcome it. The revealed word must be welcomed—like a guest.

Jesus is the " deliverance of Jerusalem." His entry into the temple marks the beginning of Jerusalem's liberation from all its enemies (1:68, 71) by God's merciful favor. Jesus himself is its deliverance (24:21). The salvation which was promised for the last stage of time is present in him.

The infancy gospel reaches its climax in this passage. In the temple at Jerusalem, both the characteristic aspects of Jesus' life were present—contradiction and acceptance in a spirit of faith, judgment and salvation, fall and resurrection. Malachi's prophecy was fulfilled: " The Lord for whom you yearn will come suddenly to his temple; see, the angel of the covenant whose presence you long for is coming now " (Mal. 3:1). This day is a day of judgment: " But who can endure the day on which he comes; who will be able to hold his ground, when he appears? He will be like the refiner's fire, like the fuller's lye " (Mal. 3:2). On the other hand, this day is also a day of salvation: " Then will the sacrifice Judah and Jerusalem offer be acceptable to the Lord, as in the days of old and the years long past " (Mal. 3:4).

THE RETURN TO NAZARETH (2:39)

[39]*And when they had done everything according to the law of the Lord, they went back to Galilee, to their own city.*

Jesus was made known at Jerusalem while he showed his obedience in fulfilling the law. His obedience will raise him to such a degree of glory and exaltation that the universe will profess its faith that Jesus Christ is the Lord (Phil. 2:11).

After his hour of glory in Jerusalem, Jesus was once more brought back to their own town in Galilee. He relinquished God's glory to return once more to the town which remained without any claim to fame or renown in the history of Israel. Nazareth was *their* town, the town of Mary and Joseph. Jesus followed his mother, and she followed her husband, Joseph. Once more he gives proof of his obedience. He " came from a woman " (Gal. 4:4). Jesus' whole life consisted in emptying himself of his divine glory by a life of obedience.

40The child grew and became strong in the Spirit; he was filled with wisdom, and God's grace rested on him.

A complete personality has need of physical and spiritual strength; it needs wisdom and God's favor. Jesus grew in physical strength and became strong in the Spirit. Wisdom took full possession of him, so that he was able to live a life in keeping with God's will. We are told also of John the Baptist as a child that he grew in body and spirit (1:80), but there is no mention of God's wisdom or grace. Jesus is greater than John—even in his childhood.

A Twelve-Year-Old Boy (2:41–52)

His Self-Revelation in the Temple (2:41–50)

41And his parents used to go up to Jerusalem each year at the Passover.

The religious atmosphere in which Jesus grew up was the piety of the Old Testament. Pilgrimages to the temple in Jerusalem were an essential part of this. " You must celebrate a feast in my honor three times a year. You must observe the feast of unleavened bread. . . . And then the feast of the harvest of the first fruits of your grain . . . At the end of the year, you must celebrate the feast of the ingathering, when you bring your produce home from the fields. Three times a year every male Israelite must appear before the Lord, the Almighty " (Ex. 23:14-17). The holy family did more than the law demanded; Mary also made the pilgrimage, although it was not obligatory for women. They took their twelve-year-old son to accustom him to observing the law. According to the instructions of the scribes, a boy was bound to all the precepts of the law when he had completed his thirteenth year.

⁴²And when he was twelve years old and they were making the pilgrimage according to the custom of the feast, ⁴³they finished their stay there. But, as they were returning home, the boy Jesus remained behind in Jerusalem, and his parents did not notice it. ⁴⁴They presumed he was with their traveling companions, and they went a day's journey before looking for him among their relatives and acquaintances. ⁴⁵And when they did not find him, they went back to Jerusalem to look for him.

The feast of unleavened bread, the passover feast, lasted seven days. No one could leave until after the second festive day, so that the holy family remained for the entire week of the feast. When the feast was over, Mary and Joseph left for home. In those days, people traveled in caravans. These were composed of groups of relatives and friends, but were not exclusive. Traveling together like this made for security and allowed a certain freedom of movement. The boy Jesus evaded the careful attention with which his mother surrounded him as a child. He " remained behind in Jerusalem."

When the first day's journey was over and the various families came together, Jesus was missing. The search began. Why Jesus decided to behave as he did is a mystery.

⁴⁶And it happened that after three days they found him there in the temple sitting among the doctors of the law, listening to them and asking them questions. ⁴⁷And all those who heard him were amazed at his intelligence and the answers he gave.

The halls of the outer court of the temple were used by the doctors of the law for their lectures. The method of teaching these rabbis followed consisted in holding disputations. According to an old Jewish proverb, a person acquired knowledge of the law by means of the investigations of one's equals and the disputes of one's pupils. Jesus was probably sitting on the floor among these teachers. His grasp of the law was confirmed by the amazement the doctors expressed. Later, he himself would be addressed as a teacher and regarded as such (10:25). His opponents would ask themselves in amazement: " How does this man know the scriptures when he was never a pupil of the rabbis? " (Jn. 7:15). Jesus proclaimed God's will in a new and direct way. He made the claim to be the only one who could teach God's will. His teaching office was already revealed to some extent in this incident in the temple at Jerusalem.

⁴⁸When they saw this, they were upset and his mother said to him : " Child, why have you treated us like this? See, your father and I have been looking for you in anguish."

Mary's words are a spontaneous expression of the sorrow and grief she felt during the long search. She is a real mother. The straightforward, down-to-earth narrative makes no effort to conceal her human feelings.

Jesus had acted in an independent way. Mary addresses him as

" child," but he was already a boy. Previously he had never done anything without his parents' knowledge, but now they had been forced to search for him in anguish. There is something mysterious about him. Why have you treated us like this? As a child, Jesus' relationship to his father and mother seemed to be just like that of any other child. But when the child began to grow up, various enigmas appeared. Jesus' assertion of his own consciousness resulted in his parents being upset.

*49And he said to them : " Why did you search for me? Did you not know that I must be in the place which is my Father's? "
50And they did not understand the word he spoke to them.*

The first words which the gospels record as coming from Jesus' mouth imply a deep consciousness of his own being. His words affirm Jesus' independence of all human limitations; he transcends all human understanding. These words indicate here and now the course his life will take. It is not without reason that the story of the finding in the temple stands between the two verses in which Jesus' wisdom is mentioned (2:40, 52). He possesses wisdom because he is the Son of God.

Jesus must be in the place which is his Father's. The temple is dedicated to God; Jesus calls God his " Father." The word used in his mother tongue was " *Abba*." This is what small children called their earthly fathers. Later in life, he would retain this form of address. He made this childlike term the foundation of his relationship to his Father, and of that of his disciples. Jesus' life was dominated by an imperative ("I must") which inspired his activity (4:43) and led him through his passion and death to glory (9:22; 17:25). This was rooted in God's will as it was expressed in scripture, and Jesus followed this unconditionally.

Jesus must be in the place which is his Father's. Although he was speaking about the temple, he did not mention it by name. With his coming, the old temple had lost its role in salvation history. Its place is taken by a new temple. This temple exists wherever the fellowship of Father and Son is realized. Jerusalem occupied a prominent place in Jesus' life. This was the city towards which he turned his face, and it was there that his Father's will was accomplished in his death and exaltation. This resulted in the rise of a new Jerusalem and a new temple (see Rev. 21:2f.).

Mary and Joseph "did not understand the word he spoke to them." The veil which concealed the abyss of God's love and of Christ's love was drawn aside only gradually. We are in constant need of the message revelation brings; we need to reflect continuously on Jesus and the events of our salvation. No matter how familiar we are with Jesus, there will always be some obscurity, some mystery surrounding him. The only access we can ever have to him on this earth is by faith, and faith is not vision.

AT HOME IN NAZARETH (2:51–52)

[51]*And he journeyed down with them and came to Nazareth and was subject to them. And his mother kept all these words in her heart.*

Nazareth was the town to which Jesus descended at the annunciation and on this occasion which marked the beginning of his work in a certain sense.

He was "subject to them"—to Mary and Joseph. Jesus proved the genuine character of his divine sonship by being obedient. By his obedience, he prepared himself for his glorification after his baptism. "We testify to these facts and also the Holy Spirit whom God gave to those who obey him" (Acts 5:32).

The events of the infancy gospel have all the characteristics which are to be found in a true revelation. No one except Jesus' mother could have witnessed the events of the infancy gospel. She was a reliable witness because she kept all these events in her heart. St. Luke did not forget her when he investigated everything from the beginning.

⁵²And Jesus increased in wisdom, as he grew up, and in favor with God and men.

What St. Luke says in this verse is confirmed by the terms he chooses. Jesus grew from babyhood (2:12, 16) to childhood (2:17, 27, 40) and to boyhood (2:43). The most important thing now is the growth he achieved in wisdom. He enjoyed the favor not only of God but also of his fellow men. As he grew up, Jesus took his place in society.

St. Luke speaks of Jesus in terms taken from the story of Samuel (1 Sam. 2:26). It was with Samuel that the prophets began: "All the prophets who have delivered themselves of their message from the time of Samuel until now proclaimed this day [Jesus' day] " (Acts 3:24; see 13:20). Jesus had to wait until the process of growth achieved its purpose; then he would make his debut as a prophet who surpassed all the other prophets in wisdom and knowledge of God.

St. John's Mission;
Jesus Begins His Public Life (3:1—4:13)

The Baptist (3:1–20)

THE BEGINNING OF THE BAPTIST'S MISSION (3:1–6)

¹In the fifteenth year of the reign of the emperor Tiberius, when Pontius Pilate was governor in Judea and Herod was prince in Galilee, while his brother Philip was prince of Iturea and Trachonitis and Lysanias prince of Abilene, ²ᵃunder the high priests Annas and Caiaphas.

Salvation history takes place in this world and on the level of its realities without being identical with what we call world history. St. John's appearance in the wilderness formed the immediate introduction to the saving event which was inaugurated with the coming of the Messiah. St. Luke indicates the date in biblical style. A sacred history is about to begin. Hosea indicates the moment in which the Lord's word came to him in similar terms: "The word of the Lord which came to Hosea the son of Beeri in the days of Uzziah" (Hos. 1:1).

The time of salvation began in the fifteenth year of the reign of the Roman emperor Tiberius (14–37 A.D.). That was the year 28/29 A.D. according to our calendar. Pontius Pilate was procurator (governor) of Judea (26–36), Herod Antipas was tetrarch (prince) of Galilee (4 B.C.–39 A.D.), while his brother Philip was prince of Iturea and Trachonitis, to the north and east of the sea of Galilee (4 B.C.–34 A.D.). Lysanias was ruler of Abilene in the Lebanon, north west of Damascus (he died between 28 and 37 A.D.). The accuracy of St. Luke's references is proved by inscriptions and ancient historians. He mentions the religious authorities together with the secular powers. The reigning high priest was Joseph Caiaphas (18–36 A.D.), but his father-in-law Annas who had been deposed from that office still enjoyed high esteem.

If St. Luke's only purpose had been to give us the date, one reference would have been enough. The first one he gives is the clearest and most precise. The other references are intended to give us an idea of the political and social situation, the intellectual world in which God's promise was fulfilled. Palestine was under foreign domination. The Roman emperor Tiberius was the supreme authority in the land. Roman historians rightly or wrongly portray him as a suspicious, cruel, and pleasure-seeking tyrant. The southern part of the country, Judea and Samaria, had been a Roman province since 6 B.C. The Jews condemned the administration of the governor Pontius Pilate as ruthless and unyielding. He was accused of engaging in corruption, violence, and theft, as well as criminal and insulting behavior, of repeated executions without trial, and of interminable and unbearable cruelty. The rulers from the family of Herod were Idumeans; they ruled only by favor of Rome. The two high priests had succeeded in retaining their office for many years by skillful diplomacy. The widespread cry for a king from David's family was easy to understand. Zechariah, among others, hoped for " deliverance from the hands of all those who hate us " (1:71).

The geographical area involved in St. Luke's references represents the territory in which Jesus was active; sacred history took place in Galilee and Judea, and north of the sea of Galilee. These areas had been incorporated more or less completely into the Roman empire. Jesus himself rarely went beyond the boundaries of Palestine but through his apostles the message he preached would one day overrun the entire world subject to the emperor Tiberius. The Acts of the Apostles continue the story of the triumphal progress of God's word which began in Palestine.

²ᵇ*God's word came to John, the son of Zechariah, in the desert,* ³*and he went all about the country around the Jordan, proclaiming a baptism of repentance for the remission of sins.*

" God's word came to John," just as it had come to the prophets of the Old Testament. The Baptist resumed the work of the great men God had sent in previous centuries. He was linked with the tradition of the prophets, not with fanatical apocalyptics, " humanistic " teachers of wisdom, pharisaic legalists, rabbinical traditionalists or the zealots who waited for the kingdom. God's word summoned him and pressed him into its service. It remained the ruling force in his life. " The Lord's word came to me: ' Before I formed you in your mother's womb, I chose you . . . You must say whatever I command you . . . I am putting my words into your mouth; today, I am giving you power over nations and kingdoms, to build up and

65

to pull down, to destroy and to lay in ruins, to build up and to plant ' " (Jer. 1 : 4–10).

St. John's field of activity was confined to the country about the Jordan, the territory comprising the southern reaches of the river. Here he wandered about, preaching. It was a small area; Jesus, on the other hand, would preach throughout Palestine. Later, the apostles would bring God's word beyond Palestine all over the world. The area covered by the word was growing.

John the Baptist was a herald; he went before his lord, crying out what must be done. The message he proclaimed was a baptism of repentance for the remission of sins. Repentance is an essential requisite. By this a man turns to God, recognizing his existence and his will. At the same time, he turns from his sins and condemns them; this is the essence of repentance.

John's baptism was by immersion in the Jordan. It was accompanied by the confession of one's sins, and was intended to set a seal on a person's determination to repent. At the same time, it assured those who received it of God's forgiveness. Consequently, it could save them from the judgment to come. The man who received this baptism was fitted and well prepared to be a member of the new eschatological people of God. It was presupposed, of course, that his repentance was genuine and that it led to a real change in his way of life. The message St. John proclaimed in this way was something new and extraordinary; what had been so long awaited was now at hand. God takes the promises he makes seriously.

⁴As it is written in the book of the sayings of the prophet Isaiah: " The voice of one crying out in the desert: ' Prepare the Lord's way, make his paths straight. ⁵Every gorge must be filled and every mountain and hill leveled; what is crooked must be made straight, and the rough roads made smooth, ⁶and all flesh will see God's salvation '."

The prophet Isaiah saw a glorious procession marching through the desert. The Lord God marched at the head of his people, leading them home from Babylon. A voice was raised in the desert through which the way led, summoning those who heard it to prepare a royal highway. This message which was addressed originally to the exiles on their return is now given a new interpretation. John is the voice crying out in the desert. The Lord—the Messiah—is coming, and his people with him. The preparation of a way is thought of in moral and religious terms; it involves repentance, turning to God, a baptism of repentance for the forgiveness of sins. This, surely, is a gigantic task—building a road through a desert. This is what conversion of heart means.

" All flesh will see God's salvation." The time of salvation was at hand. God offers it to all flesh, all mankind. Simeon's prophetic assertion was about to be fulfilled—a light to enlighten the gentiles (2:32). As the Precursor and a preacher of repentance, the Baptist's mission was directed to all ages. Repentance must prepare the way for the salvation God offers us.

THE BAPTIST'S WORDS (3:7–17)

[7]He used to say to the crowds of people who went out to be baptized by him: " Brood of vipers, who warned you that you could escape from the wrath which is coming? [8a]Bring forth worthy fruits of repentance."

It is hard for a man to bring about a real change in his life. To avoid having to do this, he will often take refuge in rites and ceremonies, under the protection of a community which is regarded as being holy, and so postpone the decision to a later date. People still sought refuge in sacred rites. They came in droves to the desert and asked to be baptized. They had themselves immersed in the river, but that was all. They did not change their lives. The Baptist reproached them: " Brood of vipers "—children of the devil! The

67

way they lived showed they were doing the devil's work, which is sin. Baptism is good, but it must lead to a different way of life.

8b *" Do not start telling yourselves: ' We have Abraham for our father.' I tell you, God can raise up children to Abraham from these stones."*

The Baptist's hearers were tempted to seek refuge in an assurance of salvation based on membership of the chosen people. They told themselves that even if one is a sinner who refuses to believe in God or obey him, he will have a share in the everlasting kingdom because he has Abraham for his ancestor. God cannot go back on the promises he made to Abraham and his descendants. They only fool themselves. God is true to his promise, but a new kind of descent from Abraham is coming into being, a relationship which is no longer based on consanguinity, but on God's intervention whereby he raises up and creates sons for Abraham. God has the power to raise up children to Abraham out of the stones that litter the desert.

9 *" The axe already lies at the root of the tree. Any tree which does not produce good fruit will be cut down and cast into the fire."*

Time is short; repentance allows of no postponement. The axe is already at the root of the tree which must be cut down. In the next instant it will be lifted up only to swing down—and the tree will be toppled. The Baptist proclaimed that this was the last moment before the Lord's coming and before his judgment.

The judgment is the harvest time; it is then the crops are gathered in. The harvest time is also a time of decision. The tree which does not produce good fruit is chopped down and burned. God's judgment which is imminent will gather up the fruits a man has produced in his life. The man who has nothing to show will incur a sentence of condemnation in the fire of hell.

"And the crowds questioned him, saying: " What must we do?"
"He answered them with the words: " The man who has two coats
should give one to the man who has none; and the man who has
food should also share it."

True repentance invariably prompts the question: What must we
do? This question shows the sincerity of a man's repentance. The
actions which show that a person has amended his life and is truly
repentant are acts of simple charity, sharing what one has with
another. " The man who has two coats should give one to the man
who has none . . ." St. John does not ask his hearers to give up
their only coat. He does not credit them with heroic virtue; he
simply expects compassion and active love for one's neighbor, a
social conscience.

"Even tax collectors came to be baptized, and they said to him:
" Master, what must we do?" "He said to them : " Do not exact
more than is laid down for you."

The tax collectors personified avaricious love of money and dis-
honesty. They were traitors to their own people who were often in
the employ of a foreign power. The way to salvation was open to
them, too; they were not " written off." They took the Baptist's call
to repentance seriously and were prepared to change their lives.
They had the essential attitude.

St. John does not ask them to give up their positions as tax
collectors. But they must not enrich themselves fraudulently. The
law allowed them a certain commission on the taxes prescribed by
the state. Therefore, they must not exact more than is allowed
them. Later, Jesus himself adopted the same attitude as John in his
dealings with the tax collector Zacchaeus.

"The soldiers also questioned him, saying : " What must we do,

69

we also? " And he said to them : " Do no violence to anyone; do not be extortionate, and be satisfied with your pay."

The soldiers were probably mercenaries from the army of Herod Antipas. Military service was forbidden to Jews. Consequently, these mercenaries must have been gentiles. The Precursor's influence extended beyond the confines of Israel. The soldiers' question presupposes an element of amazement: "And we also? " The old exclusiveness had been overcome. "All flesh will see God's salvation."

The sins which soldiers were exposed to were robbery with violence, extortion by means of false accusations, and abuse of their power. Greed was the root cause of these activities. Such excesses had to be renounced. Contentment with their lawfully earned pay must replace their lust for wealth.

Despite the imminence of God's rigorous judgment, the Baptist demands nothing extraordinary. No one is told to give up his profession, not even tax collectors or the soldiers. The Baptist does not even prescribe special practices of asceticism. This is in keeping with the words of the prophet: " With what present shall I draw near to the Lord, bowing before God on high? Shall I approach him with a burnt offering, with calves which are only a year old? Does the Lord take pleasure in a thousand rams? In innumerable streams of oil? Shall I sacrifice my first-born son for my sins, offering the offspring of my body for my soul's atonement? You have been told what is right and what the Lord demands of you: Do only what is right; practice charity and walk in humility with your God " (Mic. 6: 6–8).

[15]*The people were full of expectation, and they all asked themselves in their hearts about John, whether he might not be the Messiah.*

The people expected that the Messiah would come soon, and the Baptist's preaching strengthened their hope. The conviction was

gaining ground that John was the Christ. Certain groups repre-
s‹ ..ted the Baptist as the saviour sent by God. In the infancy gospel,
St. Luke deliberately underlines the correct relationship between
John and Jesus, as it was willed by God. John is great, but Jesus is
greater; John is a prophet and the Precursor, but Jesus is the Son of
God; he rules on David's throne forever.

¹⁶*He answered, saying to them all : " I am baptizing you with
water, but there is one coming who is stronger than I; I am not
worthy even to untie the straps of his sandals. He will baptize you
with the Holy Spirit and with fire."*

" Jesus is stronger." The Baptist realizes that he is unworthy even
to perform the most menial service for him. Slaves had to undo the
thongs of their masters' sandals; this was considered to be beneath
the dignity of a free man. What is Jesus compared to John?

Jesus' strength is indicated by what he does. John baptized with
water, but Jesus would baptize with the Holy Spirit and with fire.
To those who were prepared to do penance, the Messiah brought
the Holy Spirit in overflowing measure, that Spirit who was promised for the last stage of time. To those who refused to do
penance, he brought a sentence of destruction by fire. Jesus accomplishes God's judgment which results in salvation or condemnation.
John's baptism was a baptism with water. His work was a preparation for the final event; it was not the final event itself.

¹⁷*" In his hand is a winnowing shovel, to sweep his threshing floor
clean and gather the wheat into his granary, burning the chaff
with a fire which never burns out."*

When they had finished threshing and the corn lay mixed with the
chaff on the threshing floor, the Palestinian farmers used toss it in
the wind with a shovel. The grains of corn which were heavier fell
to the ground, while the chaff was borne away with the wind. In

this way, the threshing floor was swept clean and the chaff was separated from the grain which could then be taken to the granary, while the chaff was burned. The Messiah came to give judgment; he separates the good from the bad, admitting the good into God's kingdom and giving over those who are wicked to the everlasting fire of hell. He already has his winnowing shovel in his hand. It is this " here and now," which marks this period as the last stage of time, that gives St. John's preaching an importance beyond that of any of the prophets.

THE END OF THE BAPTIST'S MISSION (3:18–20)

¹⁸He gave these and many other warnings, and so he proclaimed the good news to the people.

St. Luke's account of the Baptist's activity is only a summary. The warnings he had for the people really formed part of the good news. John prepared the way for the eschatological salvation the people yearned for. Consequently, his message was a message of joy. The story of John's ministry marks the beginning of the gospel.

¹⁹But Prince Herod, when he was reproached by him because of his brother's wife and all the crimes he had committed, ²⁰crowned everything by shutting John in prison.

Even in the presence of the tyrannical rulers of the country, John proclaimed the message of God's judgment and refused to be silenced. Herod Antipas had violated the laws of marriage; he was guilty of numerous crimes, and had put more than one prophet to death (see Mk. 6:17f.). In his life's work, as in the fate he met, the Baptist summed up all the prophets had achieved and suffered, and surpassed them.

John's imprisonment marked the end of his work. The voice in the desert was silenced, confined to the fortress of Machaerus. The Baptist made his exit, while Jesus made his entrance. The time of the promise was at an end; the time of fulfillment had come. Between the Baptist and Jesus there was a profound division on the level of salvation history. " The law and the prophets lasted until John; from that time forward the kingdom of God is proclaimed " (16:16). " John baptized with water, but you will be baptized with the Holy Spirit " (Acts 1:5; 11:16). John's voice must continue to be heard in the church; it prepares for Jesus' coming at the end of time, which is still in the future.

Jesus Is Invested with His Office (3:21—4:13)

JESUS' BAPTISM (3:21-22)

²¹*It happened that when all the people were being baptized and Jesus, too, had been baptized and was praying, heaven opened* ²²*and the Holy Spirit came down upon him in visible form like a dove, and a voice sounded from heaven : " You are my Son. I have begotten you today."*

Jesus' baptism is mentioned only in passing; it remains in the background. The story is dominated by the divine proclamation concerning him, and by his glorification. The theophany which occurred after Jesus' baptism was preceded by three different incidents in which he lowered himself. He was just one of all the people who came to be baptized, one among many. He received a baptism of repentance for the remission of sins as if he were a sinner. He prayed as men pray when they are in need of help. The baptism of repentance and prayer prepare a man to receive the Spirit. The Father who is in heaven will give the Holy Spirit to those who ask him (11:13).

Jesus' lowering of himself in three ways is followed by a threefold glorification. Heaven opened above him. Heaven was closed, but the Jews expected that it would open at the last stage of time (Is. 64:1). Jesus is the place where God appears on earth; he is the Bethel of the New Testament (see Jn. 1:51). It was there that the gates of heaven opened and God appeared to Jacob (Gen. 28:17).

The Holy Spirit came down on Jesus. He descended in the visible form of a dove. In St. Luke's account, what happened at the Jordan was something which could be observed. The dove plays an important part in religious thought. God's Spirit hovered over the waters as the work of creation began. The image is adapted from a dove hovering over its young. God's voice is frequently compared to the cooing of a dove. When a symbol was needed for the soul, the life-giving element in man, a dove was an obvious choice, and it is also used as a symbol of wisdom. From this moment God's Spirit accomplished his messianic mission in Jesus, that mission which involved a new creation and brought revelation, life, and wisdom to men.

Jesus possessed the Spirit as one who was conceived by him (1:35). Yet, he will receive the Spirit from the Father when he has been raised to God's right hand (Acts 2:33); indeed, he is still receiving him. The Spirit was not given to him piece by piece; it was only that the great moments of his life constantly provoked a further blossoming of the Spirit he already possessed. And it is God who determines this development.

The divine voice proclaims that Jesus is God's Son. He was already this as a result of his conception by the Spirit (1:32. 35). After his resurrection, he was solemnly announced as such by the apostles (Acts 13:33).

THE NEW ADAM (3:23–38)

[23]*As he began his work, Jesus was about thirty years old, and people thought he was the son of Joseph.*

Jesus was endowed from on high with all that was necessary for his messianic office, but he also possessed the human qualifications which he needed for his mission; these he received on earth. At the beginning of his public life he was about thirty years of age. It was at the age of thirty that a priest was qualified to serve God (Num. 4:3), that Joseph was chosen by the Egyptians for his high office (Gen. 41:46), that David was raised to the throne (2 Sam. 5:4), and that Ezekiel was called to be a prophet (Ezek. 1:1). As he entered on his messianic office, which involved being a king, a priest, and a prophet all at once, Jesus had attained the necessary age. The time of growing and becoming stronger was over.

For the sublime office he was now undertaking Jesus had to be descended from the right ancestry; he needed a family tree. This was supplied by Joseph, his " legal " father. Jesus' virginal conception remained a secret. God endowed Jesus with everything he needed, so that no one could have any reason for taking offense at him.

[24]*the son of Joseph, son of Heli, son of Matthat, son of Levi, son of Melchi, son of Jannai, son of Joseph,* [25]*son of Mattathias, son of Amos, son of Nahum, son of Esli, son of Naggai,* [26]*son of Maath, son of Mattathias, son of Semein, son of Josech, son of Joda,* [27]*son of Joanan, son of Rhesa, son of Zerubbabel, son of Shealtiel, son of Neri,* [28]*son of Melchi, son of Addi, son of Cosam, son of Elmadam, son of Er,* [29]*son of Joshua, son of Eliezer, son of Jorim, son of Matthat, son of Levi,* [30]*son of Simeon, son of Judah, son of Joseph, son of Jonam, son of Eliakim,* [31]*son of Melea, son of Menna, son of Mattatha, son of Nathan, son of David,* [32]*son of Jesse, son of Obed, son of Boaz, son of Sala, son of Nahshon,* [33]*son of Amminadab, son of Admin, son of Arni, son of Hezron, son of Perez, son of Judah,* [34]*son of Jacob, son of Isaac, son of Abraham, son of Terah, son of Nahor,* [35]*son of Serug, son of Reu, son of Peleg, son of Eber, son of Shelah,* [36]*son of Cainan, son of Arphaxad, son of Shem, son of*

Noah, son of Lamech, [37]son of Methuselah, son of Enoch, son of Jared, son of Mahalaleel, son of Cainan, [38]son of Enos, son of Seth, son of Adam, son of God.

Unlike Matthew, Luke is not content merely to trace Christ's lineage back to Abraham; he traces it back to Adam and his origin from God. Jesus is the Messiah the Jews awaited, but he is also the saviour of the world. He is related not only to David and Abraham (Mt. 1:1) but also to Adam. In him the promises made to Abraham and David are fulfilled, but he is also the ancestor from whom springs a new race of men.

Luke's genealogy is made up of eleven groups of seven members each; from Jesus to Zerubbabel and from Shealtiel to David there are three groups of seven each; from David to Isaac there are two groups, and from Abraham to Adam there are three groups once more. The various periods are marked off by crucial moments in salvation history, the Babylonian captivity, the period of the kings, God's choice of Israel, and creation. First to be mentioned in each group are God, Enos, Shelah, Abraham, Admin, David, Joseph, Joshua, Shealtiel, Mattathias, and Joseph. Jesus marks the beginning of a new group, the twelfth. According to the apocalyptic division of time into twelve weeks, the last period of time begins with the world's twelfth week. Jesus inaugurates the last stage of time. To us, such interpretations may seem to be merely playing with words, but in antiquity people regarded them as expressing profound truths. We are interested in what these truths express, not in the way people arrived at their content.

JESUS IS TEMPTED (4:1–13)

[1]*Full of the Holy Spirit, Jesus returned to the Jordan once more and was led in the Spirit into the desert, [2]where he was tempted forty days by the devil.*

Jesus is " full of the Spirit." He possesses the Spirit, not merely in a certain " measure " (Jn. 3:34) like the prophets, but in all his fullness. All his journeying and activity is accomplished in obedience to the Spirit and in virtue of the power the Holy Spirit arouses in him. His baptism and the temptations are closely interrelated.

In the Spirit, Jesus was " led into the desert." There, in the uninhabited reaches of the wilderness, nothing stood between him and God. He sought peace in prayer (5:16), as well as solitary communion with his Father.

In St. Luke's account, Jesus is not driven out into the desert, as St. Mark puts it (1:12); on the contrary, he goes himself. He is not led by the Spirit, he allows himself to be guided in the Spirit. The way in which the Spirit worked in Jesus was different from that in which he worked in the Judges, for example; in Othniel (Judg. 3:10), Gideon (6:34), or Jephthah (11:29). In their case, the Spirit came upon them and equipped them to perform some great deed. When this was done, he left them. With Jesus it was different. He is not carried away by the Spirit; on the contrary, the Spirit is at his disposal.

Jesus' stay in the desert lasted forty days, and during that time he was tempted by the devil. The three temptations St. Luke describes are intended as illustrations of this mysterious and uninterrupted struggle with the enemy. Jesus proclaims God's rule and inaugurates it; this means that the enemy of God's rule is provoked to do his utmost.

²*And he ate nothing during those days, and when they were over he was hungry. ³The devil said to him: " If you are the Son of God, tell this stone to turn into bread." ⁴Jesus answered him: " It is written: ' Man does not live by bread alone '."*

Possessed by the fullness of the Spirit, Jesus went without food or drink, and after his forty days fast he was hungry. The devil took advantage of his hunger to tempt him. Calumniator that he is, the devil wished to destroy the good relations which existed between Jesus and God. This is his usual plan. The tempter took up the words God himself had used at Jesus' baptism: " You are the Son of God." You have unlimited power; with a single word you can satisfy your hunger.

Jesus' reply made it clear where the temptation lay: " Man does not live by bread alone." The sole purpose of man's existence is not to preserve his earthly life or keep it safe. The words Jesus quotes from scripture come from the book of Deuteronomy (8:3). These were the words Moses used to remind the people how God had provided for them miraculously in the desert: " He brought you low and made you endure hunger. But then he fed you with manna, with the manna which you and your father knew nothing about, to show you that man does not live by bread alone. Man lives by everything that comes from God's lips [that is, everything that comes into being by God's word]." The hunger they had to suffer was meant to teach the people of God to trust him and obey him.

Jesus is God's Son; he enjoys the fullness of power. If his Father now allows him to feel hungry, it is because he wants to lead him to place his trust in him and obey. He does not want him to use the power he enjoys as the Son of God for his own personal advantage. Jesus is the Messiah, but he is also the suffering servant.

⁵And he led him up and showed him all the kingdoms of the world at once. ⁶And the devil said to him : " I will give you all this power and its glory. They have been made over to me and I give them to anyone I wish. ⁷If, then, you will adore me, it will be all yours." ⁸And Jesus answered, saying : " It is written : ' You shall adore the Lord your God and serve him only '."

The devil now adopts the role of the " prince of this world " (Jn. 12:31), the " god of this world " (2 Cor. 4:4); he is an anti-god. Yet, even in his presumption, he had to admit his dependence: "All this has been made over to me "—by God. He enjoys, not the fullness of power, but only the measure of power delegated to him.

In a single moment the tempter conjured up " all the kingdoms of the world " and their glory before Jesus' eyes. It was Satan's intention that Jesus should be completely alienated from God by the glory he displayed before him, although it was only an empty illusion. But Jesus confronted his tempter with the words of scripture : " You shall adore the Lord your God and serve him only " (Deut. 6:13). He came to establish God's rule. He is God's servant, not the devil's.

⁹*Then he led him to Jerusalem and stood him on the pinnacle of the temple and said to him: " If you are the Son of God, throw yourself down from here. ¹⁰For it is written: ' He commends you to your angels, that they may keep you safe,' ¹¹and: ' They will carry you in their hands, so that you will not strike your foot against a stone '." ¹²And Jesus said to him in answer: " It is said: ' You shall not tempt the Lord your God '."*

The pinnacle of the temple was probably a sort of balcony which jutted out from the exterior wall of the temple high over the street. That was where the devil brought Jesus. He wanted him to throw himself down, to test the divine protection promised him by God's word (Ps. 91 : 11). In this way he could be sure that God had chosen him and that he was the Son of God; he could experience the power he enjoyed from God and with him.

Jesus exposed what was implied in such presumption. It would mean tempting God. The purpose was to provoke God and force him to intervene on his behalf, by abusing his promise of protection. However, Jesus was determined to serve God, not to exercise authority over him; to obey him, not to make him subject to himself.

According to St. Luke, the temptation which occurred on the pinnacle of the temple in Jerusalem was the last. For Jesus, all roads led to Jerusalem; his face was turned towards that city (9:51). It was there that he died, there that he was glorified. There he lowered himself as God's true servant and was obedient to the point of death. And it was at Jerusalem that he would experience God's protection in the fullest sense; God raised him from the dead and brought him to glory. He did not demand God's protection or his glorification; he waited for them.

The result of each of the three temptations was the same; Jesus persevered in obedience. He was tempted in his role as the second Adam; just as the first Adam, too, had been tried by temptation. The first Adam failed the test; the second passed it victoriously. "As the many became sinners through the disobedience of one man [Adam] so, too, by the obedience of one [Christ] the many were justified " (Rom. 5 : 19).

Jesus' temptations continue to occur in his disciples (see 22 : 28ff.). Indeed, the church as a whole spends its life in the midst of these temptations. When his followers are tempted, Jesus is there to help them; he, too, endured temptation. And he shows us how temptation can be overcome, by means of scripture which is at once a profession of faith, a prayer, and a power; it is the " sword of the spirit " (Eph. 6 : 17).

[13]*And when the devil had finished all his temptations, he went away from him, until the appointed time.*

Jesus began his public life by overpowering the devil. During the time of salvation which Jesus introduced the devil was fettered. He was powerless until the appointed time came. Wherever Jesus is active, the devil is forced to give way. But it was only until the appointed time came that Satan stopped tempting Jesus. At the beginning of the passion, we read the words: " Satan entered Judas " (22 : 3). Jesus' enemies had him in their power because the power of darkness was being revealed (22 : 53). As long as his hour had not come, his enemy could not touch him. The ruler of this world nailed Jesus to the cross, but it was precisely by means of the death he accepted as God's obedient servant that Jesus overthrew Satan's rule.

¹⁴And Jesus returned to Galilee in the power of the Spirit.

It was in Galilee that he had been born; in Galilee that his preparation for his messianic office began. So, too, his messianic work began in Galilee. Now that he is about to accomplish his mission as the Messiah, he is once more guided by the Spirit.

THE GALILEAN MINISTRY (4:14—9:50)

Jesus Inaugurates His Mission (4:14—6:16)

The Beginning in Galilee (4:14—5:11)

IN GALILEE (4:14-15)

¹⁴*And Jesus returned to Galilee in the power of the Spirit; and a report went out all over the area about him.*

By the power of the Spirit, salvation sprang from the " Galilee of the gentiles," which the Jews despised so much. Jesus' activity in the power of the Spirit caused a feeling of amazement; it inspired a report which spread throughout the whole territory. The Spirit's work covers a wide area. When Jesus brings his mission which began in Galilee to its final accomplishment in Jerusalem, his disciples will set out in the power of the Spirit and the news of him will reach the whole world.

¹⁵*And he taught in their synagogues and was praised by everyone.*

The synagogues with their weekly meetings for prayer and the liturgy of the word were the obvious place for Jesus to teach. His teaching took the form of an explanation of scripture. The promises made by the prophets were now being fulfilled. When the apostles brought the word of God to the world at large, they followed Jesus' custom. They went first to the synagogues where they announced that the promises had been fulfilled (see Acts 13:16–41).

Wherever the news of Jesus penetrates, those who hear the news echo it with their praise of him. The whole world constitutes the sphere in which the news of him will be heard; everyone—in the fullest sense of the term—will give glory to him.

In Nazareth (4:16–30)

¹⁶And he came to Nazareth where he had been brought up and went into the synagogue on the sabbath day, according to his custom, and he stood up to read. ¹⁷The book of the prophet Isaiah was handed to him and, when he opened the book, he found the passage where it was written . . .

The beginning he made was marked by this insignificant town which was without faith. It was offended by the message he preached and tried to kill him. His beginning was a beginning from nothing, from faithlessness, sin, and rejection. And yet he began.

The religious service on the sabbath day consisted of prayers and readings from scripture. The books of the law (the Pentateuch) were read consecutively, but the choice of a passage from the prophetical writings was left to the reader. Every male Israelite had the right to perform this reading and to add an explanation or a word of exhortation. As an indication that he wanted to avail of this right, Jesus stood up. This was how the ritual surrounding the scripture reading began. St. Luke describes the ceremonial followed in great detail; Jesus accommodated himself perfectly to the prescribed ritual. Scripture contains God's word. Consequently, it is fitting that it should be treated reverently and in a religious manner.

The passage of scripture which came to hand was from the book of the prophet Isaiah. It was not by accident that Jesus came upon it; it was by the inspiration of the Holy Spirit with whom he had been anointed and in whose power he acted. Isaiah was the favorite prophet of those who waited for God's kingdom in Jesus' time. Mary sensed his relevance at the annunciation; Simeon was enlightened and inspired by him, and it was through him that the Baptist realized what his mission was. The Qumran community based their lives on his writings. Jesus, too, described his mission in words taken from him.

[18]" *The Spirit of the Lord is upon me, because he has anointed me; he has sent me to proclaim the good news to the poor, to announce their deliverance to those who are in prison, to tell the blind to have sight, to let those who are bowed low go free,* [19]*to proclaim a welcome year of the Lord."*

The words are taken from Is. 61:1f. Only one line is changed. " To let those who are bowed low go free " (Is. 58:6) replaces the words: " To heal the broken-hearted." This change gives the whole passage its articulation. The first and second lines describe how the bringer of salvation was endowed with the Spirit and given a commission by God, while the other lines deal with the work he was to accomplish. The first and the last lines correspond with one another, as do the two middle lines. The former speak of the good news and its proclamation, while the latter speak of the saviour's activity. The saviour accomplishes his task by his words and deeds; he is a redeemer and a herald of victory.

[20]*And he rolled up the book and gave it to the acolyte and sat down; and the eyes of all in the synagogue were fixed on him intently.* [21]*So he began to speak to them: " Today this passage of scripture is fulfilled in your hearing."*

The reading from scripture was followed by an instruction (Acts 13:15). This is summed up in one lapidary sentence with words

84

which are as impressive as they are forceful: " Today this passage of scripture is fulfilled." Jesus proclaimed the time of salvation and ushered it in. This is what is new and extraordinary about this moment. The hallowed customs of the Jews and the words of scripture which contained a promise were now fulfilled.

" In your hearing." It was only by listening to Jesus' message that a person could know that the time of salvation had begun and that the saviour was present. This could not be seen or experienced. The message of salvation demands faith, and faith comes by listening; it is an answer to a challenge.

The welcome " year of the Lord's favor " lasted as long as Jesus was on earth. It was to this that the men of old had looked forward, and it is to this that the church looks back. This is the center of history, the greatest of all God's great deeds. In the joy and glory of this " year," what Isaiah says about it proves inadequate: " To proclaim a year of the Lord's favor and a day of vengeance for our God " (Is. 61:2). The Messiah is first and foremost a bringer of salvation, not a judge who condemns.

22And they all bore testimony to him and wondered at the gracious words which came from his mouth. They said: " Is not this Joseph's son?"

Jesus had increased in favor with God and men (2:52). Now he stood before his hearers as one who had come to the end of his period of training and had been anointed with the Spirit. Now he had begun to fulfill his mission. God's favor was displayed to the full. They all bore him testimony that his words expressed God's graciousness and won the favor of men. " The graciousness of God our redeemer has appeared for all men " (Tit. 2:11). " God was with him " (Acts 10:38). That was the first impression, the immediate experience of those who knew Jesus.

However, Jesus' hearers took offense the very next moment: " Is not this Joseph's son?" His humanity was a stumbling block; his words represented a challenge and they were scandalized. They welcomed his message, but they rejected the saviour who brought the message because he was one of themselves and he offered no proof in support of his claim to be the saviour sent by God. However, his death would eventually prove to be the real stumbling block. In the same way, people took offense at the apostles, just as they still take offense at the church and at any human being who preaches a message from God.

23And he said to them: " I am sure you will quote the proverb at me: ' Physician, heal yourself. Do here in your own home town all we have heard of as having happened in Capernaum '." 24But he said: " I tell you truthfully, no prophet is welcome in his home town."

The people of Nazareth wanted a sign that Jesus was the saviour who had been promised. The demand for a sign makes its appearance once more. Men adopted a demanding attitude towards God; they called on him to prove his prophet's mission in the way they prescribed. God demands faith; he demands that we should accept what he has disposed and give it our assent. The people of Nazareth had no faith (Mk. 6:6).

25" In truth I tell you : there were many widows in Israel in the days of Elijah when the heavens were shut for three years and six months, and a great famine came upon the whole country. 26And Elijah was sent to none of these; he was sent to a widow in Sarepta in the territory of Sidon. 27And there were many lepers in Israel in the time of the prophet Elisha and none of them was cleansed except Naaman the Syrian."

A prophet does not act on his own initiative; he must be at God's disposal, because it is God who sends him. In the case of Elijah and Elisha, God decreed that their miraculous intervention should benefit, not their fellow countrymen, but foreigners and gentiles. The people of Nazareth had no legal claim to salvation simply because they were fellow townsmen of the saviour and were related to him by blood. Similarly, Israel as a whole could not lay claim to salvation because the Messiah came from their midst. Jesus proclaimed and established God's sovereignty, and God gives salvation to the men who are the objects of his good pleasure. Salvation is a grace.

Jesus preached the message of salvation to his own countrymen first of all; he addressed himself to others only when they had rejected him. As Paul and Barnabas told the Jews: " It must needs be that God's word should be preached to you first of all. But as you have rejected it and proved yourselves unworthy of eternal life, see, we will go to the gentiles " (Acts 13:46f.).

Jesus resumed the activity of the great prophets. The impression he made on the people is described in the words: " He is a prophet, powerful in word and deed before God and all the people " (24:19). In Jesus, God visited his people with the fullness of his grace, as he had done through the prophets. But Jesus met the same fate as they.

[28]*And all those in the synagogue were filled with anger when they heard this.* [29]*They jumped up and drove him out of the town and led him to the brow of the hill on which their town was built, to throw him down.* [30]*But he passed through the midst of them and went away.*

Anyone who claims to be a prophet must prove himself by signs and wonders (Deut. 13:2f.). Jesus offered no such proof, and so the people felt obliged to condemn him as a blasphemer and stone him to death. In the first stage of the punishment of a blasphemer, the chief witness pushed the guilty person backwards off the edge of a height. The whole gathering set themselves up to judge Jesus; they condemned him and were determined to carry out the sentence immediately. The incident made it clear that Jesus' mission to his own people would be frustrated. He was expelled from the community of his own people, condemned as a blasphemer, and put to death.

However, Jesus evaded the anger of his own countrymen. He did not work a miracle, but no one laid a hand on him. The hour of his death had not yet come. His life and death were at God's disposal. Even when he was put to death, that could not prevent his being raised from the dead; it could not prevent him from going to his Father, there to live and work forever.

He left Nazareth forever and took the road towards other parts of the country. The witnesses of the great things God accomplished in Jesus were strangers, not his own countrymen. God has power to raise up children to Abraham from the stones lying in the desert.

In Capernaum (4:31–44)

³¹*And he went down to Capernaum, a town in Galilee. And he taught there on the sabbath, *³²*and they were astonished at his teaching, because his words were pronounced with authority.*

Nazareth was built on a hill, while Capernaum was by the sea. So Jesus went down. When his home town where he had grown up rejected him, he chose another town, Capernaum, as his new home (Mt. 4:13). God's word went out from Galilee. It is not without reason that we are told Capernaum was a town of Galilee. It was in Galilee that Jesus gathered his first disciples together, appointing them as witnesses for his church. They were known as " Galileans " (Acts 2:7). God's plan of salvation achieves its purpose despite its rejection by men.

Jesus adopted the same method in Capernaum as in Nazareth. He taught in the synagogue during the service on the sabbath, interpreting scripture in a new sense by showing that the promises were now fulfilled.

[33]And in the synagogue there was a man who had a spirit of an unclean demon, and he cried out with a loud voice : " Stop ! What is there between us and you, Jesus of Nazareth? [34]Have you come to destroy us? I know who you are, God's Holy One."

Jesus accompanied his authoritative words with actions which were equally authoritative. The spirit which held the possessed man in its power was an evil spirit, a demon which made a man unclean. The picture of a possessed person which we get from the gospels is not identical with that of a person suffering from a mental disease. Evil spirits wield influence over human beings. In those who were possessed, we can see the ultimate consequence of what it meant for mankind to be without salvation.

The demon could not endure Jesus' presence and he forced the possessed man to cry out. The time of salvation which had now dawned spelt ruin for the evil spirits. Jesus is acknowledged as " God's Holy One " by an angel from heaven and by the demons from hell. And what of men? " God glorified him and gave him a name which is above every other name, so that at the name of Jesus every knee should bend of those who are in heaven, on earth, and under the earth, and every tongue should confess : Jesus Christ is the Lord " (Phil. 2 : 9ff.). This shows us how we are expected to acknowledge him.

[35]And Jesus threatened him and said : " Be silent and go out of him." And the devil threw him down in their midst and went out of him without doing him any harm.

The threatening words Jesus spoke were endowed with divine power. " The pillars of heaven tottered; they shook when he threatened them " (Job 26:11). The demons, too, were forced to bow before Jesus who pronounced a divine threat against them.

Jesus scorned the profession of faith made by the unclean spirit. " Faith which is not accompanied by good deeds is dead. But perhaps someone will say: ' You have faith while I have deeds to show. Show me your faith which has no deeds to prove it, and I will prove my faith to you by my deeds.' Do you believe that there is only one God? You do well—the demons, too, believe this, and tremble " (Jam. 2:17-20). Any profession of faith must be accompanied by a life which is pleasing to God and gives him praise.

The devil resisted but his blustering was powerless. He had no power to do harm. The term St. Luke uses is a medical one. He realizes clearly what Jesus has done. Jesus enjoyed superhuman powers, powers which surpassed even those of the demons. God worked through him; he was God's Holy One and through him God manifested himself as the Holy One, the completely Other, the All-Powerful.

³⁶*And amazement came upon them all and they talked among themselves, saying: " What kind of a word is this? That it should command the unclean spirits in authority and power, and they go out?" *³⁷*And his fame spread through every place in the district.*

Jesus' display of power inspired the onlookers with a feeling of awe and amazement. They talked among themselves. They were too overcome to speak aloud. Awe and a feeling of wonder act as a prelude to faith, as do amazement and dumbfoundedness. These are so many different ways in which a man may come to acknowledge God and his revelation.

The people wondered at Jesus' word. His word was authoritative and powerful; it was charged with God's authority. What kind of word is that? Such amazed questioning opens the way to knowledge of Jesus. His powerful word called forth an echo. His fame spread through every place in the district.

38But he rose to his feet and went out of the synagogue and entered Simon's house. Simon's mother-in-law had been taken ill with a severe fever. And they pleaded with him for her. 39He stood over her and threatened the fever, and it left her. She stood up immediately and waited on them at table.

The sick woman lay on a mat, and Jesus took up a position near her head, like a doctor. He stood over her. He threatened the fever with the same word he had addressed to the demon. His word was effective and she was cured there and then. Nothing could withstand God's word when Jesus spoke it.

The woman who had been cured waited on them at table. They had a celebration and Peter's mother-in-law served them. Her cure had been instantaneous and complete. In Capernaum, a town with which he had no connections, Jesus found a new home in Simon's house. " My mother and my brother are those who hear God's word and observe it " (8:21). Simon's house was like the synagogue. In both places, God's saving action was effected by Jesus' word. The word forced its way out of the synagogue into people's homes.

40But as the sun was going down, all those who had friends who were suffering from the most varied types of illness brought them to him. He laid his hand on each of them and cured them. 41The demons, too, went out of many of them crying aloud and saying: " You are the Son of God." He threatened them and would not let them speak because they knew he was the Christ.

God's grace was in Jesus in overflowing measure. He laid his hand on each of them. The cure was effected by the power of the Spirit which Jesus possessed. By laying his hands on them, he communicated this power to them and cured them. He laid his hand on each one. This was an example of his compassionate goodness. He welcomed everyone by welcoming each one individually.

The demons tried to resist Jesus. They hoped to reduce him to powerlessness by addressing him with his own name. In antiquity, it was believed that the devil could be cast out by pronouncing his name. Here they tried to use against Jesus the magical formula people used against them by invoking their names. Now that the time of salvation had come, a struggle flared up between Jesus and the demons, but Jesus was victorious despite the efforts of the diabolical powers.

42But when it was day, going out he went to a lonely hill; and the crowds looked for him and came to him and tried to detain him, so that he might not go away from them. 43And he told them: " I must bring the good news of God's kingdom to the other towns, too; this is what I was sent for." 44And he preached in the synagogues of Judea.

Jesus refused to be detained in Capernaum. He went: we are told this twice. St. Mark speaks of the prayer Jesus offered on the mountain (Mk. 1:35) and St. Luke, too, likes to mention the times Jesus prayed alone. Here, however, he omits any mention of it. Jesus went without delay. The word forces its way into the wide world—it refuses to be detained by anyone or anything.

His field of activity was expanding; from Nazareth to Capernaum and the surrounding district and from there to Judea which meant the whole of Palestine. His message resounded in all the synagogues, but only in the synagogues, among the people of Israel. It was only when he had been raised to glory that his field of activity was freed from all limitations.

The First Disciples (5:1–11)

1It happened, however, that the people pressed close upon him and

listened to God's word. He was standing by the Lake of Gennesaret
²and he saw two boats lying by the sea. The fishermen had gone
away from them and were washing their nets. ³He went on board
one of the boats which belonged to Simon and directed him to move
out a little from the land. Then he sat down and taught the crowds
from the boat.

As dawn broke over the Lake of Gennesaret, Jesus was standing on
the shore, preaching God's word. A great crowd surrounded him,
pressing close about him. Then he went on board one of the boats
which was moored by the shore. There he sat down like a teacher,
and taught the crowds who stood on the shore from the boat. God's
word attracts people in great crowds.

The boat Jesus boarded belonged to Simon. Simon was already
known to him; he had been in his house, and had cured his mother-
in-law. He had been Simon's guest. Now he laid claim to his host's
services for himself and the people. Simon, in his turn, knew Jesus;
he knew his power to heal and had felt the force of his word. If he
followed Jesus the moment he was called, we must remember this
had been carefully prepared; it was perfectly understandable. God's
powerful word takes hold of a man in a human way.

⁴When he had finished speaking, he said to Simon: " Move out
into the deep and cast your nets for a catch." ⁵And Simon answered
him saying: " Master, we have worked hard all night and caught
nothing; at your word, I will let out the net." ⁶When they had
done this, they took a great catch of fish. ⁷Their nets were on the
point of tearing and they signaled to their companions in the other
boat to come and help them. And they came, and they filled both
boats so that they were ready to sink.

Jesus addressed the command which he gave to Peter. This had the
effect of setting him apart from the crowd and also from the other
fishermen in the boat. He gave him precedence over the others. The

long trawling-net (four to five hundred yards of it) which was really an arrangement of three nets was meant for use in deep water. It took at least four men to let it out. Jesus' command put Peter's faith to the test. From a human point of view, which was the result of long experience, it was pointless to let out the nets at that time of the day. If they had caught nothing all night, which was the best time for fishing, there was no possibility whatever that they would catch anything at that time of the morning. God's calling and choice of a man demand a faith which is prepared to dispense with reason; he must " hope against hope " (Rom. 4:18). This was the kind of faith and hope Mary had, and this was how Abraham, too, believed.

Simon realized that Jesus' word was authoritative and that it had power to achieve what could not be accomplished by human means. " Master . . . at your word." The title " master " is peculiar to St. Luke's gospel. It is really a translation of the word rabbi or teacher. St. Luke obviously chose this term to show that Jesus is a teacher whose teaching is accompanied by power and authority to command.

The faith St. Peter showed in the master's word of command was not disappointed. They took so many fish that their nets were on the point of tearing with the weight. Peter had not asked for a sign; that was why he was given a sign which was in keeping with the life he led and with the vocation he received. It was something he could grasp easily. God dealt with him as he had dealt with Mary. Salvation demands faith, but God strengthens a person's faith by means of signs.

[8]*When Simon Peter saw this, he fell down at Jesus' knees, saying: " Go away from me, Lord. I am a sinful man."* [9]*Amazement and alarm had seized him and all those who were with him, at the catch they had made together.* [10a]*It was the same with James and John, Zebedee's sons, who were Simon's companions.*

In Jesus, Simon saw God revealing himself, an epiphany. He had personal experience of the miracle, the divine power which was at work in Jesus. The divine manifestation inspired him with a consciousness of his own sinfulness and unworthiness. He was overcome with the fear of the God who is so holy, so completely Other. The admiration he felt drew Simon to Jesus, but the consciousness of his sinfulness drove him away from him. He expressed the sublimity of the experience this miracle involved for him by addressing Jesus as " Lord."

St. Luke does not use the name " Simon " on its own; he accompanies it with the name " Peter," " the Rock." It was on this occasion, when Simon took his stand on faith in Jesus' word, that the foundation was laid for the promise: " You are Peter, that is, the Rock. On this Rock I will build my church " (Mt. 16:18); for the call to strengthen his brothers: " You, when you have come back, must strengthen your brothers " (22:32); and also for the pastoral charge he received (Jn. 21:15ff.). Simon's faith prepared him for his mission as the Rock.

Amazement and alarm at the unexpected catch of fish had also taken hold of Zebedee's two sons, James and John. St. Luke mentions only these, although there must have been at least one other there to handle the nets. Simon, James, and John were the three privileged apostles, the witnesses of Jesus' most secret revelations. They were present at the raising of the daughter of Jairus, the transfiguration, and the agony in the garden. They already shared St. Peter's trade as a fisherman; they were his partners, brothers of the same trade. Jesus founded a new type of fellowship on the basis of the old.

[10b]*And Jesus said to Simon: " Do not be afraid. From now on you will fish for men."* [11]*And they brought the boats to land and left everything and followed him.*

Jesus relieved Simon of his fear and gave him a commission. This was also what had happened when the angel made God's will known to Mary. An attitude of reverence in the presence of the God who is so holy is the foundation for any vocation by means of which God wishes to reveal his sanctity and his greatness.

Up to this time, Simon had hauled fish from the sea into his net; from now on, he was to haul men into God's kingdom. Jesus' word contained a promise and it also issued a call; one day it would endow Peter with authority. Jesus' call was effective. He called those whom he chose and made them what he chose. This was the way God had dealt with the prophets. Simon and James and John brought the boat to land and abandoned their calling as fishermen. They left everything—the boat, the nets, their father, and their home. They had discovered a new means of fulfillment. They followed Jesus as his disciples. From this time on they accompanied Jesus, just as the rabbi's disciples followed their teacher and assimilated his message, his way of life, and the teaching he gave. Their lives were now completely taken up with Jesus, with God's kingdom, and with fishing for men. Simon had experienced God's revelation of himself in Jesus; he had acknowledged that he was a sinner and he had received his vocation, the saving task he was to accomplish.

The beginnings of Jesus' activity in Galilee were consecrated to Simon Peter. Jesus' home town had rejected him, but on the borders of Galilee, at the Lake of Gennesaret, Peter welcomed him and followed him. The expulsion of the unclean spirit in the synagogue, the healing of Peter's mother-in-law, and the numerous miracles Jesus worked in the evening at his house were all crowned in the miraculous draught of fishes. The various spheres of Peter's life, the place where he prayed, where he lived with his family, and where he worked, were all relieved of their distress by God's saving actions. They were freed from the influence of the devil and from illness, misery, and failure. Now he was taken away from all his old surroundings; he was to be a fisher of men on behalf of God's kingdom, in the service of Jesus and his all-powerful word.

The Power of Jesus' Actions (5:12–39)

A LEPER IS CURED (5:12–16)

¹²It happened that while he was in a town there was a man there who was covered with leprosy. When he saw Jesus, he fell on his face and entreated him, saying: " Lord, if you wish, you can make me clean." ¹³And he stretched out his hand and touched him and said: " It is my wish. Be made clean! " And immediately his leprosy left him.

Jesus was working on one of the towns which he visited while he was going about preaching (4:44). The leper stood before him, although it was in a town which he should have avoided. " The leper who suffers from this illness must tear his clothes, let his hair fall loosely, and cover his upper lip. He must cry out: ' Unclean! Unclean! ' As long as he suffers from this malady he is unclean. He remains unclean and he must be segregated; he must stay outside the camp " (Lev. 13:45f.). He was covered with leprosy. This is something St. Luke notes as a doctor. Leprosy was incurable; anyone afflicted with it was as good as dead.

In his misery, the poor man had no thought for the law, for the fact that he was excluded from the company of his fellow men, or for the bitter realization that his condition was incurable. Jesus' power meant more to him than the law or death. He acknowledged his misery by falling to his knees, while his prayer expressed his trust. He professed his belief that God's power was at work in Jesus. " You can make me clean." He implored Jesus' pity: " If you wish . . ." Jesus was his life's hope. Jesus' wish meant life to him, a life in union with God and with his fellow men.

Jesus had pity on him. " He stretched out his hand and touched him." In showing his compassion in this way, he disregarded the law. By touching him, he took him into his company and into the company of men. At the same time, he granted him communion with God. He took up the words of entreaty the leper had used and fell in with his wishes. Jesus' wish cleansed him of his leprosy and restored him to union with God, giving him the right to share in the divine worship once more.

Jesus' word made the leper clean and declared him free from stain all at once. He possessed the power both of the prophet Elisha who cleansed Naaman the leper, and also of an Israelite priest who could pronounce a person cured. He had greater power than they; by his word alone, he made a person clean and pronounced him cured.

¹⁴And he commanded him to tell no one about it, saying: " Go, show yourself to the priest and offer the gift for your cleansing which Moses commanded as evidence for them." ¹⁵But the talk of him spread still further and great crowds gathered to listen to him and to be cured of their illnesses. ¹⁶But he used withdraw to lonely places, to pray.

Jesus did not work this miracle to gain credit for himself by a boastful show. " He went about doing good and healing those who were in the power of the devil, because God was with him " (Acts 10:38).

The law prescribed that a leper who had been cured should be certified clean by a priest (Lev. 13:40); such a person was also obliged to make an offering for his cleansing (Lev. 14:1–32). Jesus was anxious that the law should be observed; he himself obeyed the law. The priests must be given evidence to show that the time of salvation had come. The prophet Isaiah had foretold that the time of salvation would bring deliverance from sickness.

The news about Jesus and his saving activity traveled further afield. Jesus forbade people to speak about him, but the word spread nonetheless. The word contained in itself a power which impelled it to spread ever more widely. Over and over again it brought crowds of people together to listen to Jesus' saving message and to witness his actions.

Jesus used to seek solitude for prayer. His activity grew out of his communion of prayer with his Father. He was active because God was with him (Acts 10:38). The union of prayer he enjoyed with his Father implied a deeper underlying union.

JESUS FORGIVES SIN (5:17–26)

17It happened one day that he was teaching and there were Pharisees and scribes sitting there who had come from every village in Galilee and Judea and from Jerusalem, and the power of the Lord was there, so that he granted healing.

Jesus' activity consisted in teaching and healing; in this he enjoyed the support of God's power. The word about his teaching and healing had spread throughout Palestine, making its way into every· village. The Pharisees and scribes who lived all over the country took note of it. Even before Jesus himself made the journey from Galilee through Judea to Jerusalem the word about him had preceded him. The news alarmed those who would later put him to death, when he reached the end of his journey.

18And some men brought another man there who was paralysed, lying on a bed. They tried to bring him in and put him down before Jesus. 19Finding no means of bringing him in because of the people, they went up onto the roof and let him down through the tiles on his bed, in the middle in front of Jesus. 20And when he saw their faith, he said: "Man, your sins are forgiven you."

Jesus was teaching in a house. The crowd was so great that it was

99

impossible to enter the house by the door to reach Jesus. Therefore, they let the sick man down through a hole in the roof. Palestinian houses had a flat roof which could be removed (Mk. 2 : 4). St. Luke mentions tiles. He was thinking of a Greek house. It will be easier for us to understand him if we picture him in a world which we understand, in which we ourselves live. St. Luke pictures him living in a Greek world.

The paralytic's sins were forgiven him. Jesus' word which announced this also effected their remission; the Lord's power was at work in him. Jesus forgave the man his sins when he saw the faith of his companions. The men had placed all their hope in him; they believed that being near him would cure the paralytic. The individual human being was taken up into the community and the community shared his burden. They had expected that Jesus would cure his body; instead, he healed his soul. According to the Jewish point of view, a physical cure depended on the remission of guilt. Was St. Luke thinking of this? Jesus heals all man's ills, sickness and sin as well.

[21]*The scribes and Pharisees began to discuss among themselves: " Who is this fellow? He is blaspheming. Who can forgive sins except God alone? "*

The man who claims something which belongs to God alone blasphemes God. God alone has the right and the power to forgive sins. Sin is an offense against God, so that he alone has power to forgive it. Their reasoning was correct. But they should also have discussed whether or not God could give this power to someone else, to whom he gave all power.

" Who is this fellow? " Even the question implied rejection. The attitude taken up by the people of Nazareth was reproduced by the scribes and Pharisees. Only faith in his divine mission could enable a man to admit that Jesus had the power to forgive sins. External appearances should never be an obstacle to such faith.

²²But Jesus was aware of what they were thinking and he gave them their answer, saying: " What are you thinking in your hearts? ²³Which is easier to say : ' Your sins are forgiven you,' or : ' Stand up and walk '? ²⁴But that you may see that the Son of man has the power to forgive sins on earth "—he said to the paralytic—" I say to you, stand up, take your bed, and go home."

Jesus had the power to forgive sins. God had given him a share in his own power. He also had the power to read people's hearts; he knew what his enemies were thinking. This is a divine power. He had the power to heal the sick, which in this case was the more difficult feat because it was something which could be checked. If he could do what was more difficult, there was all the more reason why he should be able to do what was easier. He had the power to forgive sins because he was the Son of man to whom God gave all power. Jesus was a prophet; he could read people's hearts and he had power to heal the sick. But he was more than a prophet; he also had the power to forgive sins. He was the Son of man, to whom all power had been entrusted.

²⁵And he stood up before them immediately, took up what he had been lying on, and went home glorifying God. ²⁶And amazement seized them all and they gave glory to God; they were overcome with fear and said: " We have seen an unheard of event today."

The variety of actions performed by the man who had been cured showed the joy he felt at his recovery. In everything he did he gave glory to God. This was the whole purpose of Jesus' activity. " I have glorified you by accomplishing the work you gave me " (Jn. 17:4).

Those who witnessed the miracle were moved to the depths of their hearts. They were beside themselves, overcome with fear and astonishment. Their emotion, too, prompted them to give praise to

God. Today an unheard of event occurred. The time of salvation had come. But did the people realize this?

THE CALLING OF THE TAX COLLECTOR (5:27–39)

[27]After that he went out, and he saw a tax collector called Levi sitting in the customs house. And he said to him : " Follow me." [28]And he left everything and stood up and followed him.

St. Luke once more closes his account of Jesus' powerful actions by describing how he called a disciple to follow him. This time he called a tax collector. Tax gatherers were hated because they associated with gentiles and because of their greed and arbitrary behavior. They were regarded as public sinners who had to be avoided. Yet it was one of these that Jesus called to be his disciple; he called him away from the customs house and the practice of his unclean profession to follow him.

The power of Jesus' glance and the word by which he called him was so great that the tax collector left everything he had, all that he had formerly served and had been a slave to, and became a disciple of Jesus. Jesus' call brought about a radical change in his way of life.

[29]And Levi prepared a great feast for him in his house. And there was a great crowd of tax collectors and other sinners there who reclined at table with them. [30]And the Pharisees and their scribes complained to his disciples saying : " How is it that you eat and drink with tax collectors and sinners? " [31]And Jesus answered them, saying : " It is not those who are healthy that need a doctor; it is those who are sick. [32]I have not come to call those who are just; I have come to call sinners to repentance."

At the meeting point of the old and the new life, Levi held a great reception. The meal was in Jesus' honor. Jesus, his disciples, and Levi's friends were all invited, his partners in office and others who were friends of the tax collectors. The conversation which occurred during this meal showed what it means to be a disciple of Jesus. St. Luke loves to portray Jesus as a guest at a meal. In Greek literature deep discussions were described as " symposion " (" table-talk "). St. Luke, therefore, pictures Jesus in Greek surroundings. The gospels relate history, but at the same time they " de-histori-cize " the story they tell.

The Pharisees and the scribes who shared their spirit complained. According to them eating with sinners who were disreputable people and did not keep the law was in itself a violation of the precepts of the law. But Jesus followed a different course; his goal was not to excommunicate or boycott, but to heal what was sinful. That was why he found it necessary to have contact with sinners. Far from excluding them from salvation, he went in search of them.

The approach Jesus adopted was that of a doctor. If a doctor attended exclusively to those who were in good health and stayed away from those who were sick, he would have completely misun-derstood his vocation. It was the same with Jesus. His mission was to bring healing, the healing of physical infirmities and especially the healing which results from the remission of sins. Holiness for Jesus' disciples consists not in avoiding contact with sinners, but in offering salvation to all, whether saints or sinners. It is not anxious care for one's own salvation that matters, but the love which is prepared to risk everything.

[33]*But they said to him: " John's disciples fast rigorously and give themselves to prayer. The Pharisees, too, do the same, but your dis-ciples eat and drink." [34]And Jesus said to them: " Can you expect the friends of the bridegroom to fast while the bridegroom is still with them? [35]The days will come when the bridegroom is taken away from them; then they will fast, in those days."*

Jesus and his disciples were taking part in a feast, and the Pharisees and scribes found fault with them. Their first remarks were addressed to his disciples, but ultimately they concerned Jesus himself. Those who felt a responsibility for the sanctification of the people, John the Baptist and the Pharisees, kept a strict fast and devoted themselves to prayer. The two went together; days of fasting were also days of prayer; fasting recommends a person's prayer. Fasting brings a person low, and God listens to the prayer of those who are brought low and are in need. Why did Jesus' disciples not fast? Why did he not impose new fasts and prayers on them?

The Pharisees had failed to grasp the significance of the hour that had dawned. It was something completely new, and its life was governed by new rules. A marriage was taking place and this, surely, could not be the time to fast. No one would like to see the friends of the bridegroom, the wedding guests, compelled to fast. Jesus compared the time of salvation which had now come to a marriage, a time of joy. The welcome year of the Lord had come. Such an event called for a feast, not for a period of fasting.

Christ's disciples fasted in memory of their Lord's death. The bridegroom was taken away from them by force and they fasted as a sign of grief. Christ here gives a hint of his violent death. It is as the Messiah that he is the bridegroom. His disciples would fast in those days, not only on the day the bridegroom was taken away from them, but all during the time when he was no longer visibly with them, from the moment of his " taking up " into heaven until he comes again. This period of time is marked with the sign of joy; salvation has come already. But it is also a time of sorrow because Jesus is no longer present; we are waiting for him.

The attitude of Jesus' enemies indicated here and now that he would eventually be taken away from his disciples by force. His opponents criticized him first of all in their thoughts; then they criticized him openly for undermining traditional piety and discipline. It was clear that in time to come he would be removed by force. Their rejection of him began in their thoughts; it passed into words, and finally into action.

³⁶*He also told them a parable: " No one tears a piece from a new garment and patches an old garment with it. If a person does that, the new garment is torn and the piece will not suit the old garment.* ³⁷*No one pours new wine into old wine skins. If anyone does that, the new wine will burst the skins and flow out and the skins are destroyed.* ³⁸*New wine must be put in new wine skins.* ³⁹*And no one who has drunk old wine wants new wine. He will say: ' The old is mature '."*

What makes a person Jesus' disciple? The scribes and Pharisees were convinced that religious renewal could only consist in the strict avoidance of all that was unclean and in new religious practices, such as fasting and praying. The old observances must be supplemented with new prescriptions. Jesus had other ideas. Such methods were not suitable, as was clear in the parables of the pieces of cloth and the wine in the wine skins. It is a person's interior attitude which must be renewed, not merely his outward religious practices. The novelty of Jesus' message did not consist merely in pouring something new into a container which was already old, or in stitching a new patch on to an old garment. The time of salvation involved a completely new departure, something hitherto unheard of; it involved a new birth, and it presupposed repentance and a complete change of heart on man's part. There could be no question of merely adding new prescriptions and observances to the old.

It is difficult to accept what is new. No one who has been drinking old wine calls immediately for a recent vintage. This remark is not without a hint of sadness. Nothing is more difficult than true repentance, than an interior change of heart. What is old is more agreeable. Jesus demands that a person should renounce himself. They left everything—that is the sign of his true disciples.

The Power of Jesus' Word (6:1–19)

PLUCKING EARS OF CORN ON THE SABBATH (6:1–5)

¹It happened that he was walking through the cornfields on a sabbath day and his disciples plucked some ears of corn and ate them, after rubbing them in their hands. ²But some of the Pharisees said: " Why are you doing something which it is not lawful to do on the sabbath?"

The poor were allowed to pull some ears of corn in the fields when they were hungry. " If you are passing through your neighbor's cornfield, you may pull some ears of corn with your hand " (Deut. 23 : 26). The ears of corn were then rubbed between one's hands and the grains which fell out were eaten. Some of the Pharisees saw this and warned the disciples. According to their interpretation of the law, this was an infringement of the sabbath rest. Plucking corn was a form of harvesting and this was included among the twenty-nine principal forms of work, which were further divided into subordinate activities, all of which violated the sabbath. If this happened inadvertently, the person responsible was given a warning; in addition, he had to offer an expiatory sacrifice. But if the sabbath rest was violated in spite of the presence of witnesses and a previous warning, then the penalty was death by stoning. The warning in this case was addressed directly to the disciples, but it was really meant for Jesus.

³And Jesus answered, saying to them: " Have you not read what David did when he himself was hungry and those who were with him? ⁴How he entered God's house and took the consecrated bread and ate it, and gave it to those who were with him, although it was not lawful for anyone to eat it except the priests."

The tradition concerning the conflict over the sabbath was of the highest significance to the church which was just beginning to observe Sunday, and not Saturday, as the day of rest. This change-over was in the process of being completed, when St. Luke wrote his gospel. For him the reasons for the new interpretation of the law governing the sabbath were important. These underlined the power of Jesus' word by which he made God's will known.

Jesus was familiar with the method of disputation in use in the Jewish schools. Consequently, he answered the Pharisees by asking another question himself. In so doing, he appealed to scripture (1 Sam. 21:1-7), which was acknowledged as the supreme authority. The consecrated loaves, twelve in number, were left lying for a week on a dish in the sanctuary of the temple (or of the tent) as an offering to God. When the week was over, no one could eat them except the priests. But David and his companions ate them because they were hungry and there was no other bread available. No one found fault with him for this, neither scripture, nor Ahimelech, the priest who gave him the bread, nor the scribes. Therefore, necessity can excuse a violation of the law. Jesus' disciples had not transgressed the law by plucking some ears of corn on the sabbath when they were hungry. In interpreting the law, it is God's will and not merely the letter of the law which must be considered. God did not institute such ritual laws to harass human beings. Compassion for one's fellow men means far more to him than the observance of ritual laws. The sabbath rest was not intended to prevent people helping those who were in need. It is mercy that God wants, not sacrifices (Mt. 12:5-7).

⁵He used to say to them: " The Son of man is Lord even over the sabbath."

As the Son of man, to whom God had given all authority, Jesus had the right to decide concerning the sabbath rest and its interpretation. He intervened in a domain which belonged to God alone; he claimed God's right to forgive sins and to decide concerning the sabbath rest which was a symbol of the divine repose which followed the creation of the world (Gen 2:2f.). He also intervened in the sphere of the divine worship which was offered to God's glory. He used his power to rescue human beings from their difficulties.

HEALING ON THE SABBATH (6:6–11)

⁶It happened that on another sabbath day he entered a synagogue and was teaching. There was a man there whose right hand was withered. ⁷The scribes and Pharisees watched him, to see if he would cure him on the sabbath, so that they could bring a charge against him.

St. Luke is careful to give the exact details. Jesus worked his miracles at a unique historical moment, at a definite time, in a definite place, and in definite circumstances. Jesus' life and the word he spoke on earth provide the norm for the life and time of the church, until he comes again.

According to the interpretation the Pharisees gave of it, the law permitted a work of healing on the sabbath only if a person's life was in immediate danger. A withered hand constituted no such immediate threat. What would Jesus do when he saw this man's plight? His enemies' hostility showed a marked increase. In the first dispute about the sabbath, they had merely remarked—almost by the way—that his disciples were violating the law. Now they watched him closely to see if they could catch him in a transgression and bring him before the court.

⁸But he knew their thoughts and he said to the man whose hand was withered: " Stand up and come into the center." And he raised himself and stood up.

The sick man now stood in the center of the group, like an accused person before a court, waiting for condemnation or acquittal. This was a new principle of interpretation of the law. It was no longer the letter of the law which would be decisive, but the human being who was affected by the law. The question of the sabbath concerned human beings, their salvation or their condemnation.

⁹But Jesus said to them: " I ask you whether it is lawful to do good on the sabbath or to do evil, to save a life or to destroy it?"

Who could say that the law concerning the sabbath forbade a person to do good and demanded that he should do evil? For the Jews, the sabbath was not merely a day of rest; it was also a day of rejoicing, a day for doing good. Festive meals, the study of the law, and the practice of virtue made it a feastday, a day of joy. Food had to be kept ready for needy travelers. Was all this to be forgotten? Jesus restored its true meaning to the sabbath. " It is mercy I want, not sacrifices " (Hos. 6:6).

Jesus confronted his enemies with a choice; should a life be saved on the sabbath day, or should it be destroyed? The obligation of resting on the sabbath day was based on the fact that God had rested after the work of creation (Ex. 20:8ff.). However, when we are told that God rested, it does not mean he did nothing; he took pleasure in the work he had done. " God finds joy in his creation " (Ps. 104:31). The sabbath is a day to enjoy life, to rejoice over one's work, and glorify God. Surely there could be no objection to restoring its deepest meaning to the sabbath by curing the man who was ill. No one could choose to destroy life rather than save it.

¹⁰When he had looked around on them all, he said to him: " Stretch out your hand." He did this, and his hand was restored.

11But they were completely blind to it all, and they discussed among themselves what they could do to Jesus.

Jesus looked around at the whole company. His gaze rested on each and every one of them. No one made any reply. They would not admit that they were in the wrong; yet they could not escape the force of his wisdom. The image they had formed of God compelled them to regard the letter of the law as being supreme, but Jesus made known God's will. He had a different idea of God. His God was a God of mercy who drew near to men; their God was unapproachable and exalted high above all men.

The man's hand was restored to him. The restoration of all things was one of the elements of the time of salvation. What was now beginning would one day be brought to completion. " He [Jesus] had to be taken up into heaven, until the time for the restoration of all things comes, which God has prophesied through the mouths of his holy prophets from of old " (Acts 3:21). By healing the man who was sick, Jesus showed that, according to God's plan, he was to give the sabbath back its true meaning, because he inaugurated the universal restoration. The sabbath is an image of God's great sabbath rest (Heb. 4:8ff.) which will begin when everything has been restored and brought to its completion.

Hatred makes it impossible to reason or think clearly. Jesus' enemies were completely blinded; they wanted to obstruct his activity. They discussed among themselves what they could do to him to destroy him. Who could set himself up against the power and might of God's Spirit? Jesus' enemies had no faith and so they fell victims to blindness.

THE CALLING OF THE TWELVE (6:12–19)

12It happened in these days that he went out on to a mountain to pray and he spent the night praying to God.

Once more St. Luke ends his account of Jesus' powerful actions by telling us that he called a number of disciples. His enemies were determined to destroy him, but his work would go on. At this very time, he took steps to ensure this by choosing the twelve apostles. He prepared for this crucial event by praying to God. He prayed on the mountain, isolated from all human contact, alone, and close to God. The prayer he offered lasted all night. The world was shrouded in darkness. In the presence of God who alone is great, everything else receded into the background.

13And when it was day, he called his disciples to him and chose twelve of them, whom he called his apostles.

In his prayer, Jesus was united with God; God's will was his will and it was according to God's will that he chose the apostles. From among the number of disciples who had followed him, he picked out twelve. This number was based on the number of the patriarchs who were the ancestors of the chosen people in the Old Testament. A new people of God was coming into being.

Jesus called them his apostles, his envoys. The principle of Jewish law applied to them: A person's emissary is just like the person himself (Jn. 13:16). The twelve apostles were intended to be Jesus' legal and personal representatives.

14Simon, to whom he also gave the name Peter, and Andrew his brother, and James and John, Philip and Bartholomew, 15Matthew and Thomas, James [the son] of Alpheus and Simon who was called the Zealot, 16Judas [the son] of James, and Judas Iscariot who turned traitor.

The lists of the apostles which we have in the New Testament have a number of points in common. In each case, Peter is named first, while Judas Iscariot is always last. The same names always occur in the first, fifth, and ninth places—Simon, Philip, and

James the son of Alpheus. The divisions which are formed in this way always include the same names, but the order is different. It seems, therefore, that the lists imply a certain " organization " within the apostolic college. There are three groups of four apostles each.

There are a number of distinctive features about St. Luke's version of the list. He puts the three disciples whose calling he described (5 : 1-11) in the first place. Andrew is introduced as Simon's brother (Mt. 10:2). The other Simon is given the nickname " Zealot." He was obviously a member of the faction of the Zealots who professed a fanatical form of nationalism and wanted to establish God's reign by force. The James who occurs in the third group is described as the son of Alpheus. Judas Iscariot (the man from Iscariot) is called a " traitor." St. Luke tells us very little about the background, character, or previous history of these men. It is not biographical detail that is important; it is the fact that Jesus chose them and called them, appointing them to be the patriarchs of the new people of God, and his representatives.

¹⁷*And he went down with them and stopped on a piece of level ground. There was a large number of his disciples there and a great crowd of the people from all over Judea and Jerusalem, and from the coast of Tyre and Sidon, ¹⁸who had come to hear him and to be cured of their infirmities. And those who were possessed by unclean spirits were cured. ¹⁹And the whole crowd tried to touch him because power went out from him and healed them all.*

Like Moses, Jesus came down from the mountain where he had been in communion with God to the people. God was with him. About him were his apostles, the disciples, and the people. These were three circles which formed around him. Jesus was the center and power went out from him; he had been anointed with the Spirit. Anyone who entered into contact with these circles, and through them with Jesus himself, had a share in the blessings which accompanied the time of salvation.

The area from which the crowds flocked to Jesus included the whole of Judea with Jerusalem, its capital city, and the coastal region of Tyre and Sidon. These territories are not included among the mission territories mentioned in the Acts of the Apostles. St. Luke regards the Christian communities which existed in these areas as going back to Jesus himself. The news of Jesus' activity had already swept the whole country and its influence was felt even beyond the boundaries of Palestine.

The prophets of the Old Testament were convinced that Israel, Jerusalem, and Sion were to be the repositories of that salvation to which all the nations would come as pilgrims to receive instruction, to learn the law and to share in the light of divine glory. This promise was fulfilled in Jesus. As he stood there, a power to heal and instruct went out from him. Around him were assembled the patriarchs of the new people of God who were endowed with his power and spirit. Around them stood the disciples who had heard his word and answered its call. And finally, there were the crowds who were healed when they touched him. The Spirit who had anointed him was active in all those who crowded about him. This is a picture of the church.

A Prophet Powerful in Word and Deed (6:20—8:3)

The New Doctrine (6:20-49)

Like St. Matthew, St. Luke includes in his gospel an address which is referred to as the " Sermon on the Mount." St. Luke's version reproduces scarcely a third of the version given by St. Matthew. Literary criticism has made it clear, however, that his version is not merely an extract of Matthew's. Both accounts depend on a common source which the two evangelists used to illustrate their own interpretation of the gospel.

Matthew, for his part, was careful to report the Master's words; yet he made Jesus' prophetic message sound like a lawgiver's oration. Luke, on the other hand, preserved the prophetic character of Jesus' words in a purer form. The train of thought in St. Luke is straightforward and more compact. On the whole, his version is closer to the original. He presents us with a priceless fragment of the most ancient tradition.

THE BEATITUDES AND THE WOES (6:20-26)

²⁰And raising his eyes towards his disciples, he said: " Blessed are you who are poor; yours is the kingdom of heaven. ²¹Blessed are you who are hungry now; you shall have your fill. Blessed are you who mourn now; you shall laugh."

The poor, the hungry, and those who mourn are all the same people; the poor and needy who are regarded as the least of all in this world. Jesus encourages them, addressing his message of comfort to them. Israel had experienced in its own history how God takes the part of the poor and the oppressed when they set their hope on him (Is. 49:13). It is to those who are poor and wretched that God listens above all (Ps. 86:1). God continues to act in this way in the time of salvation which Jesus proclaims. The gospel was preached to the poor and brought to them (4:18).

Poverty, hunger, and mourning for sheer destitution are oppressive circumstances, and yet Jesus pronounces a blessing on those who are poor: " It is well for you!" He congratulates them in all seriousness. God confers the greatest blessing he has promised on them—the kingdom of God. Salvation history knows of no greater blessing. When God asserts his rule, everything is well.

²²" It is well for you when men hate you, and when they cast you out and revile you, rejecting your name as something evil, because of the Son of man. ²³Be glad and rejoice on that day, for your reward in heaven is great. Their fathers did the same to the prophets."

The fourth beatitude is for Jesus' persecuted disciples. As a community, the disciples looked on themselves as a community of the poor, like Israel. They were the little flock (12:32), powerless and exposed to contradiction and persecution. Jesus' disciples professed their belief that he was the Son of man, to whom God had given all power. This belief called down on them the hatred of their enemies. They would be excluded from the society of those who frequented the synagogue; they would be insulted and their names would be removed from the list of those who belonged to the synagogue. Jesus himself experienced hatred and persecution; he was cast out by his own people and suffered a criminal's death. His disciples would endure the same suffering, for his sake.

Is the disciples' fate a reason for mourning? No. They, too, belong to those who are poor, who are hungry, and mourn, and Jesus addresses them with the words: "It is well for you." "Be glad and rejoice." Their fate is a reason for happiness. "Your reward in heaven is great." Jesus' disciple who shares the poverty of those who are persecuted receives God's kingdom and all its blessings.

[24]*" On the other hand, it is too bad for you who are rich; you have already received your comfort.* [25]*It is too bad for you who are filled now; you will be hungry. It is too bad for you who laugh now; you will mourn and weep."*

The proclamation of salvation is followed by a threat; the beatitudes are accompanied by a number of woes. In this, Jesus imitates the prophets' preaching (Is. 5:8–23). The woes do not involve a final sentence of condemnation; they are a warning cry and are intended to frighten people and bring them to their senses, making them repent.

The rich, the well-fed, and those who laugh are those who possess the goods of this world and can enjoy them. Yet Jesus addresses a warning woe to them. In Jesus' presence and before his word a complete reversal of values takes place. The rich man is endangered by his wealth. He is in a state of false security; he seeks a firm foothold for his life, not in God where it could be found, but in his wealth where it cannot be found. The poor are receptive for the good news of God's kingdom; they find salvation. The rich are deaf; they are closed and they go to ruin, because they lack nothing.

²⁶" *It is too bad for you, when people speak well of you. Their fathers spoke the same way about the false prophets."*

The last woe is addressed once more to Jesus' disciples. This time, however, it is addressed to those who escape persecution and are welcomed by men with fine words which express their appreciation and flatter those who hear them. These disciples are rich, not in worldly wealth or worldly possessions, but in spiritual riches. On a human level, they are secure; they are in no danger of having to give up their lives, their good name, or their physical well-being. However, they are in danger of no longer depending upon God for each moment of their existence. They run the same risk as those who are rich.

Jesus' true disciples follow in the footsteps of the prophets; they are exposed to persecution and rejection by their fellow men. Those who encounter no opposition must take heed. They are in danger of imitating the false prophets; they met with no opposition, because they flattered people and left men at peace with the God of Israel. But what fate did they meet with?

Even a person who is a disciple, who has faith and is a member of the church, must take the beatitudes and the woes as so many calls addressed to himself. He must be always striving to accomplish the reversal of values these brief sayings demand. They demand a reappraisal of all human values and call for the overthrow of all the secure refuges a man has constructed for himself.

THE PRACTICE OF CHARITY (6:27-36)

[27]" But to you who are listening I say: Love your enemies! Do good to those who hate you! [28]Bless those who curse you ! Pray for those who do you wrong."

The rich to whom the woes were addressed were not present at the Sermon on the Mount. Jesus turned once more to his disciples who were listening to him. He spoke to them authoritatively : " But I say to you." His word was a proclamation from God; he spoke as one who had authority, not like the scribes and Pharisees (Mt. 7:28).

Jesus reduced the law, the fulfillment of God's will, to the commandment of charity : " You shall love the Lord your God with your whole heart and your whole soul, with all your strength and with all your senses, and your neighbor as yourself " (10:27). The way to love of God with one's whole heart has been cleared by the beatitudes and the woes. Now St. Luke speaks about love for one's neighbor.

The commandment to love one's neighbor was not unknown in the Old Testament: "Love your neighbor as yourself " (Lev. 19:18). Jesus picked this commandment out from among all the others and endowed it with an importance surpassing that of any other commandment. He gave it a new interpretation; a man's neighbor is every human being, even his enemies. It is from this radical interpretation of the precept of love as love for one's enemies that the moral injunctions of the Sermon on the Mount take their origin in St. Luke's version.

The words " your enemies " refer to the disciples' own enemies, those who calumniate and persecute them, and to the enemies of each individual disciple. The love which Jesus commands means doing good to a person, blessing him and interceding for him. To love means to live for a person . . . even for one who hates or curses or ill-treats us.

Love for one's neighbor is not merely a matter of forgiving injuries we have suffered. Jesus says nothing about forgiving; it is taken for granted. It is clear that Jesus' true disciple will do everything his enemy demands. A Christian requites hatred by doing good; he blesses those who curse him and prays for those who ill-treat him. The man who loves his enemy is not content merely to place himself at his service by returning good for evil; he also takes God into his service by praying to him for the benefits he himself cannot provide. In a disciple there must be nothing which is not completely penetrated with love for his enemy; his actions, his desires, his words must all be penetrated with this love, as well as his heart, for it is there that his prayer is offered.

[29]" *To the person who strikes you on the cheek offer the other cheek also; do not refuse your coat to the man who takes away your cloak.* [30]*Give to everyone who appeals to you, and do not ask the man who has taken what is yours to give it back.*"

It is hard to love one's enemy. We defend ourselves against injustice and, if we have been wronged, we are eager for revenge. We are determined to put an end to malice by fitting retribution. " What you have done to me, I will do to you " (see Mt. 5 : 38). But Jesus prescribed that evil must not be returned for evil; on the contrary, we must not resist evil; we must overcome it by doing good. These principles are valid both for personal injuries we receive: " To the person who strikes you on the cheek . . .," and for the loss we sustain in our belongings: " To the man who takes away your cloak . . ."

Jesus' disciples must give proof of unlimited generosity. "Give to everyone who appeals to you," without considering their race, their creed, their personal attitude, or their worth . . . simply give. But Jesus goes even further; property which has been taken by force or fraud must not be demanded back. The man who has suffered loss in this way must not look for compensation; he must not take his belongings back. The question is, does this mean that injustice is to be regarded as a right?

The examples Jesus gives seem so extraordinary, so paradoxical, and so shocking, because people behave among themselves, in fact, according to completely different norms. They expose the irreligious character of a man's behavior if he has not been seized and transformed by God's sovereign power. When we oppose evil and return evil for evil, we justify ourselves by saying that evil must be uprooted. But Jesus proclaimed that evil must be overcome by good. He inaugurated God's kingdom. The sum total of all the good which is realized in God's kingdom will result in the victory of good over evil.

Jesus' manner of speaking is graphic and pointed. He wanted to disturb his listeners, to shake them, and wake them up, so that he could transform them. The examples he gives are examples of an attitude to which he calls his disciples. He is not giving a lecture about moral obligations, so that he does not have to discuss all the ifs and buts. Neither is he promulgating a new code of laws made up of four articles: first, to the man who strikes you on the cheek . . .; second, to the man who takes your cloak . . . That would be to misunderstand the meaning of Jesus' message. His examples are intended as illustrations of a certain attitude. It is this attitude he demands, and his disciples must live up to it in the various circumstances of their lives; they must translate it into action.

[31]" *As you wish men to treat you, so you must treat them, in the same way.*"

How is love of one's enemies to be practiced? How must a Christian treat his neighbor, including his enemies? Teachers of wisdom and doctors of the law among both Jews and gentiles had spoken about this in the " Golden Rule." Tobit in his old age handed on this teaching to his son: " Do not do to anyone else what you do not like yourself " (Tob. 4 : 15). The Jewish scribe Hillel says the same: " Do not do to your neighbor what you yourself would dislike; that is the whole of the law; the rest is only a commentary on this." The rule was a commonplace of Greek sapiential literature. The Stoics expressed it in the words: " Never do to anyone else what you would not like anyone to do to you." A man carries the code and the measure of his conduct towards his fellow men in himself. His own wishes and his own needs show him how he should behave.

Jesus gives a new version of the Golden Rule: " As you wish . . . so you must treat them, in the same way." The rule the others gave was that a person must never do anything to his neighbor which he would not like to have done to himself. The rule Jesus gives is that a man must do good to his neighbor, including his enemies. That is the great difference. It is not merely a question of not doing evil; we must do good. Jesus' true disciple can never be content with simply not doing what is wrong; he must do good, all the good he would wish for himself. Jesus sets up a man's self-love as the norm and the measure of the love for one's neighbor which is ready even to embrace one's enemies. " You shall love your neighbor as yourself."

³²" *If you love those who love you, what thanks is that to you? Even sinners love those who love them.* ³³*If you do good to those who do good to you, what thanks is that to you? Even sinners do the same.* ³⁴*If you lend to someone from whom you hope to receive something in return, what thanks is that to you? Even sinners lend to sinners, to receive the same in return.*"

Jesus tells his listeners that they must love others when the others show no responsiveness and do not repay their love. They must love, because that is God's will. " When you give alms, your left hand must not know what your right hand is doing, so that your almsgiving may be in secret. Your Father who sees in secret will reward you " (Mt. 6: 3f.).

Love finds its expression in doing good, in lending. The man who loves comes into his own wherever distress is found. The love Christ is thinking of is active love: " Little children, we must not love only in words, with our lips; we must love in deed and in truth " (1 Jn. 3 : 18). Love can be commanded because it is active love. It is capable of being developed in the man who is open to his neighbor and his needs. The man who is adapted to his neighbor has the strength to love.

Jesus promises a reward to such love. " What thanks is that to you?" God acknowledges a man's deeds; he shows favor to those whose conduct is pleasing to him, and so he rewards them for their love.

[35]" *Rather, love your enemies and do good and lend, without hoping for anything in return. Then your reward will be great, and you will be sons of the Most High; he, too, is kind to the wicked and those who are ungrateful.*"

"Without hoping for anything in return ": that is the motto of Christian love. Jesus' disciples look for no recognition from men; they do not seek praise; they want nothing in return. Love is not calculating. It rises from the depths of a man's heart and blossoms forth. When a Christian lends, he does not do so in the hope of recovering his property, but only from a desire to help. Love for one's enemies must renounce the hope of receiving anything in return; that is why it is the most authentic form of a disciple's love.

It is God's will that moves Jesus' true disciple to love, his sovereign power, as well as Jesus his master and the word he preached.

The disciple who obeys the command to love his enemies receives a great reward. He is called a " son of the Most High." The man who obeys the command to love his enemies shares Jesus' sonship and his royal power.

Divine sonship is not only something to be hoped for at the end of time; it is granted here and now when a person shows love for his enemies. Unselfish love which is not merely a return of love makes Jesus' disciple like God himself. God is " kind to the wicked and those who are ungrateful." The true disciple becomes a son of the Most High who is exalted high above all human affairs in his infinite goodness.

[36]" Be merciful as your Father is merciful."

A man is merciful if he allows himself to be touched by the misery of his fellow men. He is open to his neighbor's needs; he intervenes to help those who are afflicted with a heavy burden.

The Father's own mercifulness shows Christians what they must do. Jesus demands what the Jews used call the " imitation of God." " As God clothed those who were naked (Gen. 3:21), so you too must cloth the naked. As God visited a man who was sick (Gen. 18:1), so you too must visit the sick . . . As God is merciful and gracious, you too must be merciful and gracious and give to everyone without any reward . . . As God is kind . . . you too must be kind."

Love has two norms by which to test itself and guide its conduct: the desire of a man's own heart—" Love your neighbor as yourself "; and the mercifulness shown by our heavenly Father. These two norms are really one; a Christian is a son of the Most High; he is God's image. Jesus restored God's image in man by proclaiming the supreme sovereignty of the Most High who is our all-merciful Father.

37a" And do not judge and you will not be judged. Do not condemn and you will not be condemned."

Mercy and love towards our fellow men begin when we refuse to set ourselves up as judges over them. The man who looks first to see whether his neighbor deserves mercy or love, whether he is " worthy," sins against the commandment of love by that very fact. It is pity for one's neighbor's needs that inspires love to give.

37b" Forgive and you will be forgiven. 38aGive and it shall be given to you; a good measure, pressed down and shaken up and overflowing, will be given into your lap."

The sins and offenses others have committed against us could be an obstacle to the practice of mercy and love. Jesus shows us two ways to overcome this; forgive (" Do not condemn ") and give. Then the barriers obstructing the I-Thou relationship will be dismantled; this is the result of not condemning. Giving, on the other hand, helps to build a bridge between the two.

Here once more Jesus' demand is imposed subject to the threat of judgment. " And you will be forgiven," and " it shall be given to you." God's attitude as a judge will be determined by our own behavior. The outcome of the judgment is in our own hands. " Forgive us our sins, as we also forgive those who are in our debt " (11:4).

38b" For it is the measure you yourselves have used that will determine the amount you receive in return."

God's giving is without measure, but he gives only to the man who has been generous himself. We can also say that he forgives without measure, but only in the case of a man who has shown forgiveness in his turn.

Jesus' words about love for one's enemies contain a reference to the last judgment. But what they evoke is not God's just punishment; it is his infinite goodness. All these sayings of Jesus follow the same pattern, but when he demands that we should give, the promise " and it will be given to you " is overloaded. In this way, the emphasis is transferred from God's severity to his goodness, from his judgment to the happiness he gives, from his threats to his promises, from fear of him to hope in him.

The concluding phrase contains a note of warning once more—measure for measure. The man who gives little will receive little; he who gives generously will receive generously. Here the picture of God's generosity is referred to once again. God's unfathomable mercy at the judgment is subject to certain conditions. The man who gives to his neighbor and forgives him will receive God's gifts and his forgiveness in full. He who does not give or forgive cannot hope for God's forgiveness or for his gifts.

True Holiness (6:39–49)

³⁹ᵃ*He also told them a parable.*

This rubric which serves to introduce a story marks the beginning of a new part of the discourse. A parable is the correct title; in fact, Jesus told them five short parables. They were intended to make people think. To the prophetic (6:20–26) and exhortatory (6:27–38) words he had already spoken, Jesus now added a number of sayings in the form of parables.

³⁹ᵇ*" Can a man who is blind lead another blind man on his way? Will they not both fall into the ditch? ⁴⁰The disciple is not greater than his master; each one will be taught like his master."*

Jesus intended the parable of the blind leader for the Pharisees.

They pretended to lead the people to true holiness. They had studied the law with painful anxiety, and they did their best to keep it. Yet they were blind leaders; they were closed to God's greatest revelation; God's word as it was proclaimed by Jesus could not reach them. Jesus' disciples were now to take the place of these blind leaders.

"The disciple is not greater than his master." This saying was verified in the scribes' schools. There the teacher handed on what he had received; the disciple had nothing else to do but to receive what was handed on to him. Jesus' disciple hands on what he himself has received from Jesus. How could he do justice to his responsibility to others if he himself was not thoroughly grounded in Jesus' word, if he had not made it his own?

[41]" *How do you see the splinter in your brother's eye, when you do not see the beam in your own eye?* [42]*How can you say to your brother: 'Brother, wait. I will take out the splinter which is in your eye,' when you do not even see the beam in your own eye? Hypocrite, take the beam out of your own eye first and then you will be able to see to take the splinter out of your brother's eye."*

Fidelity to his message demands that a disciple should correct those who are at fault or in error; he should be prepared to help them to overcome their faults. Jesus' words presuppose that his disciple feels this anxiety for his brother, his partner in the faith. Such correction involves certain risks. One is that the person who is correcting his brother may not have a true estimate of his fault; self-love distorts the truth. The parable of the splinter and the beam illustrates this in glaring colors. The most insignificant faults of another seem great, while a person's own faults, even when they are serious, seem small. A person is capable of correcting another only when he is free from all self-righteousness and is no longer influenced by the urge to dominate.

A further risk inherent in such correction is the danger of hypocrisy. The man who corrects another thereby implies that he is determined to vanquish evil in the world. If he fails to achieve this in himself as well, there is a fatal dichotomy between his inward and his outward attitude. He is a leader in the struggle against evil in others—but in himself? "Take the beam out of your own eye first." Begin by correcting yourself first; then the way will be clear to correct others.

[43]" *There is no good tree which bears bad fruit, and again there is no bad tree which bears good fruit.* [44]*Each tree is known by its fruit. Figs cannot be picked from thorns or grapes plucked from brambles.*"

The danger of hypocrisy can be overcome only when a person's outward behavior and his inward attitude are at one. His exterior actions, his words and his deeds, are good when the interior source from which they come is good. For the scribes and Pharisees, an action was good if it was in keeping with the law. Jesus, on the other hand, pronounced a man's actions good if they spring from an interior attitude which is good. A man's heart, the seat of his thoughts, his desires, and his emotions, is the source from which flow his plans for good or evil; this is the seat of his decisions in the moral order, the origin of all his words and actions. " It is from within, from the heart, that evil designs come, adultery, stealing, murder . . ." (Mk. 7:21ff.). But when is a man's heart good?

Everything that man says or does shows what kind of a person he is interiorly. They reveal his heart as surely as the fruit reveals the species and the quality of a tree. Brambles will not bear figs.

[45]"*A good man brings forth what is good from the treasure of goodness in his heart, while an evil man brings forth evil from*

his store of evil. It is from his heart's overflow that his mouth speaks."

In this passage, Jesus employs a different image. A man's heart, the seat of his moral and religious decisions, is compared to a treasure. The question is, when is a man's heart a treasure which contains only what is good and from which only what is good can come out? When is a person's inner self good? When is his conscience properly formed? The gospel makes it clear that it is not enough simply for a person to live up to the demands of his innate human nature. It is only when a man has been fully instructed by Jesus his master that his heart is good. When Jesus' word has been welcomed into a man's heart, when God's rule and God's holiness have completely possessed it, then it becomes a treasure overflowing with all that is good. Here once more we see that the basic demand Jesus makes is that a person should repent and be converted.

[46]*" Why do you call me: 'Lord, Lord,' when you do not do what I say?"*

Jesus' disciples addressed him as " Lord." This was the title with which their disciples addressed the scribes. For the disciples who followed him, Jesus was their rabbi, their master and teacher. But this was not the only sense in which he was their Lord. For them he was far more. It was God who spoke through him. The title " Lord " expresses all that is most sublime and exalted in dignity. Anyone who reads the Old Testament in Greek will find that the divine name Yahweh is there translated " Lord." All this is implied when Jesus quotes his disciples as calling him " Lord, Lord." Jesus who delivered the Sermon on the Mount is the Lord.

The Lord has the right to dispose of others; he gives the orders and he is the judge. His word is endowed with a God-given power to command. Certainly, it would be an extraordinary contradiction to address Jesus as Lord and not carry out his word or do his will, when they are well known to us. His question, therefore, is intended to make his hearers wake up and think.

⁴⁷" *If a man comes to me and listens to my words and carries them out, I will show you what he is like.* ⁴⁸*He is like a man who is building a house. He has dug deep and excavated and laid the foundation on rock. When the flood came, the river broke against that house, but it was not strong enough to shake it, because it was solidly built.* ⁴⁹*On the other hand, the man who hears my word but does not carry it out is like a man who built a house on the ground without any foundation. The river broke against it and the collapse of that house was great.*"

St. Luke has arranged both parables in a Greek setting. His description of the construction of the house differs from that of St. Matthew (Mt. 7:24-27). St. Matthew says only: " He built his house on rock "; " he built his house on sand." In St. Luke's version, the builder digs a foundation, carefully and laboriously, or simply builds on the ground without any foundation. St. Matthew describes the subsequent disaster in a genuinely Palestinian fashion: " The rain fell in torrents and the floods came and the storms raged "—the winter rains which fall in Palestine. St. Luke changes this to a " swollen river in spate." The incarnation continues in the way God's word is handed down; God's word is adapted to human beings, it comes down to them, to penetrate them and the world in which they live completely.

The parable and the words which precede it make it clear beyond all doubt that the Sermon on the Mount must be put into practice. Our salvation or condemnation will be decided by the obedience or disobedience we have shown to the message contained in this discourse. The concluding words: " The collapse of that house was great," go beyond the parable and apply to the reality it represents. The man who hears Jesus' word and does not obey it will suffer a terrible disaster at the last judgment.

Jesus' Saving Activity (7:1—8:3)

THE CENTURION AT CAPERNAUM (7:1-10)

¹When he had finished all his words in the hearing of the people, he went to Capernaum. ²A centurion's servant who was very dear to him was sick and on the point of death. ³But when he heard about Jesus, he sent some of the elders of the Jews to him and begged him to come and heal his servant. ⁴They appeared before Jesus and begged him insistently, saying to him: " He deserves that you should do this for him. ⁵He loves our people and he built the synagogue for us."

As a border town, Capernaum possessed a tax office (Mk. 2:13f.) and a garrison. Herod Antipas, like his father, had mercenaries from all over the world serving in his army, Syrians, Thracians, Germans, and Gauls. The centurion mentioned here was a pagan. His servant (" boy ") was seriously ill and he left nothing undone to help him. As a pagan he felt unworthy to present his petition to Jesus himself and so he sent some of the Jewish elders to intercede for him. In his humility, he acknowledged that by God's providence salvation was to come to the gentiles through the Jews. The compassion he displayed, together with his humility and his obedience, had prepared him for the message of salvation Christ brings.

The centurion was one of those pagans who could no longer be satisfied with polytheistic myths. The wisdom of the philosophers failed to still his religious yearnings, and so he adopted the monotheism of the Jews and the moral law which followed from it. He was numbered among those who feared God; he believed in the one true God and joined in Jewish worship. However, he had not yet gone over to Judaism completely. He sought the salvation which God offers. His faith in the one true God, his love and veneration for him, found expression in his love for God's people and in the care he bestowed on the synagogue which he had built. He expressed his attitude in his deeds.

The elders of the Jews were the leading members of the community. They regarded Jesus as a man in whom God gave proof of his favor towards his own people. They were convinced that God showed his favor in this way only to his own people. Yet they hoped that he would make an exception in favor of the centurion because of all he had done for God's people, and be gracious to him even though he was a pagan. They believed that belonging to Israel was an indispensable condition for salvation (Acts 15:5). However, the conditions of admission to God's kingdom and eternal salvation were laid down in the beatitudes. Blessed are the poor, the hungry, the mourners. There is nothing there about belonging to Israel or to the synagogue. Jesus is a prophet whose message is addressed to all men including pagans; in this way, he resembled Elijah and Elisha.

6So Jesus went with them. When he was already near the house, the centurion sent some friends to tell him: " Lord, do not put yourself to any trouble. I am not worthy that you should enter under my roof. 7That is why I did not even think myself worthy to come to you, but say only a word and my servant will be healed. 8I, too, am a man who is subject to authority. I have soldiers under me and I say to one: ' Go,' and he goes, and to another: ' Come,' and he comes, and to my servant: ' Do that,' and he does it."

The centurion believed that Jesus enjoyed a special relationship with God. As an unclean and sinful pagan, he regarded himself as unworthy to stand in his presence. Peter had been overcome with similar emotions at the thought of God's holiness which he encountered in Jesus. He could not bear to be near him. When a man turns to God who is all-holy, he experiences his own sinfulness. This is one of the results of turning to God and of that repentance which is the way to salvation. " Repent! The kingdom of God is close at hand."

The Jewish elders thought that Jesus would have to be present to cure the man who was sick. The centurion, on the other hand, ascribed this power exclusively to Jesus' word. Speaking from his own experience, he describes this word as an authoritative word, a word of command. Such a word effects what it expresses. It is always charged with saving power quite independently of the presence of the one who speaks it. This word is enough to confer healing and banish the powers of corruption. On the other hand, the centurion does not dissociate his word from the totality which is Christ. In his word, it is Jesus' person and his influence which are present.

⁹But when Jesus heard this, he was amazed at him. He turned to the people who were following him and said: " I tell you, not even in Israel have I found faith like this." ¹⁰And those who had been sent returned to the house and found the servant cured.

" Not even in Israel . . ." These words reproduce what St. Matthew wrote: " Truly, I tell you, I have not found faith like this in anyone in Israel " (Mt. 8 : 10). Throughout its long history, the law and the prophets had been at work preparing Israel for the coming of the Messiah. He came, but he found no faith. This pagan believed and found what he was looking for; he was responsible for the cure of his servant. In the beatitudes, the Sermon on the Mount revealed the basic attitude which is necessary if a man is to attain salvation. And what was this? They demand a frame of mind, an openness for God, which anyone can acquire no matter whether he is a Jew or a gentile. Jesus' word has power to bring salvation to everyone, if it is welcomed in a spirit of faith.

The servant who was sick was cured; he was saved from certain death. He is mentioned only at the beginning and the end of St.

Luke's account, but he is always there in the background. The destructive powers which were bringing the sick man to his death were surmounted by the compassion of his master and his love for Israel and its God. The Jews' intercession, the humble faith of the centurion, and above all Jesus' all-powerful word, were effective in his behalf. This is true, too, of the church in which the centurion's attitude is incarnated. It is with a profound insight that the church uses the centurion's words as a prayer when Jesus approaches the faithful in the Eucharist to bring them salvation.

THE RAISING OF THE YOUNG MAN (7:11–17)

11And it happened later on that he was going into a town called Nain and his disciples and a great crowd of people went with him. 12As he drew near the gate of the town, a dead man was being car-ried out, the only son of his mother who was a widow, and there was a great crowd from the town with her.

Nain was on the road leading from the sea of Galilee past Mount Tabor, through the plain of Esdraelon, to Samaria. St. Luke speaks of a town, but it was really only a small village. There at the gate of the town two processions met; a procession whose leader was the giver of life, and a procession led by death. In a sermon preached after the first Pentecost, St. Peter told his listeners: " You rejected the holy and the just man, asking instead for the pardon of a mur-derer [Barabbas]. You killed the leader of life whom God has raised from the dead, as we now testify " (Acts 3 : 14f.).

The dead man was his mother's only son, and she was a widow. Her husband and her son had died prematurely. A premature death was regarded by the Jews as a punishment for sin. It was her son who had made life bearable for the widow. In him she could find comfort, protection, and support. The depth of her misery aroused the compassion of great numbers of the townsfolk who accompanied her. They could console her, but had no power to help her.

¹³When the Lord saw her, he was touched with pity for her. He said to her: " Do not weep." ¹⁴And he went up and touched the bier, while the bearers stood still. And he said: " Young man, I say to you, get up! " ¹⁵And the dead man sat up and began to speak, and he gave him to his mother.

Jesus was touched with pity. He proclaimed God's mercy and brought it to those who mourned and wept. God asserts his rule by showing mercy to those who are afflicted.

The body lay wrapped in a linen cloth on a bier. Thinking in Greek terms, St. Luke says Jesus touched the coffin. This was a sign to the bearers to halt. Jesus then called out to the dead man as if he were alive. His call gave him back his life. " God makes the dead live and calls what does not exist as if it were already in being " (Rom. 4:17). By means of his all-powerful word, Jesus is the " author of life " (Acts 3:15).

The young man was restored to life; he sat up and began to speak. " Jesus gave him to his mother." By raising the dead man to life he had proved his power and his mercy; his power was used in the service of his mercy. Both power and mercy are signs of the time of salvation.

He gave him to his mother. These are the words used in the book of Kings (1 Kings 17:23) where we are told that Elijah raised the son of the widow at Zarephath from the dead. Jesus is a prophet like Elijah, only he excels him. Jesus raised the dead man by his all-powerful word; Elijah was forced to have recourse to prayer and tedious effort.

¹⁶Fear gripped them all and they praised God saying: "A great prophet has risen among us. God has visited his people." ¹⁷This

*word concerning him spread through the whole of Judea and the
entire surrounding country.*

The onlookers' praise mentioned two saving events. One was that
a great prophet had arisen. God had intervened decisively in the
course of history; Jesus was a great prophet. The other was that
God had visited his people with his grace. The prophecy which the
Baptist's father made in his canticle of joy was being fulfilled:
" Praised be the Lord, Israel's God. He has visited his people and
brought them redemption. He has raised up a horn of salvation
for us in the house of David his servant " (1:68f.). Jesus' renown
spread throughout the whole of Palestine and beyond to the surrounding districts. The word about him possessed a dynamism
which impelled it to fill the whole world. All those who heard it
passed it on.

JOHN THE BAPTIST AND JESUS (7:18–35)

St. Luke here combines three incidents preserved by tradition to bring
out Jesus' importance by comparing his mission with that of John the
Baptist. The Baptist inquired about Jesus' mission (7:18-23), while Jesus
made a statement concerning the Baptist's mission and indirectly about
his own (7:24-30). He also pronounced on the attitude of the people towards the Baptist and towards himself (7:31-35).

*18His disciples told John about all this. And John summoned two of
his disciples to him 19and sent them to the Lord, saying: "Are you
the one who is to come, or must we wait for another? " 20When
these men came to him, they said: " John the Baptist sent us to you,
to ask: 'Are you the one who is to come, or must we wait for
another? ' "*

John was in prison. The news of Jesus' preaching and of the powerful acts he performed reached him through his disciples. The result

134

was that he sent two disciples to the Lord, to ask him whether he was the Messiah or not.

Who was Jesus? St. Luke is the only evangelist to say in this context: "He sent them to the Lord." In these words, he expresses the entire belief of the early church concerning Jesus. The profession of faith the early Christians made was: "Jesus Christ is the Lord" (Phil. 2:11). This was what God had made him after he had accomplished his work on earth. First he suffered and died; then God raised him from the dead and glorified him. The long road which led from the Baptist's preaching to the resurrection and the descent of the Holy Spirit culminated in recognition of this. The title "Lord" which St. Luke uses here shows us where this road was bound to end and where it ended in fact.

For John the Baptist, the "one who was to come" was a messianic figure, not God himself. He referred to Jesus as the one who was to come. The one who was to come was Israel's great hope: "Only a little while yet and he who is to come will come. He will not delay" (Heb. 10:37). The Baptist had described the one who was coming as a judge who already had his winnowing shovel in his hand; he would baptize with fire and the Spirit; he would pass sentence and give new life. What had become of him? The Baptist told his disciples to ask: "Are you the one who is to come, or must we wait for another?" This was the question St. Luke was interested in; he was not interested in the Baptist's state of mind which prompted it. Who was Jesus?

²¹*At that time, Jesus cured many people of their illnesses and their scourges, and of evil spirits. He gave many who were blind the gift of sight.* ²²*And he said to them in answer: "Go and tell John what you have seen and heard. The blind see, the lame walk, the lepers are made clean, the deaf hear, the dead rise up and the gospel is preached to the poor.* ²³*It is well for the man who is not scandalized at me."*

The facts spoke for themselves; together with God's word as it was spoken by the prophets they made it clear who Jesus was. The disciples whom the Baptist sent were witnesses of the miracles of healing Jesus worked. Jesus inaugurated the restoration of all things; he freed those who were suffering from sickness and misery; he brought reconciliation with God and broke the power of the evil spirits.

The significance of this in salvation history was indicated by the instructions Jesus gave John's disciples. These were formulated in words taken from Isaiah, the prophet whose writings inspired the longing for salvation prevalent in Jesus' time. " Then the deaf will hear the words of scripture, the eyes of the blind will see through the darkness and shadow " (Is. 29:18). " Then the eyes of the blind will open, deaf ears will be unsealed; the cripple will leap like a deer, and the dumb man's tongue will sing a joyous song " (Is. 35:5f.). " The Spirit of the Lord and Master rests upon me. The Lord has anointed me; he has sent me to tell the good news to the poor " (Is. 61:1). Jesus acted on man's behalf in the place of God himself. He came, not as a king and a judge but as God's servant who was to take away man's guilt and cure his illnesses. He came as a messenger of joy, to preach the gospel to the poor, as a high priest who reconciled the human race and united it with God.

The form in which the one who was to come finally appeared was a cause of scandal to some. " It is well for the man who is not scandalized at me." The image of the one who was to come which John's disciples and the Pharisees had formed for themselves had to be compared with the facts as God had ordained them and with God's word as it was spoken by the prophets. It is well for the man who does not close his heart to all that God achieves in Jesus, even when it does not correspond with the ideas he had formed for himself.

[24]*When John's messengers had gone away, he began to speak to the*

crowds about John. " What did you go out into the desert to see? A reed swaying back and forth in the wind? *²⁵Or what did you go out to see? A man dressed in soft clothing? See, those who live in luxury and dress in fine clothes are to be found in kings' palaces. ²⁶But what did you go out to see? A prophet? Yes, I tell you, and more than a prophet."*

In popular language which was at once vivid and unadorned, Jesus addressed a number of forceful questions to his listeners, to make them reflect and think about the Baptist's mission. Anyone who arrived at a clear grasp of this would easily be able to understand the significance of Jesus' activity.

Who was John? An ascetic? A prophet? The people regarded him as a prophet who proclaimed God's will (Mt. 21:26). They all looked on him as a prophet (Mk. 11:32). His father Zechariah had foretold that he would be a prophet of the Most High (1:76). A commission of inquiry sent by the Sanhedrin asked him : " Are you a prophet? " (Jn. 1:21). His preaching reproduced that of the older prophets; he proclaimed God's avenging judgment and demanded a radical change of heart as he spoke of the salvation to come. It was as a prophet that he stood up to the ruler of his country (Mk. 6:17ff.); he behaved towards him as Samuel had behaved towards Saul (1 Sam. 15:10ff.), as Nathan had behaved towards David, or as Elijah had behaved towards Ahab (1 Kings 21:17ff.). Jesus confirmed the impression the people had got of John. Yes, he was a prophet. But this was not enough. With the full consciousness of his authority, Jesus told the crowds : " I tell you, he is more than a prophet."

²⁷" This is the one concerning whom it is written : ' See, I am sending my messenger on before you; he will prepare your way.' ²⁸For I tell you : among all those born of women, there is none greater. But the least in God's kingdom is greater than he."

137

In John, the words of the prophet Malachi were fulfilled: "See now, I am sending my messenger on ahead, to prepare a way before me" (Mal. 3:1). That is the version given in the original text. The version given by St. Luke adapts the prophecy to the reality. In his version, God is shown speaking to someone else, someone who is sent by him; he comes in God's name and inaugurates the last stage of time. "I am sending my messenger on before you." John was the man sent by God to prepare the way for the saviour whose coming had been promised for the end of time. He brought the long line of prophets to an end and he excelled them all. He was the prophet who stood on the threshold of the messianic era.

Deliberately and with full authority, Jesus described him as the greatest of men. For him, a man's greatness consisted in the service he rendered to the salvation which God offers. John prepared the saviour's coming. The story of his childhood had already mentioned his greatness. His birth was announced by an angel and it was surrounded by prophets and by the joy salvation brings. From the first, he possessed the Spirit and was consecrated to God; he surpassed Samuel and came on the scene like an Elijah. He was chosen out from among all men, and he was superior to all the great figures of salvation history.

But John's greatness was immediately limited. "The least in God's kingdom is greater than he." It was Jesus himself who was the least. He became the servant of all men and made himself small before John when he received baptism from him. He came, not as a ruler, but as God's lowly servant. In the minds of many of John's disciples, he was less than John, and yet it was he who brought God's kingdom. In him, the time of fulfillment dawned and the time of waiting in which John lived came to an end. Jesus was the greatest in being the least. God's kingdom dawned in him who was the least.

29"And all the people who heard him and the tax collectors gave God his due. They received John's baptism. 30But the Pharisees and the scribes frustrated God's plan for them, when they refused to be baptized by him."

John was a baptist; it was by means of his baptism of penance for the remission of sins that he prepared the way for the one who was to come. It was God himself who had appointed this baptism as the way to salvation for all men. The whole people had need of it; they were offered this chance of being cleansed.

The people were despised by the scribes and Pharisees because of their ignorance of the law, as were the tax collectors who were regarded as reprobates and sinners. Yet it was they who gave God his due. They bowed to his saving design; they were converted and received John's baptism as they did penance for their sins. The scribes and Pharisees, however, rejected John's baptism and so frustrated God's plans for their salvation. The outlaws and the sinners accepted God's offer of repentance, while the scribes and Pharisees turned it down. Those who had been expelled by the Pharisees were received into the community of salvation. The separatists who regarded themselves as the community of salvation scorned the opportunity of entering into it which repentance offered them. God's offer of salvation was intended for all men, but it demanded that all men should be converted. The way to salvation is marked out for all by God's design; no one can decide it for himself. John the Baptist's activity gave rise to divisions among those who heard him. He inaugurated the judgment which was to come, and so he introduced Jesus' mission.

31" With whom, then, shall I compare the people of this generation? Who are they like? 32They are like children who sit in the market place and call out to one another, as they say: ' We played the flute for you and you did not dance. We sang a lament for you and you did not weep'."

Why did people reject God's plan of salvation? Why was John, and eventually Jesus, too, rejected? The parable of the obstinate children gives the answer. A group of children were playing in the market place of a town. Some wanted to play a wedding, while others were determined to play a funeral. The first group played on a flute and invited the others to dance, but the others remained obstinate. Then they played a lament; they sobbed and wept, but the others now wanted to play a wedding. Who could satisfy such obstinate people? In the same way, men want to change what God has disposed in his divine plan. It is their own self-centeredness which prevents them from accepting salvation. Repentance turns a man away from himself towards God and his will. The way to salvation consists in turning away from oneself and turning towards God.

[33]" John the Baptist came; he did not eat bread or drink wine, and you say: ' He has an evil spirit.' [34]The Son of man came; he ate and drank, and you say : ' He is a friend of tax collectors and sinners '."

The obstinate attitude of Jesus' contemporaries was demonstrated in their condemnation of both John and him. They found the Baptist too ascetical and declared he was mad. They regarded Jesus as not being sufficiently holy and decided he was a worldling who made friends with tax collectors and sinners. St. Luke omits the ugly words: "A drinker and a glutton " (Mt. 11 : 19).. John came as a messenger of repentance, while Jesus came to bring salvation to all, and especially to those who were looked upon as being lost and had no hope in Israel.

[35]"And wisdom received its due from all its children."

To us, God's ways in salvation history may seem impenetrably mysterious. Yet they are not arbitrary; they are an example of God's wisdom. Only a person who is a child of wisdom can recognize God's wisdom for what it is in all he does. To do this, we can say a person must be born of wisdom; he must be transformed and penetrated by it; he must think and judge as it does.

When the ordinary people recognized John as the Precursor of the Messiah and were not scandalized in Jesus, it was not the result of any human effort; it was a gift given them by God; God communicated his wisdom to them. That was why Jesus could give thanks in the words: " I give you praise, Father. . . . You have hidden this from those who are wise and clever and revealed it to those who are insignificant" (10:21). Human wisdom is incapable of understanding and accepting God's plan of salvation. God himself must make us a gift of his wisdom and revelation.

The two sayings: " It is well for the man who is not scandalized at me," and: " Wisdom received its due from all its children," are complementary. A purely human outlook is bound to be scandalized at God's plans for our salvation, but divine wisdom gives them their due. If a man is to be able to recognize that the coming of John and Jesus marked the beginning of salvation, he must have a share in this divine wisdom; he must be prepared to renounce his own human ideas. He must be converted and change his outlook; he must take God, not himself, as the measure of all things. He must get out of himself and allow God's word to give him light; he must lay aside all human wisdom and become a child. God caused the gospel to be preached to those who are poor.

THE SINFUL WOMAN (7:36–50)

St. Luke is the only evangelist who tells us that Jesus was sometimes invited to dinner by the Pharisees. He likes to write about the conversations they had at table. On these occasions, they discussed the various points which separated them, the correct attitude towards sinners (7: 36ff.), the laws concerning ritual purity (11:39f.), and the sabbath rest

(14:1ff.). Their disputes became a subject for conversation at table (14: 7ff.). The atmosphere of St. Luke's gospel differs from that of St. Matthew; it is a Greek atmosphere which is more human and inviting.

[36]One of the Pharisees invited him to dine with him, and he went into the Pharisee's house and reclined at the table. [37]And then a woman who was a sinner in the town learned that he was reclining at table in the Pharisee's house. She took an alabaster flask full of anointing oil [38]and stood behind him at his feet weeping. She began to wash his feet with her tears and she dried them with the hair of her head. She kissed his feet again and again and anointed them with the oil.

Jesus reclined at the table. He was a guest at a festive meal in the Pharisee's house. He also availed of the opportunity to teach, and Simon addressed him as master. Jesus' approach differed from that of the Baptist. John lived a life of severe asceticism in the desert far from everybody. Anyone who wanted to hear him had to make the pilgrimage out to him. Jesus worked in the towns where people lived and in their homes, at receptions and festivities. John summoned men before the judgment; Jesus brought them salvation.

The house where a banquet was held was open even to those who were not invited. They could look on and enjoy the spectacle, and even join in the conversation. That was how the woman who was known in the town as a sinner could make her way in. She seems to have been a prostitute.

The woman showed unlimited reverence for Jesus. She wept, overcome by emotion in the depths of her soul. Kissing a person's foot was a sign of the most humble gratitude, such as a man might show to someone who had saved his life. She loosed her hair, although it was considered shameful for a married woman to do this in the presence of a man. And she dried Jesus' feet with her hair. She forgot herself and gave herself up completely to the feeling of gratitude towards God, refusing to spare herself. What was the reason for all this? Jesus would later touch on the story which led up to this outburst of heartfelt emotion.

[39]Seeing her, the Pharisee who had invited him said to himself: " If this fellow here were a prophet, he would know who this woman is that is touching him and what kind of a woman. She is a sinner." [40]And Jesus answered and said to him: " Simon, I have something to say to you." And he replied: " Speak, Master." Jesus said: [41]"A creditor had two debtors; one owed him five hundred silver pieces, the other fifty. [42]But because they had nothing to pay him back, he remitted both debts. Which of these two will love him more? " [43]Simon answered and said: " I suppose the man whom he let off more." And Jesus said to him: " You have judged correctly."

Simon had heard that the people said Jesus was a prophet. Now, however, he had come to his own conclusion. Jesus could not be a prophet; a prophet has the power to read people's hearts and he will have nothing to do with sinners. Simon formed his idea of a prophet according to the teaching of the Pharisees, according to his own wisdom, not according to God's thoughts or God's wisdom.

However, Jesus had a prophet's ability to read men's hearts. He knew what Simon was thinking. Simon despised the woman as a sinner and set himself up as her judge. What are we to think of this? Jesus was a prophet; he knew men's hearts and was familiar with God's plan. The parable he spoke fitted the situation. The guilt of sin is compared to a debt. Which of the two who had their debts remitted will love their creditor more? The parallel would have been even closer if Jesus had asked : " Who will be more grateful? " There was no word for " thanks " in Aramaic. Gratitude finds its expression in the desire to give in return for what we have received, in love. The sinful woman at Jesus' feet showed her heartfelt gratitude by the many signs she gave of her love.

The second part of the parable should have given Simon cause for thought—the man who was in debt for a sum of fifty silver pieces and was let off. He, too, was guilty. But he was not conscious of his guilt and so he did not love much. We are reminded of the saying about the splinter and the beam in the Sermon on the Mount.

⁴¹And turning to the woman, he said to Simon: " Do you see this woman? I came into your house and you gave me no water for my feet. But she washed my feet with her tears and dried them with her hair. You gave me no kiss ⁴⁵but from the moment she came in she has not stopped kissing my feet over and over again. ⁴⁶You did not anoint my head with oil, but she anointed my feet with anointing oil. ⁴⁷And so I tell you, her sins—numerous as they are—are forgiven, because she loved much. The person to whom less is forgiven feels less love."

The Lord's gaze rested on the penitent woman and he asked Simon, too, to look at her. She was to be used to illustrate Jesus' teaching. The woman loved much. Washing a guest's feet, giving him a kiss of greeting, and anointing his head, were the ordinary tokens of hospitality, and she had fulfilled them personally in a spirit of humility and devotedness. She washed Jesus' feet with her tears and dried them with her hair; she anointed him with expensive oil which she had obtained specially for this; instead of kissing his head, she kissed his feet. She loved much, with a love that involved her personally, to the depths of her heart. And what of the Pharisee? He had not shown Jesus even the normal signs of hospitality and courtesy. This woman's love overflowed with gratitude for God's overflowing goodness—and Simon despised her as a sinner! She emptied and renounced herself; God was everything to her.

" Her sins were forgiven because she loved much." It is true that love and sin are incompatible. " Love covers a multitude of sins " (1 Pet. 4:8). " We know that we have gone over from death to life, because we love the brethren " (1 Jn. 3:14). " The man who loves will be loved by my Father " (Jn. 14:21). Love blots out sins. Her sins—numerous as they were—were forgiven, because she loved much.

In the light of the parable itself, we should have expected the conclusion to be: Because much was forgiven her, she loves much. Why did Jesus say: "Her sins are forgiven, because she loved much"? A mysterious saying such as this is intended to make us think. The sinner's love was at once the reason for, and the result of, the forgiveness she received. She knew from what Jesus said that he had authority to proclaim the forgiveness of sins. Consequently, she was moved to love, and because she loved she received forgiveness. Jesus' word about the forgiveness of sins effected what he expressed. To be effective, however, his word must also inspire love; sin cannot be forgiven without love. This love which Jesus inspires in a sinner gives him the power to love. Love is the characteristic of the new life he enjoys and sin is submerged in it.

The person to whom less is forgiven feels less love. Does this mean that a person must commit many sins, so that when they are forgiven he will love all the more? Such an inference would be like the one St. Paul rejects as nonsense in the Epistle to the Romans: " Let us remain in our sins, so that God's grace may be all the more plentiful (and show itself in all its power) " (6:1). This saying is not addressed to Simon the Pharisee; it is the reverse side of the saying which precedes it and which it is intended to clarify. The self-righteous person who thinks he has little or no need of forgiveness is in danger. He does not realize his guilt, and so there is nothing to impel him to welcome the gospel of God's mercy longingly, in a spirit of joy and gratitude. He may all too easily lack the overflowing love which is heralded by God's kingdom. Jesus had a blessing for the poor, while he told the rich: " It is too bad for you!" Simon was in danger because he despised the sinful woman and looked on himself as a just man. Because he was a just man, his love was weak.

Jesus did not do away with the distinction between greater and lesser guilt. He called sin by its own name. But in his struggle against sin, he followed different tactics, tactics unlike those of the Pharisees. They excluded sinners from the people of God who were meant to be holy, and separated themselves from them. Jesus, on the other hand, proclaimed and brought forgiveness. He made sinners holy and enrolled them once more among the people of God. He did this by preaching that love which is at once a gift and a command. This is love for Jesus such as the sinful woman had and, through him, for God. It is also love for one's brother, as it is implied in the parable of the pitiless servant who was deprived of the forgiveness he had received because he did not forgive his brother and had no love for him. It is in love that the way is prepared for forgiveness; in God's love for the sinner, in the sinner's love for God and for his fellow men.

[48]And he said to her : " Your sins are forgiven." [49]And those who reclined at table with him began to say to themselves : " Who is this who even forgives sins? " [50]But he said to the woman : " Your faith has saved you. Go in peace."

Jesus now affirms that her sins were forgiven. They had already been forgiven and they remained so, but Jesus now proclaimed this openly and set the final seal on it. It was faith that brought the woman salvation, but the remission of her sins was attributed to her love. " Much was forgiven her because she loved much." She was made capable of such love because she listened to Jesus' word and applied it to herself, welcoming it in a spirit of faith. Faith and love are closely linked, but both are concerned primarily with Jesus. In those days, no one had ever thought of a love for Jesus which could honor him and offer him grateful worship, while at the same time it was without real faith and failed to make a man a believer, first and foremost.

The Women Who Followed Jesus (8:1-3)

¹In the period that followed, he traveled from town to town and from village to village, heralding and proclaiming the gospel of God's kingdom, and the twelve were with him.

St. Luke loves to portray Jesus as a guest and as a tireless traveler. Jesus proclaimed the gospel, the message of victory. He acted as the herald who announced the coming of God's kingdom. Everything he did was in the service of this message; his actions were so many signs that God's kingdom was being inaugurated; they were an expression of this kingdom.

He was accompanied on his journeys by the twelve. Through him they heard and learned everything which they later announced to the people and effected among them. Jesus and the twelve formed the nucleus of the new people of God.

²And some women who had been delivered from evil spirits and from illnesses, Mary whose name was Magdalene, from whom seven devils had been driven out, ³and Joanna the wife of Chuza, one of Herod's stewards, and Susanna, and many others who provided for them with their own means.

Women, too, were among those who followed Jesus. The rabbis excluded women from their disciples. To them they seemed incapable of studying the law. "The man who teaches his daughter the law teaches her debauchery." The center of the circle which gathered about Jesus was not the law but Jesus himself; he came to bring salvation to the poor and the despised, to the outcasts and those who were ignorant of the law. The women among his followers bore witness to his intention and to his mission. Jesus made his teaching and the salvation he brought available to women.

The group of women who followed Jesus included some who had been delivered from evil spirits and illnesses. In St. Luke three names are prominent. Mary Magdalene from whom devils had been driven out, Joanna the wife of Chuza, one of Herod's stewards, and Susanna. These women give us an idea of the widespread influence Jesus' ministry had in Galilee. They realized that he was a saviour. St. Luke does not tell us that they were specially called to be Jesus' disciples. These women had no mission to teach or work miracles. They provided for Jesus and the twelve with their own means.

The service these women performed out of their own resources was a great help in furthering God's word, not only in Jesus' time but also in the future. The numerous women who helped the preachers of the gospel with the means at their disposal took their inspiration from them; Lydia (Acts 16:14), Priscilla (Acts 18:2), Syntyche and Evodia (Phil. 4:2), Chloe (1 Cor. 1:11), and Phoebe (Rom. 16:1f.).

In Galilee, Jesus assembled the witnesses of his activity. They followed him as he went about preaching, and later they would stand by the cross (23:49). Mary Magdalene, Joanna, and others would be informed of the resurrection by the angels and sent to bring the news to the apostles (24:10).

The regulations governing contemporary Jewish practice make it clear that women were not regarded as members of the community. They were allowed to take part in divine worship, but they were not obliged to do so. The divine worship could be celebrated only if at least ten men were present; women were not counted. These Galilean women, on the other hand, were founder-members of the church, and St. Luke provides a memorial to them: " The eleven apostles persevered with one mind in prayer, together with the women and Mary, the mother of Jesus, and his brethren " (Acts 1:14).

148

More than a Prophet (8:4—9:17)

In His Words (8:4–21)

A Parable (8:4–15)

Jesus pronounces the parable of the sower (8:4–8). Its explanation is a gift from God (8:9–10) which is granted primarily to the disciples (8:12–15). According to St. Mark, the parable of the sower opens Jesus' discourse by the lake, but St. Luke has nothing about this. In Mark, the lake is the center of Jesus' activity as a teacher, whereas in Luke Jesus appears by the lake only once. St. Luke's presentation of the facts is subordinated to a salvation history idea. Jesus' work was confined to the interior of the small country of Palestine; after the descent of the Holy Spirit, his disciples would abandon the inland country and take to the sea, to bring God's word to the whole world. The time of salvation marked by Christ's life was confined to Palestine and it was limited by the duration of his life; the time of the church encompasses the entire world and lasts until Christ comes again. But Christ's life was the center of all ages; it marked the fulfillment of the old age and the foundation and root of the age that was to come.

⁴*When a great crowd had gathered and people came to him from one town after another, he addressed them in a parable.* ⁵*"A sower went out to sow his seed. As he sowed, some fell on the path and was trampled on, and the birds of heaven ate it up.* ⁶*Other seed fell on the rock and when it sprouted it withered, because it had no moisture.* ⁷*Other seed fell among thorns and the thorns grew up with it and choked it.* ⁸ᵃ*Still other seed fell on good ground and grew and bore fruit a hundredfold."*

Jesus had a particular sower in mind. The autumn rains were over and it was now between the middle of November and December. The sower carried the seed in a sack suspended at his waist or in a fold of his clothing which he had drawn up. He went out to the field which had not yet been ploughed. The ploughing was done when the sowing was over; in this way, the seed was covered with earth. It was " his own seed " which he sowed; it contained an element of his own life and destiny.

The seed's fate depended on the ground it fell on. The field was in the hill country overlooking the sea of Galilee. While it lay fallow, a number of paths had been beaten across it. In many places, the soil scarcely covered the underlying limestone and the thistles grew shoulder-high. " Some fell on the path." The sower did not have to worry where he sowed the seed; the path, too, would be ploughed in when he was finished. St. Luke had not grown up in Galilee, and so he writes: The seed " was trampled on." In addition, the birds came along and ate it. He describes these with the biblical phrase: " The birds of heaven " (Gen. 1 : 26). " Other seed fell on the rock." The thin layer of soil covering the rock warmed up quickly and the corn sprang up luxuriantly; but it soon withered. The soil was so thin that it could not retain sufficient moisture. Some seed also fell " among the thorns and thistles." When the sowing was complete, these would be ploughed into the earth. As the seed germinated, the thistles would grow with it, thick and strong. They would soon choke the new growth.

St. Luke altered the text of the source he followed on numerous points. He was anxious that they should grasp the truth contained in the parable; he was not interested merely in reproducing it word for word. The gospel was intended primarily as a means of proclaiming the faith to particular people in a particular situation; it was not meant to be merely a literal account of all that was said and done. However, St. Luke was careful not to touch up his source too much. His regard for what was history prevented him from altering the image notably; on the other hand, the kerygma permitted any change which served the gospel's purpose. The gospel must remain alive.

[8b]*When he had said this, he cried out: " Let him hear who has ears*

to hear with." ⁹However, his disciples asked him what this parable meant. ¹⁰He replied: " It is granted to you to know the mysteries of God's kingdom, but the others know them only in parables, so that they see without perceiving and hear without understanding."

Jesus called on his listeners to attend to his word; he wanted them to reflect on it wholeheartedly. " He cried out." He was a herald, a messenger of the time of decision. The crowd was still present when his disciples asked him to explain the parable. Here St. Luke seems to be deliberately correcting the impression given by St. Mark. They requested an explanation of the parable, not only for themselves, but also for the people.

The kingdom of God is a " mystery "; it is God's design which was hidden from past ages (Mt. 13 : 35), but was now revealed at the last stage of time. Jesus inaugurated God's kingdom; in him, the mystery of the kingdom was present. Anyone who realized that it was Jesus who introduced the final event would also grasp the mystery of the kingdom. Such knowledge is a gift from God, not a result of one's own insight.

The realization that God's kingdom had come in Jesus set the disciples apart from the rest of the crowd. They were granted an insight into the parables which spoke of the kingdom. To the others, they remained a mystery, so that they saw without perceiving and heard without understanding. People saw but they did not perceive the essential point. The essential point was the realization that God's kingdom was already present and that it was Jesus who introduced the last stage of time.

The prophet Isaiah had said that there would be some who would see without perceiving, and listen without hearing. Why was it that the disciples understood the parables of the kingdom, while the others failed to do so? The evangelist was not writing a study of the psychology of belief or unbelief; he merely indicated the ulti-mate theological reason for these attitudes. So he based it on God's plan as it appears in scripture. However, God condemns no one to unbelief without some fault of his own. If a man sees without perceiving or listens without hearing, it is because he is impervious to the light of God's word.

The gulf between the disciples and the others was not insurmountable. They asked Jesus to explain the parable for them and for the people. They would pass on the explanation they received from him to the people. Through them, the grace of understanding would be given to the others, too, if only they were receptive and did penance.

11" *This is what the parable means. The seed is God's word.* 12*Those on the path are those who listened to the word; but then the devil comes and takes the word away from their hearts, so that they do not believe and are not saved.* 13*Those on the rock are those who, when they hear the word, receive it gladly, but have no root. They believe only for a time and in the time of temptation they fall away.* 14*What fell among the thorns represents those who listened to the word and are choked by the cares, the riches, and the pleasures of life, so that they do not bring their fruit to maturity.* 15*What fell on good ground represents those who receive the word with a good and noble heart and bear fruit in patience."*

" God's word " is the word about God's kingdom; it is the gospel, the good news of Jesus Christ who inaugurated God's kingdom. As a word which comes from God, it is endowed with power; it grows and it is active. The ultimate fruit this word produces is eternal salvation.

For the word to achieve its purpose and bear fruit in a man, it must be united with him in a life-giving communion. Instead of the words: " Those on the path are those . . . ," we should have expected something like: " The seed which fell on the path represents God's word." The unexpected turn of phrase is obviously inspired by the idea that those who hear the word are at once the ground in which the seed is sown and also the seed which must grow to maturity. The word enters into a union with the man who hears it; it changes him and transforms him completely.

The growth and fertility of the seed were endangered. The danger came from the devil, from inconstancy, from the temptation to fall away, from the cares of everyday life, from wealth, and from the desire for pleasure. These are still the major obstacles which prevent God's word from achieving its full growth.

The word achieves its optimum growth when three conditions are fulfilled. A man's heart must be beautiful and good. There is an echo here of the Greek ideal of nobility of life (" *kalokagathia* ": " moral beauty and goodness "). The noble man is the man who adapts himself to the divine will. Natural goodness in a man is the best preparation for an effective influence of God's word in his life. Then the word must be welcomed; a man must hold fast to it despite temptation and threatening difficulties. He must " bear fruit in patience," day after day, perseveringly and courageously. The word is meant to be lived and to be put into practice, despite all opposition.

While the word is preached and listened to, the enemies of man lie in wait; they are determined to destroy the word and prevent it from growing. Anyone who brings God's word to the world must reckon with these opponents, and the man who receives the word will not be spared either. The battle rages at every stage of the word's growth, immediately it is received, while it is growing, and before its final success. It is not without reason that the last phrase of the parable is an exhortation to patience.

HEARING THE WORD IN THE RIGHT WAY (8:16–18)

[16]" *However, no one strikes a light and puts it under a cover or*

hides it under a bed. He puts it on the lampstand, so that those who come in can see the light. [17]For nothing is hidden which will not be revealed; nothing is secret which will not be known and come out into the open."

When Jesus explained the parable of the sower a light was lit, understanding dawned. The disciples were to use this knowledge like a man who has lit a lamp. He does not put it under a cover or hide it under a bed; he puts it on a lampstand where everyone can see it. The man who has received God's word with its lightgiving power is bound to use it in the service of others.

[18]*" Be careful, then, how you listen. The man who has something already will be given more, and the man who has nothing will have even what he thinks he has taken from him."*

The disciples were to proclaim what they had heard. Otherwise, they would find themselves in the same position as a businessman; if he has the resources, he will be able to add to his fortune, because this gives him the possibility of a greater turnover and bigger earnings. If he has nothing, not only will he earn nothing—he will lose even the little he thinks he has, because it is dwindling all the time.

Religious knowledge which is not professed, lived, and proclaimed to others is only an empty show; it dwindles constantly. Living by the knowledge of the gospel and proclaiming it to others make a man grow in knowledge and in faith.

JESUS' RELATIVES (8:19–21)

[19]*His mother and his brothers came to him and could not get to him because of the crowd. [20]Then he was told : " Your mother and your brothers are outside. They want to see you." [21]He answered*

and said to them : " My mother and my brothers are those who hear God's word and do it."

Jesus was hemmed in by the packed crowd. His mother and his brothers wanted to see his miracles, to see him. But this is not the important thing. Once Jesus Christ had taken his seat at the Father's right hand, no one could meet him personally any more; we cannot see him with our own eyes or watch what he is doing. Jesus himself told us what the important thing is: " to hear God's word and do it." We possess God's word. " It is well for the man who has not seen and yet has believed " (Jn. 20:29).

The man who hears God's word and puts it into practice becomes " Jesus' mother and brother." It is not blood relationship that associates a person with Jesus; it is hearing God's word and keeping it. The church is built up by God's word; God's word is its soul; the church is the fruit God's word bears.

Jesus' mother is presented in the infancy gospel as good ground which hears God's word and keeps it. She is the Lord's servant; she heard God's word and placed herself at his disposal (1:38). She kept every word spoken about her child in her heart and reflected on it (2:19). She brought the word to Elizabeth and her proclamation of it multiplied it so much that it overflowed in the " Magnificat." She had a noble heart which held fast to the word and bore fruit in patience. Mary was Jesus' mother, not only because she gave him human life, but also because she heard God's word and put it into practice.

In His Actions (8:22–56)

A STORM IS CALMED (8:22–25)

22It happened one day that he boarded a boat with his disciples and said to them : " We will cross over to the far shore of the lake."

*And they pushed off. ²³And while they were on their way, he fell
asleep. A storm of wind came down on the sea and they were
swamped with water, so that they were in danger. ²⁴ªThey went to
him and cried: " Master, master! Get up. We are sinking!"*

The disciples were in grave danger. The Lord, the only one who
could come to their aid, was asleep. Blowing from the hills, the
storm broke with devastating power on the warm low-lying valley
and the lake. The boat was filled with water. In their desperation,
they roused Jesus. However, they did not utter a word of reproach,
simply: " We are sinking! "

²⁴ᵇ*But he stood up and threatened the wind and the raging waters,
and they subsided and there was calm. ²⁵And he said to them:
" Where is your faith?" But they felt afraid and they wondered,
saying to one another: " Who is this, that he commands even the
wind and the water, and they obey him?"*

God's power was revealed in Jesus. It is God who stills the roaring
of the sea and calms its waves; when the nations rage, he curbs
them (Ps. 65 : 8). It is he who " controls the boisterous sea. When its
waves rise up, he brings them to rest " (Ps. 89 : 10). The experience
past generations had had of God was now repeated in Jesus: " They
cried to the Lord in their distress and he freed them from their
affliction. He calmed the storm; the sea's waves were stilled "
(Ps. 107 : 29ff.).

In Jesus the disciples had God's kingdom present with them, to
bring them salvation. But they were on the point of despairing.
Where was their faith in him? It was he who had made them
put out to sea. He gave the order and entrusted them with this
mission. He was still with them. It was his word which gave the
command, and so they should not be afraid to take the risk.

The disciples clearly had some inkling of the truth; they were afraid and astounded. A feeling of reverence and awe held them captive. The questions they asked were addressed to themselves, not to Jesus. The wind and the waves obey him; he is a master and has the right to command. But what kind of a master is he? What earthly master has power to impose his will on the unchained forces of nature? Only God can command them with such power that they obey. Who is Jesus?

THE POSSESSED MAN AT GERASA (8:26–39)

[26]And they sailed on to the country of the Gerasenes, which is on the other shore, opposite Galilee. [27]But when he had stepped out onto the shore, a man from the town came to him who was possessed by demons. For a long time, he had gone without clothes and lived, not in a house, but in the tombs.

The land of the Gerasenes was pagan country and it was regarded as being in the devil's power. It was there that the disciples were to be initiated into Jesus' power over the demons. Jesus did not work any miracles in this pagan country; he merely saved the man who was possessed. The journey was intended to make his disciples realize that the concerted might of the devil could not withstand him, even on the devil's own ground.

The devil's power was revealed in the possessed man in all its horror. He spurned life itself and deliberately spent his time where others were overcome with revulsion and death made its home.

[28]But when he saw Jesus, he screamed and fell down before him, crying with a loud voice: " What can there be between me and you, Jesus, Son of the Most High God? I beg you, do not torment me." [29a]For he was commanding the unclean spirit to go out of the man.

The demons tried to defend themselves against Jesus. They knew that he had power over them. They forced the possessed man to go down on his knees before Jesus. In antiquity, the rules of magic prescribed that a man should lower his eyes before the approach of the deity and look at the ground, to be able to exercise more effective control over it. The demons tried to achieve this with the magic formula: "What is there between me and you?" We have nothing in common; you go your way and we will go ours. Shouting out Jesus' name was intended as a charm to ward him off and destroy his power. That was why they cried out: "Jesus, Son of the Most High God," and begged him, imploring his compassion : "Do not torment me." They appealed to his supreme power and at the same time to his human emotions. This shows us how Jesus appeared in the demons' eyes.

[29b]*For it had often seized him, and he was chained hand and foot and held in custody, but he broke the chains and was driven out into the wilderness by the demons.* [30]*Jesus asked him: "What is your name?" He replied: "Legion," for many devils had entered him.* [31]*And they begged him not to command them to go back into the abyss.* [32]*There was a herd of swine there, a great number of them, feeding on the hills; and they begged him to allow them to go into them, and he allowed them.* [33]*The demons then left the man and went into the swine and the herd rushed down the steep incline into the sea and was drowned.*

St. Luke loves repetition and here he describes the possessed man's misery once more. The superhuman power of the demons was manifested in the strength and the brute force of which the demoniac was capable. He was possessed by demons. This seems quite harmless, and yet they had often seized him and carried him off with them, abusing him as a helpless instrument of their restlessness. In his fits of delirium, he burst the chains which bound him and rushed out into the wilderness. What power had purely human bonds to check the unrestrained strength of a man who was possessed? Human custody and all human efforts were powerless.

The name " Legion " revealed the demon's terrible power. In the Roman army, a legion numbered about six thousand men. The possessed man was in the grip, not merely of one demon, but of a great number of them. A Roman legion was a well-organized and closely knit striking force, each unit of which had its allotted place. Rome's legions dominated the entire Mediterranean world. The demons, therefore, formed a kingdom, a kingdom which was in opposition to God.

By revealing their name, the demons acknowledged Jesus' superiority and at the same time abandoned the possessed man. They admitted that Jesus had power to command them; he was their judge, the Lord who set the final seal on their overthrow. In his presence, they were reduced to powerlessness; they could no longer do anything except admit their helplessness and beg for mercy.

Then a third indication of the demons' power was seen. The entire herd of swine into which the demons had entered rushed down the hillside and was drowned in the sea. In the demonology prevalent in antiquity, frenzied behavior among animals was attributed to the demons. It is true that the demons wield a certain power, but it is used in the service of chaos and destruction. God's kingdom embraces the whole of creation. After his defeat in the temptations in the desert, Satan was forced to recognize God's supreme dominion over the world. The demons pleaded with Jesus to allow them to go into the swine. They, too, acknowledged Jesus' power over all creation.

34When the swineherds saw what had happened, they fled and brought the news to the town and to the countryside. 35And the people went out to see what had happened. They came to Jesus and found the man from whom the demons had gone out sitting *there at Jesus' feet, fully clothed and restored to his senses, and they were afraid. ³⁶Those who had seen it told them how the possessed man had been saved. ³⁷And the whole crowd from the territory of the Gerasenes begged him to leave them, because they were seized with great fear. He boarded a boat and returned.*

Jesus stood in the center of the scene with the man who had been saved sitting at his feet like a pupil, fully clothed and in complete possession of his senses. He had recovered his true nature through Jesus. His power to command the demons cleared the way for the restoration of order and profound peace. Jesus is a liberator, a saviour in whom ruined creation is once more restored to its due order. This order was visible in the man sitting at Jesus' feet and listening to his word.

Those who witnessed the incident were terrified and took to their heels; they told everybody what had happened. Those who heard the news went out to see for themselves. The upheaval affected the whole territory of the Gerasenes and the entire population went out to Jesus, where they were seized with fear. The repercussions of Jesus' activity were becoming more and more widespread. However, his power on this occasion had a sinister effect; it inspired fear, not hope. Jesus' power appears uncanny and terrifying to anyone who does not realize that he is a saviour who frees men by means of God's word.

The crowd wanted to have nothing to do with this frightening stranger who was superior to all the sinister powers of the demons. For a few moments, it had become clear that there are other powers and influences at work behind the ordinary events of this world. Man, too, is drawn into this mysterious world. " Put on God's armor, so that you will be able to withstand the devil's attacks. Our battle is not against flesh and blood; it is against the powers, the spirits of evil in the heavens " (Eph. 6: 11f.). For us, Christ is God's armor.

³⁸But the man from whom the devils had gone out pleaded with him to let him remain with him. However, he sent him away saying: ³⁹" Go home and relate what God has done for you." And he went off through the whole town, proclaiming what Jesus had done for him.

The man who had been saved wanted to become an apostle, one of the twelve. Being with Jesus was the essence of the apostleship which the man sought. But his request was rejected.

At the same time, Jesus did not refuse him everything: " Go home and relate all that God has done for you." Anything implying that he had been sent by Jesus, or that he had a commission from him, was carefully avoided. His sphere of activity was to be his own home, his family; his preaching was to take the form of relating the facts. He was to speak, not about Jesus, but only about God. However, the man enlarged on it all, so that he preached a genuinely Christian message. The whole town was his field of activity; he did not merely relate what had happened, he proclaimed it, crying out as a herald, like the apostles. He spoke, not about what God had done for him, but about what Jesus had done. The Christian message burst forth with primeval power even in a man whom Jesus tried to restrain. When Jesus has risen from the dead and been raised to glory, the gentiles themselves will be apostles. Jesus was not content to vanquish the power of the demons who held mankind in captivity; he made those who had been captives preachers of God's kingdom and witnesses of his power over the devils.

His Power over Illness and Death (8:40–56)

⁴⁰When Jesus arrived back, the people welcomed him; they had all been waiting for him. ⁴¹And a man came there whose name was Jairus; he was the president of the synagogue. He fell at Jesus' feet and implored him to come to his house. [41]He had a daughter, an only child who was about twelve years old, who was on the point of death.

The people of Israel waited for Jesus and welcomed him; the gentile crowds, on the other hand, had sent him away. By means of salvation history, God had prepared Israel for the redeemer who was to come; the pagans had no liking for him.

In the presence of death and its power, Jairus, the president of the synagogue, was helpless. St. Luke's choice of words reflects his deep sorrow; an only child, her father's darling, twelve years old. She had just reached maturity, the age for marriage, and now she was on the point of death. All human power was here reduced to powerlessness. Jesus was her father's last hope.

[43]*As he went the crowds pressed about him. A woman who had been suffering from a hemorrhage for twelve years, and had spent her entire fortune on doctors without finding anyone to cure her, [44]came up behind him and caught the fringe of his garment, and the flow of blood stopped immediately.*

St. Luke once more introduces his account of the incident by saying that the people accompanied Jesus. The people had been waiting for Jesus, their great helper, and now they had him in their possession. They had welcomed him warmly and now they pressed close on him.

Once more, a suffering human being emerged from the mass of the people. This time it was a woman who had a sad history of past illness. She had been ill for twelve years with a hemorrhage. Apart from being ill, this meant she was ritually unclean and ostracized by everyone. She had spent her entire fortune on doctors, but no one could cure her. It was a tragic verdict—incurable.

Her only remaining hope was Jesus. She could not approach him apart from the crowd like Jairus, and fall at his feet to tell him of her plight. She was unclean and she made others unclean. She came up behind Jesus in the crowd and caught the fringe of his clothes. According to the law, Israelites were bound to have a fringe on the edge of their garments, to remind them of all the Lord's commandments (Num. 15:38f.). Jairus had asked Jesus to go to his house. He probably thought he could only work a cure by laying his hands on his daughter. The woman merely sought to make contact with Jesus, even if what she touched was only the outer edge of his clothes.

" The flow of blood stopped immediately." Here St. Luke speaks as a doctor. Without a word, without treatment of any kind, the cure was effected by a simple touch which medical science had sought in vain for years. As a doctor, St. Luke tones down the harsh judgment St. Mark passed on the medical profession: " Despite the doctors, the woman's condition became much worse " (Mk. 5:26).

⁴⁵And Jesus said : " Someone has touched me." As they all denied it, Peter said : " Master, the crowds are all about you. They are pressing in on you." ⁴⁶And Jesus said : " Someone touched me. I know that a power has gone out from me." ⁴⁷The woman saw that she could not remain hidden. She came, trembling, and threw herself before him and explained in the presence of all the people why she had touched him and how she was immediately cured. ⁴⁸But he said to her : " Daughter, your faith has saved you. Go in peace."

Jesus knew what had happened. " Someone has touched me. A power has gone out from me." It was not merely the physical contact which worked the miracle; it was the power which Jesus had at his disposal. He alone had knowledge of this; neither the crowd nor Peter knew anything about it. Jesus was a Lord and master in a far deeper sense than Peter suspected. He had commanded the waves and now he commanded the flow of blood.

The woman who had been cured abandoned her anonymity. She realized that in Jesus God was near. She knew she could not remain hidden and she trembled with fear in the presence of the divinity which was manifested. She fell down before Jesus. She proclaimed what had happened to her as God's doing in the presence of all the people. Under God's power which Jesus exercised over her, even this shy retiring person was able to proclaim God's wonderful action in the presence of the people.

It was by her faith, not by touching Jesus' clothes, that the woman was cured: "Your faith has saved you." It is faith which brings a person into saving contact with Jesus, our redeemer and saviour. Her faith had won her a peace for which the healing of her illness was only an outward sign.

⁴⁹While he was still speaking, one of the servants of the president of the synagogue came and said: "Your daughter is dead. Do not bother the master any more." ⁵⁰Jesus heard it and answered him: "Do not be afraid. Only believe, and she will be saved." ⁵¹When he came into the house, he let no one go in with him except Peter, John, and James together with the child's father and mother. ⁵²They were all weeping and lamenting her. But he said: "Do not weep. She is not dead. She is only asleep." ⁵³And they laughed at him, because they knew she was dead.

Jesus' power was not limited even by death. He was prepared to raise the girl from the dead if her father was prepared to believe. "Only believe and she will be saved." Faith is a condition of salvation. "Have faith in the Lord Jesus and you will find salvation, you and your household" (Acts 16:31).

Jesus wanted to perform this miracle in the presence of only a small group of witnesses. This included three of the apostles, Peter as the first among them, the two brothers James and John, and the girl's parents. When the Lord rose from the dead, he appeared, not

to the people at large, but only to the witnesses appointed beforehand by God (Acts 10:41). Not even all the apostles were initiated
into this mystery of God's kingdom, because it looked forward to
Jesus' passion, death, and resurrection.

At the burial of even the poorest Israelites there had to be at least
two flute players and a female mourner to chant a lamentation for
the dead. This was sung in the form of a responsory, to the accom-
paniment of hand clapping, the beat of tambourines, and wooden
clappers. The lamentation began after the person's death at his
house and it continued until the burial. Everyone joined in the
mourning and beat their breasts as a sign of their sorrow. Jesus
stopped the lamenting. "The girl is not dead. She is only asleep."
He looked on death with God's eyes and it was as God's mouth-
piece that he spoke. When it was confronted with God's might,
death lost its power. "They laughed at him," because they knew
she was dead. It never even occurred to the crowd that Jesus could
have power over death.

*54But he took her hand and cried out, saying : " Maiden, arise! "
55And her spirit returned to her and she arose, and he directed
that she should be given something to eat. 56Her parents were beside themselves, but he commanded them to tell no one what had
happened.*

The restoration of the child to life as a result of Jesus' word and
action is described in three different ways. " Her spirit [soul] returned to her." At death, the soul is separated from the body. Before
his own death, Jesus prayed: " Into your hands I commit my
spirit " (23:46). The girl arose. The power of life filled her body.
Then she had to be given something to eat. Eating is conclusive
proof of the reality of a person's life. What happened in the case of
this child would also happen when Jesus rose from the dead. His
spirit returned to him, he arose, and he ate and drank in the presence of his disciples.

165

The command not to mention what had happened seems to have been directed only to the parents, and not to the three apostles who were present. It was natural that they should make known what was hidden. They were to proclaim the mysteries of God's kingdom and make them known. These included the resurrection of the dead, of which Christ's own resurrection was the forerunner.

Jesus had demonstrated his might against powers which left human beings powerless. He calmed the unchained forces of nature and broke the demon's power; he vanquished death with all its strength and cured an incurable illness. He was able to do this because God's power was at work in him; in him God appeared on earth. On two occasions, St. Peter gave him the title " Master," and the demons addressed him as the Son of God. He was a liberator and a saviour. These three miracles brought Jesus' activity in Galilee to a climax. What was there left for a man to fear now if only he had faith?

The Activity of the Twelve (9:1-17)

JESUS SENDS THEM OUT (9:1-6)

¹*He called the twelve together to him and gave them power and authority over all evil spirits and [the power] to heal sicknesses.* ²*And he sent them out to proclaim God's kingdom and grant healing.*

Jesus " called the twelve together to him." Together they formed a unity which was centered on him. Now he wanted to work farther afield by their means. That was why he gave them the power and authority he himself enjoyed (4:36). He sent them, as he himself had been sent, to proclaim God's kingdom and to heal the sick; this was to be a sign that it was at hand. This was the first sign that the apostles were to be separated from their master.

³And he told them: " Take nothing on your way, no staff nor wallet nor bread nor money. And you are not to have two garments."

Jesus deprived the apostles of everything an ordinary traveler would refuse to go without, a walking stick, a traveling bag, food for the journey, money and a change of clothes. They were in God's service; he would provide for them. The mission they had received was to be their sole concern.

⁴" Once you have entered a house remain there and go on from there. ⁵Wherever they do not welcome you, leave the town and shake the dust off your feet in witness against them."

Jesus presupposed that the apostles would go into the people's houses to accomplish their mission. They must not change from any house where they had been made welcome. Their only desire was to be the accomplishment of their mission. The house where they stayed was to be a center of activity. God's word knows no rest. It had compelled Jesus to go ever farther afield, and it was also the driving force behind the apostles.

The apostles were to waste no time on those who did not receive them. Before leaving pagan country and entering the Holy Land, the Jews shook the dust from their feet. The apostles' mission was equivalent to a sentence of judgment. In the case of towns which rejected them, they would be witnesses for the prosecution. Their activity marked the beginning of the last stage of time.

⁶They set out and passed through village after village, proclaiming the gospel and doing works of healing everywhere.

The plan of campaign which Jesus had initiated in Nazareth and put into effect in Galilee was extended to the country at large by the apostles. St. Luke was particularly interested in the way in which the gospel was brought to the wide world. They went through village after village; they were almost systematic in their thoroughness. The verse ends with the word " everywhere." The whole country was filled with the news of God's kingdom which dawned in the apostles' preaching and their powers of healing.

HEROD'S OPINION OF JESUS (9:7–9)

⁷Prince Herod heard of all that was going on and he was at a loss, because some were saying: "John has risen from the dead," ⁸while many others said: " Elijah has appeared," and still others that: " One of the old prophets has risen up."

Jesus' fame penetrated to the court of the prince of the country, Herod Antipas. Who was Jesus? This was the question which the people, the courtiers, and the prince asked themselves.

Herod's entourage formed various conclusions. The different opinions concerning Jesus current among the people all had one point in common, namely, that Jesus was the prophet whose coming was expected before the last period of time. It seems, however, that no one dared to maintain that in him God had raised up a new prophet. So it was suggested that one of the former prophets had been raised from the dead and had appeared once more.

⁹But Herod said: " I had John beheaded. Who, then, is this man, about whom I hear such reports?" And he tried to see him.

Herod did not believe what people said about a prophet rising, or being raised, from the dead; neither did he believe what he heard about a man who had been taken away appearing again. Herod's explanation was quite simple: " I had John beheaded." He cannot be alive again. A man who is dead is dead.

Yet the question remained: Who was Jesus? His incredible achievements in word and action alike cried out for an explanation. But where was it to be found? Herod's only hope was if he could have personal experience of some miracle of his (23:8); " he tried to see him." Personal observation, he hoped, would enable him to come to a firm decision. He wanted to see Jesus at work, to see him personally and speak to him. But it is the way of faith, not the way of experimental investigation that leads to knowledge of Jesus.

The Apostles' Return; The Miracle of the Loaves and Fishes (9:10–17)

¹⁰And the apostles came back and told him what they had done. He took them and withdrew alone in the direction of a town called Bethsaida.

What was the result of Jesus' more widespread activity in the person of his apostles? The question concerning Jesus was thrown wide open. It caused unrest at all levels of society, and even in the royal court. The apostles returned and told Jesus all they had done. What had they achieved? What was the result of their activity in Galilee? He withdrew alone, taking the apostles with him. Herod was a serious threat. He had beheaded John the Baptist. The way St. Luke presents the facts they appear as an allusion to Jesus' own trial. The people had not arrived at a true understanding of Jesus. His most elaborate missionary venture had not met with the success which could have been expected. The result was that he withdrew into solitude on the farthest border of the land of Israel near Bethsaida, northeast of the sea of Galilee.

¹¹However, the crowds noticed it, and they followed him. He welcomed them and spoke to them about the kingdom of God, and he cured those who were in need of healing.

Before this, Jesus had sought out the people, either personally or by means of his apostles. Now it was the people who sought him out. In a previous passage we were told that the people welcomed him; now it is he who welcomes the people. He did not abandon his activity; he spoke to them once more about the kingdom of God and performed miracles of healing. Yet a certain reserve made itself evident: "He cured those who were in need of healing." However, the entire incident was steeped in the Lord's unfailing goodness. He welcomed the people cordially and he continued speaking to them and healing the sick unwearyingly until it was evening and the day was drawing to a close.

[12]*The day began to draw to a close. Then the twelve approached him and said: " Let the people go, so that they can go to the villages and farms round about, to look for somewhere to stay, and to get food. We are in the wilderness here." [13]But he told them: " You give them something to eat." And they replied: " We have no more than five loaves and two fishes, unless we are to go and buy food for all these people." [14]There were about five thousand men there. But he told his disciples: " Make them sit down as at table, in groups of about fifty." [15]And they did so, and made them all sit down.*

The people had to be provided with food and shelter in the desert. The solution to this problem proposed by the apostles was: " Let them go." They felt that they were responsible for them. But was that the correct solution—to send them away from Jesus? The correct solution could only be in their coming to Jesus.

Jesus inspired the apostles to provide for the people. " You give them something to eat." But how? Why not go out and buy food for the whole crowd? But where were they to find the money? The disciples admitted their inability to deal with the situation. They could only confess their helplessness; but this in itself was a necessary factor. The kingdom is given only to the poor and helpless.

Jesus told them to divide the people into groups of fifty each, as for a meal. He wanted to celebrate a festival meal. The celebration of the paschal meal was approaching when this miracle took place; therefore, sitting together as at table was very appropriate. Memories of Israel's wonderful past and hopes for its future were bound to be aroused. The multitude who had been inspired in part by the apostles' preaching was now assembled and organized as the community of God's kingdom.

¹⁶*But he took the five loaves and the two fishes, looked up to heaven and blessed and broke them, and gave them to the disciples to put before the people.* ¹⁷*And they all ate and had enough. And the pieces which they left over were taken up, twelve baskets full.*

Jesus presided over the crowd like the father of a family. In this capacity he took the bread and fish in his hands, and blessed them, breaking the bread. The people were already linked together as a community and arranged according to the ancient order of the Israelite camp; by feeding them in the way he did, Jesus now fashioned them into a community which would share in the eschatological meal. He himself described the fellowship which exists in God's kingdom as a meal (22:30). The four actions he performed at the beginning of the meal are underlined, because the early church saw in the miracle of the loaves an allusion to the eucharistic celebration and its accompanying rite. The feeding of the multitude in the wilderness was an anticipation of the time of salvation. This became a reality in the meal which the Lord celebrated with his apostles before his passion and it finds its full accomplishment in the kingdom which is to come.

Jesus blessed the bread. In St. Luke's version, he did not give thanks over it, as was the Jewish custom; instead, we are told he blessed it. In this way St. Luke attributes the feeding of the multitude with a few loaves to Jesus' blessing. The disciples then distributed the food; Jesus gave it to them to put before the people. It was Jesus who gave it, but the disciples distributed it. Everything comes from him; the apostles are the mediators whom he sends out. They proclaim the gospel; they heal the sick, and give the people food in plenty.

They all had enough. The pieces which remained over were collected in baskets. Each of the apostles filled one of these baskets. The time of salvation with its overflowing abundance had dawned.

This event brought the Galilean ministry to a climax. Jesus was the saviour promised for the end of time. But was he acknowledged as such?

The Suffering Messiah (9:18–50)

Messiah and Suffering Servant (9:18–27)

ST. PETER'S PROFESSION OF FAITH (9:18–20)

¹⁸*It happened that while he was praying alone, his disciples were with him. And he questioned them, saying : " Who do the people say I am? " ¹⁹They answered and said: " John the Baptist, but others say Elijah, and others a prophet from the past who has risen up."*

Before confronting his disciples with serious decisions, Jesus used to pray in solitude. He had done this before choosing the apostles (6 : 12), and he did it now, as he prepared to initiate them into the mystery of his mission (9 : 18). Later, he would behave in the same way before they experienced his passion and death (22 : 32f.).

Jesus' question was intended to pinpoint the conclusion which resulted from his activity in Galilee; it also laid the foundation for what still had to be done. The teaching he gave concerning God's kingdom in general was now concentrated on his own mission and the role he was to play in salvation history. Jesus' disciples were aware of the popular ideas concerning him which had reached Herod's court, and they quoted these to him.

²⁰*However, he said to them: " But you, who do you say I am?"*
Then Peter answered, saying: " You are God's Anointed."

The apostles had often been confronted with the question which Jesus now put before them. It had already occurred to them in the amazement and terror they had experienced on several occasions, and in the titles with which they addressed Jesus, " Teacher," " Master," " Prophet." For the moment, they had quoted the people, but the question Jesus put to them demanded a clear and unambiguous answer. " But you, who do you say I am?"

In his profession of faith St. Peter describes Jesus as " God's Anointed " which also means the " Christ " or the " Messiah." This title is connected with Isaiah's prophecy: " The Spirit of the Lord and Master is upon me, because the Lord has anointed me, to bring the gospel to the poor " (Is. 61:1).

THE PASSION IS FORETOLD FOR THE FIRST TIME (9:21–22)

²¹*Then he spoke to them threateningly and forbade them to tell this to anyone, saying:* ²²*" The Son of man must undergo a lot of suffering and be rejected by the elders and the high priests and scribes; he must be put to death and be raised up on the third day."*

Visibly moved, Jesus forbade the apostles to tell anyone what Peter had said. His profession of faith needed to be completed in one essential point: " The Son of man must . . . be put to death." Jesus avoided the title St. Peter had used, " God's Anointed "; instead, he spoke of the " Son of man," as he described himself. " The Son of man must undergo a lot of suffering; he must be rejected and put to death." There is an echo here of various references made by the prophets to the servant of Yahweh: " He bore our illnesses and took our sorrows on himself " (Is. 53:4). " Men despised him, and avoided him, a man of sorrows . . . we hid our faces from him; we scorned him and regarded him as of no worth " (Is. 53:3). " He was taken away unlawfully and without anyone to champion him. Is there anyone who troubles himself about his fate, now that he has been cut off from the land of the living and brought to death for our enemies?" (Is. 53:8). It was in his suffering that the servant fulfilled God's design which was expressed in scripture. That was why it had to be so. Isaiah gives the true explanation of the servant's suffering and death: his suffering and death were an atonement. The Son of man suffered and died on behalf of the many, on behalf of all (see Is. 53:12). But on the third day he would be raised up again. " From out of this wretched life he sees the light. Indeed, by his knowledge, he satisfies many . . . that is why I gave him a share among the great; he distributes his spoils among the strong " (see Is. 53:11f.).

Jesus' Galilean ministry was introduced with the passage from scripture concerning the saviour who was anointed with the Spirit (Is. 61:1). In his profession of faith Peter took up this prophecy once more. Jesus then completed it by referring to Is. 53 which deals with the suffering servant who atones for the sins of others. Jesus' mission and his work can be understood only in the light of God's word. As the Son of man, he is at once the eschatological saviour and the suffering servant.

His Disciples Must Imitate His Suffering (9:23–27)

[23]*But he said to everyone: " If anyone wants to come after me, he must deny himself and take up his cross day by day and follow after*

me. ²⁴The man who is determined to save his life will lose it; and he who is determined to lose his life for my sake will save it. ²⁵What good will it do a man if he gains the whole world and destroys or harms himself?"

Jesus' true disciple must go after him; he must follow him. But Jesus was going to meet his passion and death; therefore, his disciple, too, must be prepared to walk the path of suffering and death for Jesus' sake. True discipleship means imitating Jesus' suffering.

St. Luke adds the phrase " day by day " to Jesus' words about taking up the cross. Martyrdom is an event which occurs once and for all; imitating Jesus in his suffering is something which must be undertaken day by day. " Through many tribulations must we enter God's kingdom " (Acts 14:22). Anyone who professes his faith in Jesus and lives by his word, doing God's will as he revealed it, is bound to encounter opposition from within and without. Men will hate Jesus' disciples and subject them to abuse for the Son of man's sake (6:22). If God's word is not to be choked, a man must say no to all anxious cares, to wealth, and to the desires of his passions.

Jesus seeks to encourage his disciples to imitate his suffering by a very prosaic, almost commercial approach. Anyone who wants to follow Jesus, the suffering servant, must be prepared for martyrdom; he must be ready to endure great distress and harm to himself. Following Jesus in this way confronts a man with a choice. On the one hand, he may keep his earthly life safe and satisfy his longing for experience; on the other, he stands to gain eternal life and true fulfillment of his longing for life in God's kingdom. The man who has no desire to follow Christ in his suffering cannot enter God's kingdom either.

How is man to choose? The important thing is that he should save himself. What good does it do him " if he gains the whole world," but destroys himself in the process? St. Luke uses two expressions: " destroys or harms himself." Here, too, he adapts what

Jesus actually said to the everyday experience of Christians. Not everything that is incompatible with following Jesus or obeying his message destroys eternal life; numerous actions merely harm it. But a Christian must have a sober estimation of things and renounce even what can harm this life.

²⁶*" For, if a man is ashamed of me and my words, the Son of man will also be ashamed of him, when he comes in his own glory and that of his Father and the holy angels. ²⁷But I tell you truthfully, there are some of those who stand here who will not taste death before they have seen God's kingdom."*

The thought of the Son of man who is coming as a judge is meant to give us the strength to follow the Son of man who took up his cross. Jesus was crucified; he was treated as a criminal, abandoned and cast out by his own people. In antiquity a Roman citizen could not be crucified; crucifixion was the lot of disreputable persons, of slaves and deserters. Anyone who professes himself a follower of this Jesus and takes his word as his rule of life exposes himself to the same disgrace as Jesus. A man will naturally defend himself against loss of reputation and slander. Consequently, he may be tempted to be ashamed of Jesus and his words, abandoning him and falling away from him. Jesus spoke these threatening words to preserve us from falling away and denying him. It is by following Christ in his shame, and professing our faith in him, that we will be saved at the judgment.

In his prophetic discourse, the threatening words Jesus used are followed by a promise of salvation. The man who takes his stand by Jesus and his word will see God's kingdom and experience it. This promise was so certain that Jesus could say that some of those who were listening would not taste death before they saw God's kingdom. God's kingdom was already present (17:21); Jesus' preaching had inaugurated it. However, it was not yet visible.

Some of the disciples who were there—Peter, James and John—would see God's kingdom revealed in Jesus' glory, when he appeared before them on Mount Tabor. These witnesses saw God's kingdom revealed in Jesus. They are our guarantee that Jesus will come one day in God's glory and be seen by everyone.

The Revelation of the Suffering Messiah (9:28–43)

THE TRANSFIGURATION (9:28–36)

²⁸*About eight days after this exchange, he took Peter and John and James aside and went up on to a mountain to pray.*

The transfiguration looks back to Peter's profession of faith in Christ and the prophecy of the passion which followed it. The transfiguration was a concrete representation and confirmation of what Jesus had said. A mountain is the traditional site for such divine manifestations.

The three disciples whom he took with him had also witnessed the raising of Jairus' daughter from the dead. At a later date, they would witness his mortal agony in the garden of Gethsemane. Before they saw him in his final agony, he granted them the vision of himself as victor over the power of death. It is probable that he did not take anyone else with him up the mountain because his glorification was intended to remain a mystery of faith until he comes again in his Father's glory. In the same way, after his resurrection from the dead, he appeared only to the witnesses God had appointed beforehand.

²⁹*As he prayed, the appearance of his face was altered and his clothes shone a dazzling white.*

The splendor of the light was a symbol of the divine world.

" You clothe yourself with light, as with a cloak " (Ps. 104:2; 1 Tim. 6:16). God's glory shone forth like a lightning flash and penetrated Jesus' entire being, even his clothes. He was revealed as God's Christ (" Anointed "), as he will come one day in sovereign power, surrounded by the glory of his majesty. The reality in which Peter has professed his faith was now revealed.

God glorified Jesus as he prayed. From his baptism, through the transfiguration, to his resurrection, the same theme constantly recurs; the way to glory is the confession of one's own nothingness in prayer.

³⁰*And see, there were two men speaking with him, Moses and Elijah.* ³¹*They were in glory as they appeared, and they spoke of his departure which he was to accomplish in Jerusalem.*

The splendor of the divine glory enveloped the two men who appeared, showing that they were heavenly persons. The evangelists describe them as Moses and Elijah. It was said of both of them that they had been taken up into heaven. They were both " prophets, powerful in word and action," and both were closely connected with the Messiah who was to come. Elijah prepared the way for him, while Moses was regarded as his prototype, as the scribes used say: The second saviour (the Messiah) will be like the first (Moses). Both Elijah and Moses had suffered greatly. The Acts of the Apostles portray Moses as a servant of God who was misunderstood and rejected (Acts 7:17–44). Elijah complained to God that his enemies wanted to take his life (1 Kings 19:10).

The two great prototypes of the Messiah spoke of his " departure which he was to accomplish in Jerusalem." They confirmed the prophecy he had made concerning his passion and death at Jerusalem. That Jesus was to suffer and die was part of God's plan, the plan he had made known in the scriptures, the law, and the prophets so long before. Jesus' departure in Jerusalem forms the center of salvation history. It was to this central point that the great men of old looked forward, and it is to this that the church looks back. His departure in Jerusalem marked the beginning of the last stage of time, for this is to bring to completion what began with his death.

³²But Peter and those who were with him were weighed down with sleep. When they awoke, they saw his glory and the two men who were standing there with him. ³³And as they were about to leave him, Peter said to Jesus: " Master, it is good for us to be here. We will make three huts, one for you and one for Moses and one for Elijah," but he did not know what he was saying.

Is there a connection between the mountain of the transfiguration and the Mount of Olives where Jesus' passion began? In both places the three chosen disciples and witnesses fell asleep while Jesus was praying. " When he rose from his prayer and came to his disciples, he found them asleep, overcome with sorrow " (22:45). On the mountain of the transfiguration, they awoke to see his glory; on the Mount of Olives, the Lord himself woke them and the traitor came on the scene immediately (22:47). The way to glory leads through suffering. Only those who keep watch and pray can understand this way.

Peter wanted to preserve the vision in three huts. When God comes to men, he lives in a tent. This was what he had done in the desert, when he lived in the tent of the covenant among his people. This is also the figure used to describe his presence in the last stage of time: " See, here is God's tent among men. He will live with them and they will be his people, and God himself will be with them " (Rev. 21:3). Peter thought that God's sovereign rule had already begun, that the messianic age was at hand; God and his saints had come among his people, and so it was good for the three disciples to be there; they could put up the tents. This was the image of God's great saving acts which Peter had formed in his human mind.

The apostle "did not know what he was saying." The glory of the Messiah had appeared in Jesus, but only for a few moments. It could not yet be made to last. First he must travel the road to Jerusalem, where death awaited him. His disciples were in the same position; they could not preserve this glory either. They, too, must journey onwards; they must depart through death. This law held good, not merely for the three disciples, but for all those who would be Jesus' disciples in the whole life of the church. We cannot yet hold him fast (Jn. 20:17); we must continue to journey onwards in patience by a constantly renewed decision in favor of God's word.

[34]But as he said this, a cloud formed and overshadowed them. They were overcome with fear, as they disappeared into the cloud. [35]And a voice resounded from the cloud saying: "This is my Son, the Chosen One. Listen to him."

A cloud was the traditional sign of God's presence when he came to punish or to bestow his favors on men. A cloud had accompanied the people of God on their journey through the desert (Ex. 14:20), and it enveloped Mount Sinai when God came down in the form of fire to reveal his will (Ex. 19:16ff.). The temple was filled with a cloud when it was being dedicated; in it, God's glory descended on the building (1 Kings 8:10ff.). The prophets had described the dawn of the last stage of time as being shrouded in clouds. The cloud which enveloped Jesus, Elijah, and Moses was a sign that God was present in the divine glory Jesus enjoyed, in anticipation of the last age of time. "The glory of the Lord will be seen and the clouds, as they were seen by Moses" (2 Mac. 2:8).

God proclaimed that Jesus was his Son, the Chosen One. The prophecy Isaiah made concerning God's servant was fulfilled in him: "See, this is my servant, whom I have drawn to myself, my

Chosen One, in whom I am well pleased. I have laid my Spirit on him; he brings truth to the nations " (Is. 42:1). Jesus' enemies would later mock him as he hung on the cross with the words : " Let him save himself, if he is God's Christ, the Chosen One " (23:35). They rejected his claim to be the Messiah because of his passion. Christ was God's Chosen One, not merely in his passion or despite his passion, but because of his passion.

" Listen to him." God's words reëchoed what Moses had already said about the prophet who was to come. "The Lord your God will raise up a prophet like me from among you, from the brothers of your own tribe. You must listen to him. The rule is valid for everyone: The man who does not listen to this prophet will be uprooted from the people " (Acts 3:22f.; Deut. 18:15, 19).

³⁶*And when the voice had sounded, Jesus was found alone. They kept silent and said nothing to anybody at the time about what they had seen.*

The glorious manifestation did not last long. Jesus was found alone. " He was in the form of God and did not consider it robbery that he should be like God. Yet he emptied himself, took the form of a slave, and was found in the likeness of men " (Phil. 2:6f.).

As long as Jesus was with them, the disciples " said nothing to anybody about what they had seen." They had seen God's kingdom and its mysteries. The greatest of these mysteries was that the glory of the kingdom had dawned as a result of Jesus' death; and that the saviour brings us salvation by means of his passion. At that time, who would have been capable of believing this mystery?

THE CURE OF THE POSSESSED BOY (9:37–43a)

³⁷*When they had come down from the mountain on the following*

day, it happened that a great crowd came to meet him. ³⁸*And there a man called out from the crowd and said : " Master, I beseech you, look at my son. He is my only child.* ³⁹*A spirit seizes him and he screams without warning. It pulls him this way and that, foaming at the mouth; it wears him down and will scarcely let him go.* ⁴⁰*I begged your disciples to drive it out, but they were not able."*

A father called out to Jesus from the crowd, addressing him as a teacher, " Master." He wanted Jesus to look at his son. He was an only child, like the widow's son at Nain (7 : 12) and Jairus' daughter (8 : 42). St. Luke describes the boy's condition with the professional competence and interest of a doctor (see Mk. 8 : 18). The symptoms of his illness showed three phases : The evil spirit seized the boy (first phase), and immediately cried out through him, pulling him this way and that, while he foamed at the mouth (second phase). Finally, he threw him to the ground; when the attack was over, the victim was tired, worn out, and exhausted (third phase). These symptoms indicated epilepsy. The doctor in him did not betray St. Luke into yielding to the temptation to include a scientific medical investigation in his gospel. He attributes the illness to evil spirits. St. Luke gives us the gospel as it is, a gospel which proclaims the advent of salvation and does not go in for medical diagnosis.

The misery of father and son was intensified by their failure to find help where they had hoped to find it. Despite the power and authority they enjoyed, the apostles who had stayed behind were unable to help them. Why was this?

⁴¹*But Jesus answered and said: " Oh unbelieving and perverse age! How long will I still be with you and have to bear with you? Bring your son here."*

Jesus was still subject to the influence of the transfiguration. The

Father had revealed his messianic dignity; he had exalted him above all others as the chosen Son of God and summoned all men to believe in his word. But what confronted him now? The demons with their destructive activities, the disciples with their weak faith, and the people who were unbelieving and perverse (Acts 2:40). In virtue of God's glory and power, Jesus held man's destiny in his hands. At the same time, however, he complained about the people's indifference. He was the Son of God, his suffering servant. The people failed to comprehend his way, so that it filled him with "dismay" (Mk. 14:33). Yet he was ready to show pity. "Bring your son here." As God's Anointed and his chosen Son, he was determined to bring salvation, to remain open to the people's misery.

⁴²Even as he was coming forward, the devil tore him and pulled him this way and that. But Jesus threatened the unclean spirit and cured the boy, giving him to his father. ^{43a}They were all amazed at God's majesty.

The demon was cast out and the boy's illness was cured, so that his father was comforted. God's majesty was revealed in what Jesus did. People called Jesus " master " and acknowledged that he made God's majesty visible.

The Way of the Suffering Messiah (9:43b–50)

JESUS FORETELLS HIS PASSION A SECOND TIME (9:43b–45)

^{43b}While they were all wondering at everything he did, he said to his disciples : ⁴⁴" Take in these words with your ears : ' The Son of Man will be given up into the hands of men '."

They all wondered at everything he did. This was the final result

183

of Jesus' Galilean ministry. Once more, a sharp distinction is made between all the people and Jesus' disciples. The disciples were not to allow themselves to be carried along by the hope the people entertained. They were not to look forward to still greater miracles; instead, the Son of man was to be given up into the hands of men who would do what they liked with him. Who was it that gave him up? God! This was his plan. While everyone else wondered, Jesus fixed his eyes on the divine plan. There is no mention of the resurrection in this prophecy.

45They did not understand this word; it was hidden from them, so that they could not grasp it, and they were afraid to ask him about it.

The words of the prophecy were clear, but what they expressed was mysterious and obscure. The Son of man would be given up into the hands of men. The Messiah, who enjoyed the fullness of power, was to be handed over to the arbitrary will of men. This was what God had disposed. " The Lord let the guilt of us all fall on him [the suffering servant]" (Is. 53:6). Why did Jesus' path to glory have to lead through his passion? Why did this have to be the way his disciples and his church must follow? The disciples were afraid to ask him about this word. Internally, they refused to face the thought of Jesus' death, but they realized that Jesus would reject such an attitude (Mk. 8:32).

DISCIPLESHIP IN THE LIGHT OF THE PASSION PROPHECY (9:46–48)

46The thought occurred to them, who was the greatest among them. 47But Jesus, fully aware of the thought in their hearts, took a child and placed him beside him. 48He said to them: " Whoever welcomes this child in my name welcomes me, and whoever welcomes me welcomes him who sent me. In fact, whoever is least among you all, he is great."

The desire to be greater than others, to rule over them and have them at one's disposal, is deeply rooted in the thoughts of a man's heart. This was true of Jesus' disciples too. But they were careful not to say what they were thinking about in their own minds; the desire to rule is kept hidden, concealed under a mask.

Jesus brought the small child close to him and gave him a place of honor at his side. He placed him over the disciples, giving him precedence before them. All eyes were fixed on him. Then he made a wonderful promise to anyone who would welcome a small child and was prepared to serve him. If anyone wants to be great, he must place himself at the service of the very least. It is serving, not ruling, that makes a man great; serving those who are small and despised.

The child must be welcomed in Jesus' name. This is not merely an act of human kindness; it is an action which should be characteristic of Jesus' true disciple. When Jesus' disciple lowers himself and serves others, he does it in imitation of Jesus who also abased himself.

If Jesus was delivered into the hands of men, it was so that those who were the least of all the helpless and unredeemed, might be made welcome, that they might find shelter with God. If a man adopts Jesus' outlook, not only does he give himself up as a slave into the hands of men; he also ensures that Jesus will welcome him; he finds shelter and fellowship with God. It is the church which is God's fellowship in Jesus. " It is he [Christ] who appointed some as apostles, others as prophets and evangelists, others as pastors and teachers, to equip the saints to perform every service for the building up of Christ's body " (Eph. 4:11f.).

THE STRANGER WHO EXORCIZED (9:49–50)

[49]*But John answered: " Master, we saw a man who drove out*

demons in your name and we restrained him, because he did not
follow you with us." ⁵⁰*But Jesus told him: "Do not prevent him.*
The man who is not against you is for you."

The answer the disciples made to Jesus' discussion on the need
to serve others was a display of ambitious anxiety to preserve their
exclusive status. Even one of those who were closest to Jesus failed
to understand what he had said about becoming little. This was
John, whom St. Luke often mentions in conjunction with St.
Peter, and who always precedes his brother. The necessity of
following Jesus who gave himself up into the hands of men to be
at their service is a constant source of fresh surprises concerning
the thoughts of people's hearts.

Among the Jews, there were people who cast out devils from
those who were possessed through prayer (exorcists). On witness-
ing the success the disciples had in driving out demons in Jesus'
name, one of these exorcists tried to do the same without becoming
a disciple of Jesus. The invocation of Jesus' name proved effective
even outside the narrow circle of his disciples.

The stranger who practiced exorcism incurred the disciples' dis-
pleasure. They regarded their position as an indication that they had
been chosen to be above everyone else. To them, the outsider's
activity seemed to lessen their own exalted rank. They were determined to give the orders, not to serve. They complained: He does
not follow—in our company. But anyone who champions Jesus
and his work must not be prevented from doing so, even if he is
not a disciple. God's choice of a man is not intended to serve his
ambition or self-seeking; it is intended to serve Jesus and the salvation of those who are troubled. The man who is chosen to follow
Jesus is chosen to serve.

The stranger who exorcized was not an opponent of the apostles.
He invoked Jesus' name. Therefore, he should have been regarded
as an ally. The apostles' attitude should have been determined by

objective impartiality, not by ambition, by the desire to further Jesus' work, not by anxiety about their own standing.

Jesus here uses a proverb which was current at the time of the civil war in Rome: " We have heard you saying that we [Pompey's supporters] regard all those who are not with us as our enemies, and that you [Caesar] regard all those who are not against you as being on your side." Jesus acknowledges that Caesar's saying was right. The stranger who exorcized acted like one of his disciples, in Jesus' name. He extended the sphere of its influence. " If only Christ is proclaimed, in whatever way it may be, whether as a pretext or in all truth, I am glad of it " (Phil. 1:18). There was no place for jealousy here. St. Luke's version of the saying: " The man who is not against you is for you" is different from that given by St. Mark who says: " The man who is not against us is for us." In this version Jesus includes himself with his disciples; in St. Luke's version he is separated from them. In their meditation on Jesus, the faithful had become more and more conscious of his exalted dignity. Obviously, we have need of both versions. We need to be reminded of our union with Jesus and we need to keep a reverential distance. We need to draw near to him trustingly, and to be respectfully conscious of what separates us.

Jesus' Galilean ministry was at an end. The brief account of the stranger who exorcized underlines many aspects of this period once again. Jesus was recognized among the people—even among the Jewish exorcists who did not follow him—as one who was able to save men from the power of the demons. The exorcisms which used to be performed by invoking God's name were now performed in Jesus' name. Jesus' message and his work were destined to break all bounds and take everyone into their service.

THE JOURNEY TO JERUSALEM (9:51—19:27)

The journey to Jerusalem is mentioned in three noteworthy passages. Jesus turned his face steadfastly towards Jerusalem (9:51). He journeyed from town to town and from village to village, teaching and making his way towards Jerusalem (13:22). As he journeyed towards Jerusalem (17:11), he passed right through Samaria and Galilee. It was at Jerusalem that the decisive phase in the saving event took place; the passion and the resurrection are intimately connected. The phrase St. Luke uses to express this union is Jesus' " taking up " (9:51). Jesus' teaching discourses (11:1—13:21; 14:1—17:20; 17:20—19:27) are linked with the accounts of his journey (9:51—10:42; 13:22-35; 17:11-19). They are situated in a framework which bears no relation to any particular place or time, so that they are of perennial significance. As he journeyed towards his goal, Jesus taught his disciples the " ways of life " (Acts 2:28).

The Beginning (9:51—13:21)

The Wandering Master and His Disciples (9:51—10:42)

JESUS IS REFUSED HOSPITALITY (9:51-56)

⁵¹*It happened that as the time for his taking up was coming to an end, he set his face steadfastly and journeyed towards Jerusalem.*

God had fixed a definite duration for Jesus' life on earth, and the passage of time was now bringing this period to an end. Jesus' life ended with his " taking up." The expression refers both to his death and his ascension. Its twofold sense expresses exactly what awaited Jesus in Jerusalem: suffering and death, passion and glorification, resurrection and ascension. Jerusalem was preparing to kill Jesus, but by God's design this also meant that his glory, too, was being prepared.

Jesus "set his face steadfastly towards Jerusalem." He knew what was waiting for him there and nothing could turn him aside from the way. Jesus also knew the glory which awaited him at Jerusalem, so that he went his way with joyful confidence.

52And he sent messengers before his face who came to a Samaritan village, to prepare a place for him to stay. 53But they would not receive him, because his face was fixed on Jerusalem, as he traveled onwards.

The shortest way from Galilee to Jerusalem leads through Samaria. This was the way Jesus chose, when he had set his face towards Jerusalem. The messengers were intended to find lodgings for his party. He was accompanied by a great crowd; the twelve were with him, together with a large number of women, and a group of disciples from whom he later chose seventy.

Bitter religious and national animosity existed between the Samaritans and the Jews. The Samaritans were descended from the Asiatic tribes which were settled in Israel, the Northern Kingdom, when it was overrun by the Assyrians in 722 B.C. and also from the indigenous population which remained on. They had adopted the Israelite faith in Yahweh, but had built a temple of their own on Mount Gerizin. The Jews despised the Samaritans as half pagans and avoided contact with them (Jn. 4:9). Hostile attacks frequently occurred between the two groups. When the Samaritans heard that Jesus was on his way to Jerusalem, their hostility was aroused and they refused to let him stay with them.

54When James and John, the two disciples, saw this, they said: "Lord, do you want us to call down fire from heaven to destroy them?" 55But he turned and rebuked them. 56And so they went to another village.

James and John were indignant because Jesus had been turned away. They recalled that Elijah had called down fire from heaven on those who insulted him, and the fire came down and destroyed them (2 Kings 1:10–14). Jesus was greater than Elijah (9:19, 30). Surely the contempt the Samaritan village had shown for Jesus had to be punished. It was clear that the disciples found it very hard to grasp the idea of a suffering Messiah. In spite of all he had said, they asked Jesus if they could pronounce a curse on these people.

Jesus rebuked the disciples. This rebuke is explained in the words given in many manuscripts: "Do you not know what spirit it is you share?" The disciples must share Jesus' outlook. He was anointed to bring the gospel to the poor and to give sight to the blind (4:18). The Son of man came, not to destroy men's lives, but to save them (19:10). The apostles were sent to save, not to destroy, to forgive, not to punish. In the spirit of Jesus, they were to pray for their enemies, not to curse them (23:34).

"They went to another village." We are not told whether it was a Samaritan village or some village in Galilee. The road Jesus took was not important, only its goal; it was not his rejection by men, but his taking up by God that mattered.

JESUS CALLS A NUMBER OF DISCIPLES (9:57–62)

57As they were on their journey, one of those on the road said to him: "I will follow you wherever you go." 58And Jesus told him: "The foxes have holes and the birds of heaven their nests. The Son of man has nowhere to lay his head."

Like the rabbis' pupils, this unknown man chose his own teacher. His decision to become Jesus' disciple at the very moment when he had been rejected on his way to Jerusalem showed unqualified generosity. "I will follow you wherever you go." He divined

instinctively the basic attitude Jesus demanded of those who followed him—the submission which is ready for anything.

"The Son of man has nowhere to lay his head." Being Jesus' disciple means sharing his lot. This is something to be remembered.
Jesus' true disciple must be prepared to journey, to be turned away,
and to go without the security of a home.

[59]*To another he said: " Follow me." But he said: " First let me go
and bury my father."* [60]*But he told him: " Leave the dead to bury
their dead, but you must go forth and proclaim God's kingdom."*

This time it was Jesus himself who called the man to be his disciple.
This was the usual thing. "He called those whom he wished "
(Mk. 3:14). "It was not you who chose me, it was I who chose
you " (Jn. 15:16). The man in question was willing to follow him,
but not immediately. Burying the dead was a serious obligation
among the Jews. Even priests and Levites had to do it for their
relatives, although they were strictly forbidden to contract ritual
impurity by contact with a corpse. This obligation dispensed a man
from all the other obligations of the law. Therefore, the man's
request for a postponement seemed fully justified.

Yet Jesus would not allow him to make any delay. He demanded
unquestioning obedience. The answer he gave seems lacking in
respect for the dead; it was completely foreign to man's natural
instincts, and would seem almost criminal in the eyes of a pious
Jew. In one sharp, pregnant phrase, Jesus gives the reason for his
refusal: "Leave the dead to bury their dead." The call to become
Jesus' disciple transfers a person from death to life. Anyone who
is not a disciple of Jesus and refuses to accept his message concerning God's kingdom and eternal life is in a state of death. The
man who attaches himself to Jesus has passed over to life through
the power of the message he brings concerning God's kingdom.
These are two worlds which no longer have anything in common.

Once a man has become a disciple there is only one thing left for him to do: "proclaim God's kingdom." This is the all-important thing. The proclamation of the kingdom takes precedence over everything and brooks no delay. Jesus was on his way; his mission to proclaim the kingdom of God could not be postponed. He kept his face turned steadfastly towards his taking up. The glory which awaited him freed him from all the bonds imposed by respect for the dead. It is more important to proclaim life to those who are spiritually dead, and to rouse them, than to bury those whose bodies are dead.

⁶¹Another man said : " I will follow you, Lord, but first let me go to take leave of those who live in the same house with me." ⁶²But Jesus told him : " No one who puts his hand to the plough and looks back is fitted for the kingdom of God."

The third candidate offered himself spontaneously as a disciple, as the first had done. He addressed Jesus as " Lord " and showed himself ready to acknowledge Jesus' unlimited right to dispose of him, giving him unquestioning obedience. The first of the three disciples was prepared to follow Jesus wherever he went; the second heard the call of Jesus' lifegiving and vivifying power; the third acknowledged Jesus as the Lord. The man who is determined to be Jesus' disciple must follow after him; he must be seized by God's creative summons and place himself completely at Jesus' disposal.

Ready as he was to follow Jesus, this person, too, asked for a certain concession. He wanted to take leave of the members of his household. He made the same request Elisha made of Elijah, but Jesus refused him permission.

The replies Jesus gave the three disciples all demand the renunciation of any home a man may have in this world. A home offers a man a place to lay his head; a home is characterized by respect for one's father and mother; a home means security in the company of those with whom it is shared. Like Jesus himself, his disciples must depart; they must go on their journey without delay and without interruption. Jesus kept his face turned towards Jerusalem where death awaited him. But that was not all; God's glory also awaited him there, man's true home.

The Seventy (10:1–24)

JESUS APPOINTS THEM AND SENDS THEM OUT (10:1–16)

¹After this, the Lord appointed seventy others and sent them out, two by two, before his face to every town and village where he himself wanted to go. ²He told them : " The harvest is great but the laborers are few. Pray, therefore, to the Lord of the harvest that he will send laborers for his harvest."

It was vitally important for the early church to realize that the twelve were not the only ones who had been entrusted with such missionary activity; Jesus had given a similar commission to another group. Besides the twelve, there were others who could be called apostles; they, too, helped to fulfill Jesus' mission.

The number seventy corresponds to the seventy nations which, according to the list of peoples given in the Bible (Gen. 10), go to make up the entire human race. Jesus laid claim to the whole of humanity, as did the message he preached. The scribes believed that the law had been offered originally to all nations, but only Israel accepted it. The last age of time saw God's original plan accomplished and brought it to perfection.

" The harvest is great." The human race is compared to a harvest which must be gathered into God's kingdom. The mission field which confronted Jesus in Palestine was only the beginning of a far greater harvest which embraces the whole world. Jesus knew the great numbers of people who have good will. It was an enormous task and an urgent one, but there were only a few laborers. Even zealous and willing men often lacked the complete dedication necessary, as the calling of the disciples showed.

God is the Lord of the harvest. Everything concerning it is in his hands. Admission into God's kingdom is his work; it is an effect of his grace. It is God, too, who calls a man to be a disciple. That was why Jesus appealed to his disciples to pray that God would inspire men with their spirit, enabling them to cooperate wholeheartedly in bringing others into his kingdom. God wants us to pray for the gifts he gives us. Praying for laborers to be sent out for the harvest would remind the apostles and disciples that it was through God's grace they themselves had received their vocation and their mission.

[3]" *Go! And see, I am sending you out like sheep among wolves.* [4]*Carry no purse for money, no knapsack or shoes; greet no one on the way.*"

" Go." This one word describes their mission. It is a mission to set out, to journey, and to act. This was a surprise preparation for their task: " Go!" Their first and most important qualification was that they were sent by Jesus himself.

The disciples were stripped of all human means. They were sent out " like sheep among wolves." Israel had always regarded itself as a " sheep among seventy wolves." But the Israelites were also convinced that their great shepherd would watch over them and keep them safe. The seventy whom Jesus sent out were the nucleus of the new Israel. God's kingdom was promised to those who were gentle and defenseless (Mt. 5:3ff.). The disciples who were sent by Jesus were to be poor. If a person has no wallet, no knapsack, no sandals, he *is* poor. Poverty is a condition for admission into God's kingdom (6:20), and the mark of those who preach it. " Greet no one on the way." Undivided dedication to their mission would allow them no time for the long drawn-out and ceremonious forms of courtesy in use in the East.

⁵" In whatever house you enter, say first of all: ' Peace to this house.' ⁶And if there is a son of peace there, peace will rest upon him; if not, it will come back to you. ⁷Remain in the same house, eating and drinking what they have. The worker is worthy of his reward. Do not move from house to house."

Their method of evangelizing was to be simple and straightforward; they were to visit people in their houses. The message of Christianity spread from household groups to the town as a whole. " Peace to this house " is at once a greeting and a gift.

In return for the gifts the disciples brought, those who were sons of peace would show them hospitality. They were to make the first house where they were welcomed their home. " Remain in the same house. Do not move from house to house." The great desire of those who were sent must be to preach the message of God's kingdom. Their personal well-being and the treatment they received from those who were to provide for them could not be the decisive factor. Anyone who is constantly changing his lodgings shows that what he values most highly is his own comfort, not God's word.

The disciples were to eat and drink what was put before them, without worrying whether they were an excessive burden on their hosts. Their mission was not to be hindered by any temporal cares. What they received was nothing more than their due return for the much greater gift which they brought with them. " The worker deserves his reward " (1 Tim. 5:18). " If we have carried out a spiritual sowing on your behalf, is it much if we reap a harvest in the material [earthly] gifts you give?" (1 Cor. 9:11). On the other hand, the disciples were to be content with what was put before them.

⁸"And when you enter a town and they make you welcome, eat what is put before you, ⁹and heal the sick, telling them: ' The kingdom of God has come close to you.' ¹⁰But if you enter a town

and they do not welcome you, go out into their streets and say:
¹¹'The very dust from your town which has clung to our feet we
shake off before you. But you must know this. The kingdom of
God is at hand.' ¹²I tell you, Sodom's fate on that day will be more
bearable than the fate of that town."

The disciples' mission was directed at homes and at towns. A town
which made them welcome gave proof of its good will. The disciples could then accomplish the work for which they had been
sent. "Eat what is put before you." They were not to worry
whether the food was ritually clean or not. It seems this is the way
St. Luke takes these words, although it is unlikely that Jesus meant
them this way. Such freedom of conscience was of basic importance
for the church's mission to the gentiles. The disciples were given
a commission to heal the sick. This was intended as a means of
preparing the people for the hour of salvation history which they
proclaimed; it provided factual proof that this hour had dawned
in all its force. Their preaching was to proclaim the message for
which their actions had prepared the people: "The kingdom of
God is at hand."

But what if a town refused to welcome the disciples? Then they
were to anathematize the place and withdraw from it publicly (in
the streets) and solemnly. The Jews used to shake the dust from
their feet when they left pagan territory and were about to tread on
the holy land of Palestine.

The man who rejects the preaching of God's kingdom and in this
way closes his heart to Jesus draws down a sentence of condemnation on himself. The outcome of this judgment is more frightful
than the sentence of condemnation passed on Sodom. The sentence
inflicted on that immoral town was proverbial, but the guilt of
those who reject Jesus and the blessings of God's kingdom surpasses even Sodom's guilt. The disciples' preaching offered those
who heard it an extraordinary grace; it confronted their consciences

with a choice, the ultimate consequence of which would be a sentence of salvation or condemnation.

¹³" *It is too bad for you, Chorazin, too bad for you, Bethsaida. If the powerful actions performed in you had been performed in Tyre and Sidon, they would have done penance long ago, sitting in sackcloth and ashes.* ¹⁴*But Tyre and Sidon will be better off at the judgment than you.* ¹⁵*And you, Capernaum, were you not raised high as heaven? You will be thrust down to the realm of the dead.*"

These three towns, Chorazin, Bethsaida, and Capernaum, formed a triangle on the north-eastern shore of the sea of Galilee. It was there that Jesus had been most active, and the miracles which revealed his divine power were particularly prominent there. Capernaum had been the center of his activity and it was with reference to this town that Jesus repeated the words Isaiah spoke concerning the king of Babylon: " You say to yourself: ' I will go up to heaven. Higher than God's stars I will place my throne, setting myself on the mountain of the gods in the extreme north. I will climb above the heights of the clouds and be like the Most High.' How you have fallen! Down to hell, to its deepest pit " (Is. 14:13–15). Jesus had raised Capernaum to the rank of " his own town " (Mt. 9:1). He had offered it salvation, power, and glory, an offer which he also made to the other towns. He had exalted them in his desire to give them a share in God's glory. The miracles he performed there were intended to make them think. They were to recognize God's will and make it the center of their lives, opening their hearts to repentance. But the three towns failed to meet the conditions involved in God's offer of grace. Jesus threatened them with judgment; the greater the grace that was shown them, the more stringent would be the demands made of them at the judgment.

Tyre and Sidon were pagan towns which the Jews regarded as

being completely given over to worldly interests. They had not received the grace which was offered to the Galilean towns. Jesus knew that they would have repented in sackcloth and ashes if God had visited them with his offer of grace. Precisely because God knows they would have put this grace to much better use he will judge them leniently, while passing a harsh sentence on the towns of Galilee with inexorable justice.

In the sentence of condemnation which Jesus foretold for these Galilean towns, any town can see what will happen to it if it rejects the messengers he sends. Jesus spoke these words as he was leaving Galilee where he had labored in vain. His efforts were intended to bring them salvation, but instead they constituted a sentence of condemnation because they refused to listen to his appeal for repentance.

16"The man who hears you hears me; the man who scorns you scorns me. And the man who scorns me scorns him who sent me."

Those who are sent take the place of the one who sends them. It is Jesus himself who comes in his messengers and God comes in Jesus. To welcome the messengers' words or reject them is to welcome Jesus' words or reject them; it means welcoming or rejecting God's own words. No one can remain neutral when confronted with God's word. The man who is not for Jesus is against him; the man who does not listen to the word, welcoming it and obeying it, scorns it.

THE SEVENTY DISCIPLES RETURN (10:17-20)

17The seventy came back rejoicing and said: "Lord, the demons themselves are subject to us in your name." 18But he told them: "I saw Satan falling from heaven like a lightning flash."

Of all that they had experienced on their missionary journeys, the seventy mention only one item, the power they had exercised over diabolical forces. " Even the demons obey us." It was not only that sicknessess obeyed their command, or that men obeyed God's word; the greatest thing was that the powers of Satan were subject to them. They returned rejoicing. They had had personal experience of God's kingdom which dawned in Jesus. They addressed him as " Lord." The invocation of his name had given them control over the demons. Through the Lord, the power his messengers enjoyed penetrated even into the realm of the dominions and powers who exercise their restrictive influence on the world unseen by men's eyes. It was not only earthly reality that was subject to Jesus' power and that of his disciples; their powers extended even to the spheres which influence the course of earthly events to some extent.

When the disciples cast out the demons with power, it was a visible sign of the victory of God's kingdom over the powers of Satan. " I saw Satan falling from heaven like a lightning flash." Jesus constantly regarded casting out evil spirits as a sign that Satan's power was broken. When was it broken? Jesus' words say nothing about this, but they do make it clear that the defeat suffered by Satan was decisive. The way it is put reminds us of Isaiah's words about the downfall of the powerful Babylonian monarch Nebuchadnezzar. " You were thrown down, you who conquered the nations! How you fell! Down to hell, to its lowest pit " (Is. 14 : 13ff.). This victory over Satan was a result of Christ's death on the cross and his glorification : " Judgment is now being passed on the world; now the prince of this world is being cast out " (Jn. 12 : 31).

[19]" See, I have given you twelve power to walk on snakes and scorpions, and over all the might of the enemy, and nothing will harm you. [20]Yet, you should not rejoice too much that the spirits are subject to you; rather, rejoice that your names are written in heaven."

The twelve shared in Jesus' victory over Satan. St. Luke was anxious to extend what was true of the twelve apostles to the seventy disciples and to all those who cooperate in Jesus work. They have power over snakes and scorpions. Because of their vicious nature and the threat to life they constituted, these were the very things which were regarded in the Bible and in biblical language as Satan's agents. The saviour whose coming was expected would free men from snakes and scorpions, and from all evil spirits. Protected by God's angel, the Messiah would walk on vipers and adders; he would trample down lions and dragons (Ps. 91:13). When Jesus sent out the twelve he gave them a share in this power. It was given to them permanently; no longer were they to be at the mercy of Satan's power; they were to be subject to God's rule.

The inauguration of God's kingdom was really a greater source of joy than the power to command evil spirits and the collapse of Satan's rule. The apostles' greatest source of joy was that they had been chosen out and predestined for *eternal life*. In antiquity it was customary for a town to keep a list of its citizens. Those whose names were included in it enjoyed all the privileges the town had to offer. A similar list was also supposed to exist in heaven which was regarded as God's dwelling place. This included the names of all those whom God had chosen; it was like the Book of Life. The greatest possible source of joy is to be able to share in God's kingdom, to enjoy eternal life and have fellowship with God.

Jesus' Cry of Joy (10:21–24)

²¹*In that same moment, Jesus cried out for joy in the Holy Spirit and said: " I praise you, Father, Lord of heaven and earth, because you have hidden this from those who are wise and clever and revealed it to the little ones. Yes, Father, so it seemed good in your sight."*

The disciples' return and their account of what they had done was an occasion for giving thanks (10:21), for making a fresh revelation (10:22), and for offering praise to God (10:23f.). Jesus cried out for joy at the very moment they came back. He was filled with the joy which was characteristic of the last stage of time, the time of salvation, which was announced in his victory over Satan and the communication of eternal life. As the saviour, Jesus had been anointed with the Spirit; consequently, it was in the Holy Spirit that he cried out for joy and prayed. His prayer was subject to the influence of the Holy Spirit. This was the way Zechariah (1:67), Elizabeth (1:41), and Mary (1:47) had prayed. Jesus' whole life was dictated by the Spirit. " All those who are guided by God's Spirit are sons of God " (Rom. 8:14). It was as God's Son that Jesus offered his prayer of thanksgiving and made a fresh revelation as he gave praise to God.

Jesus' prayer of thanks began with a form of address and closed with a protestation. The reason for his thanksgiving occurs between the two. The address contains an expression of praise and thanks; Jesus praises God and in so doing he gives him thanks. He gave his interior assent to what God had disposed; in words of praise he states that his will was at one with the divine will. " I praise you " —I accept your will wholeheartedly. The best way to praise God and give him thanks is to be devoted to his will.

All Jesus' prayers which have been handed down to us in scripture begin with the word " Father." This is a translation of the Aramaic term " *Abba* " (Mk. 14:36), a term of endearment young children used to address their fathers. Jesus spoke with God his Father in tones of unparalleled intimacy. At that time, no one would have dared say " *Abba* " to God, although the term Father (" *Ab* ") was used In the present verse, this intimate form of address is accompanied by the reverential title " Lord of heaven and earth." God is the creator of all, and everything is at his disposal. Confidence and reverence are the two pillars of prayer.

It was God who had hidden, God who had revealed. In the praise Jesus offered, it is this revelation, not the concealment, that is in the forefront. However, God does not give his revelation to everyone, and by that very fact he conceals it from some. What was it that he had hidden and revealed? This, that is, the mystery of the kingdom of God (8:10) and the fact that it had come in Jesus; Satan's defeat and the fact that God had chosen some for his kingdom. This was what God had hidden from those who were wise and clever and revealed to children, to little ones who had no understanding, and to those who were regarded as of no account. In Jesus' time, the wise and the clever were the scribes; they described themselves as those who were learned and wise. The children were those who belonged to the " accursed people " of the country; they knew nothing about the law, had no education, and consequently made no effort to avoid sin. That was why a scribe in Jesus' own day could say: " An uneducated person has no horror of sin; and an *am ha arez* [a person who did not have a scribe's knowledge of the law] is not a virtuous person." The experience of the early church was that God's choice in revealing or concealing his mysteries followed the same lines. There were not very many who were rich, wise, or well-born in the church at Corinth (1 Cor. 1:26ff.); it was made up largely of those who were poor, ignorant, and of low birth, of those who counted for nothing in this world.

The final words of Jesus' prayer of thanks take up the opening thought once more and reassert it. The phrase " Yes, Father," is a joyful repetition of what he had already said. Jesus takes nothing back; instead, he embraces God's plan with his entire will in a spirit of praise and thanks. " So it seemed good in your sight." It was God's design, based on what seemed good to him, that decided Jesus' will. True prayer ends with an expression of assent to God's will which represents the victory of the divine will over the will of the person praying and in surrender to God's good pleasure.

²²" *Everything has been given over to me by my Father. No one knows who the Son is except the Father, or who the Father is, except the Son and anyone to whom the Son wishes to reveal it.*"

In this verse Jesus' prayer becomes a revelation and he speaks about his relationship to God. Everything had been given over to him by the Father. The message he preached was something which had been given over to him, but what God had given him was not merely a message; he had also given him the reality and the power that went with it. In his role as the Son of man, God had given everything over to Jesus, the fullness of power and all the wealth of the world, the entire human race. "All power has been given to me in heaven and on earth " (Mt. 28:18). Because he said yes to his will, the Father gave Jesus what Satan had offered him in the temptation. The Father loves the Son and has given everything into his hands to do with as he pleases (Jn. 3:35).

Jesus and the Father are united in intimate fellowship. No one knows who the Son is except the Father, and no one knows who the Father is except the Son. If we know a person, it means that we are occupied with him; we influence him and are influenced by him; we profit by him and benefit him in return. We enjoy a certain fellowship with him which affects both our lives. The Father knows the Son and the Son knows the Father, because they both live in intimate communion. Jesus and God know one another; the Father knows who the Son is, and the Son knows who the Father is. The Son's conscious life is determined by the communion he enjoys with the Father, while the Father's life is determined by his communion with the Son. This verse is a " pearl " among all the statements concerning Christ which refer to Jesus' relationship to God. Its content finds expression in many passages in St. John's Gospel: " I am the Good Shepherd. I know my sheep, and my sheep know me, just as the Father knows me and I know the Father " (Jn. 10:14f.).

" Anyone to whom the Son wishes to reveal it " also has know-ledge of the Father. Jesus had authority to share his knowledge of the Father with others. The Son could reveal it to anyone to whom he wished to reveal it. Of himself, man could never attain this knowledge. When Jesus revealed to a man that God was his Father, and this in a unique way involving the most intimate possible fellowship, he thereby gave him a share in the fellowship he himself enjoyed with his Father; he gave him a share in eternal life. " This is eternal life, that they should know you and him whom you have sent " (Jn. 17:3).

23And turning to his disciples alone, he said: " It is well for the eyes which see what you see. 24I tell you: many prophets and kings wanted to see what you see and did not see it, to hear what you hear and did not hear it."

The disciples were the only ones to whom the Son had revealed who the Father was. He had initiated them into the mystery of his unique relationship to the Father. " It is well for the eyes which see what you see." The disciples must never forget the grace God had shown them in revealing the knowledge of the Messiah and the dawn of the time of salvation to them. These words echo the joy felt by the early church, which handed them down to us, at the thought of the gift of faith she had received. What was hidden from those who were wise and clever was revealed to children, to those who were least of all. It was well for the disciples, because they were poor and of little account.

" To hear what you hear." It is not enough merely to see. Seeing must be accomplished by hearing. Jesus can be seen properly only when we hear what revelation has to say about him. It is seeing the events as they took place in history and hearing what God's revelation says about them that gives a Christian the knowledge which will make him truly happy.

Disciples in Word and Deed (10:25-42)

Jesus went about the country doing good and proclaiming God's word. The disciples' preparation for their mission consisted in a charity which was truly universal (10:25-37) and in the word which they heard by listening to Jesus (10:38-42).

LOVE FOR ONE'S NEIGHBOR (10:25-37)

²⁵*Then a scribe approached to try him and said: " Master, what must I do to inherit eternal life?"* ²⁶*But he said to him: " What is written in the law? How do you read it?"* ²⁷*And he replied saying: " You shall love the Lord your God with your whole heart and your whole soul, and with all your strength and in your whole mind, and your neighbor as yourself."* ²⁸*And he said to him: " You have answered correctly. Do this and you will have life."*

Jesus had spoken of victory over Satan; the disciples themselves had had experience of God's kingdom; their names were inscribed on the roll of citizens in heaven. They had been told that they were fortunate because they had lived to see the time of salvation. What could be more obvious, then, than the question: What must be done to enter eternal life? This was something to be really concerned about. This was the burning question the rich young man had asked Jesus (Mk. 10:17). The scribes' disciples asked their masters the same question: " Rabbi, teach us the ways of life, so that by following them we can attain the life of the world to come."

The scribe put the question to Jesus to try him. He approached him as a teacher and was anxious to see what answer he would give to this burning question. He framed the question the way it appeared to the Jews and asked what actions must be performed. It was the actions prescribed by the law which brought a person to salvation. For the Jews, the important thing was what a man did, not his interior disposition. On what actions, on what commandments, did salvation depend? The scribes mentioned six hundred and thirteen precepts (two hundred and forty-eight commandments and three hundred and sixty-five prohibitions).

The answer to the scribe's question is contained in the law, the written law of scripture. Jesus took the answer from the law in which God's will is revealed; it is the law that shows the way to eternal life. The scribes had tried to reduce the multiplicity of precepts and prohibitions to a small number of laws which would sum them up. One way to do this was the " Golden Rule": Do not do to your neighbor what you yourself find unpleasant; that is the whole law. Everything else is only a commentary of this (Rabbi Hillel, c. 20 B.C.). Another scribe regarded the commandment to love one's neighbor as the essence of the law (Lev. 19:18). The scribe who put the question to Jesus summed up the whole law in the commandment to love God (Deut. 6:5) and one's neighbor (Lev. 19:18), as Jesus himself had done (Mk. 12:28). This way of summing up the law must not have been unknown among the Jews in Jesus' time. Jesus acknowledged that the scribe was right in regarding these two precepts as the essence of the law. The truths of revelation are meant to be synthetized and presented systematically, so that they can be made to serve the Christian life.

The Jews in Jesus' time made a solemn profession of faith in the one true God every day, in the morning and at evening. In so doing, they recalled the commandment to love God (Deut. 6:5) and dedicated all the powers of their souls to him, affirming their determination to live for him without reservation. This commandment binds a man to God in the very depths of his being, and the commandment to love one's neighbor (Lev. 19:18) is connected with it in this verse. A person's love for his own self is set up as the norm of his love for his neighbor.

This has numerous implications. It means that love must be a man's basic attitude. It is not the man who is self-centered that fulfills God's will and lives up to his image in himself; it is the man who lives for God and for his neighbor. God must be man's center. He must love him with his whole soul and with all his strength. Love of self and love for one's neighbor are both taken up into this total consecration of oneself to God. He must put it into practice. " Do that and you will have life."

²⁹*But he was determined to vindicate himself and he asked Jesus : " And who is my neighbor? "*

The Pharisees were very anxious about their standing. They were always vindicating themselves. " The Pharisee stood there and prayed in his heart with the words: ' O God, I thank you that I am not like the rest of men. . .' " (18 : 1). Jesus reproached them with wanting to vindicate themselves in men's eyes (16 : 15). Was the scribe to be blamed for asking what must be done to attain eternal life, when he already knew? Were there not plenty of other problems which needed to be solved, although the most important precepts were clear enough? In this verse, the scribe puts a question which had never been answered clearly. Who is my neighbor? How far does the obligation to love one's neighbor extend? According to the law, it extended to all Israelites and to those foreigners who lived among the people of Israel (Lev. 19 : 34). In later Judaism, this love for strangers was restricted to full proselytes, pagans who had adopted the Israelite faith in one God and observed the law, including circumcision. The Pharisees excluded the ordinary people who were ignorant of the law from the precept of charity. The opponents of one's own party were also excluded. The law, therefore, left numerous questions unanswered. Only Jesus' Spirit could give the correct answer.

³⁰*Jesus began to speak saying : " A man went down from Jerusalem to Jericho and fell in with robbers. They stripped him and inflicted injuries on him and went off, leaving him lying there half dead."*

Jesus tells a story. There are four other such stories in St. Luke. The parables compare God's behavior with man's; God's actions are explained by comparing them to what men do. In these stories, however, it is a man that is held up to us, so that we can compare our conduct with that of the man whom Jesus shows us and clarify our moral judgments.

Attacks by brigands on the Jerusalem-Jericho road were common from antiquity to modern times. " A man went down." We are told nothing about his nationality or his religion. He was simply a man; that was enough to give him a right to be loved. The robbers may have been partisans, fanatical zealots who hid in the caves and secret hideouts of the district and lived by stealing. However, from their own countrymen they used never to take more than they needed and they were careful, above all, not to endanger their lives, unless they themselves were attacked. In this case, the robbers' victim was pitifully mistreated; stripped, injured, abandoned, half dead. He had obviously defended himself when he was attacked.

[31]*"As it now happened, a priest came that way and, when he saw him, he passed by on the other side.* [32]*In the same way, a Levite came to the place and, when he saw him, he passed by on the other side.* [33]*But a Samaritan who was going that road came to him and, when he saw him, he was seized with compassion.* [34]*He went up to him and bound his wounds, pouring oil and wine into them. Then he put him on his own pack animal and brought him to an inn, where he cared for him.* [35]*Next morning he took out two silver pieces and gave them to the innkeeper, saying: ' Take care of him and if you spend more than this, I will repay you when I come back '."*

Jericho was a Levitical city. The priest and the Levite (a temple servant or singer) had fulfilled their office in the temple at Jerusa-

lem and were on the way home. St. Luke's repetition of the phrase :
"And when he saw him, he passed by," is very effective. We are
not told why the priest and the Levite passed by. Perhaps they
thought the man was already dead, and not merely half dead.
In that case, they would be reluctant to touch the corpse because it
would make them ritually unclean (Lev. 21:1). Perhaps they were
afraid they themselves would be attacked by the brigands. Or it
may be that they were unwilling to be delayed. Whatever the
reason, anxiety for their own comfort proved stronger than their
pity for the poor man by the roadside, if they felt any pity for him
at all. As a priest and a Levite, they served God; they were men
who should have been models of obedience to the commandments
of love for God. But what about love for one's neighbor? Worship
and the virtue of compassion were completely separated.

The Samaritans were the national enemies of the Jews. They had
no dealings whatever with one another, and their hatred was
mutual. Once more, Jesus repeats the phrase: " when he saw him,"
but then comes the sudden reversal: " he was seized with compassion." His sympathy did not remain ineffective. The Samaritan
reacted in the way any human being would be bound to react in
such circumstances. Jesus carefully enumerates the six different
acts of charity which are calmly taken for granted. By means of
these, the Samaritan helped the man, not merely for the moment,
but until he was recovered. Two silver pieces, the sum given to the
innkeeper, represented two days wages for a laborer. This was not
much; in Italy about the year 140 B.C. board and lodgings for a
day cost one and one-third silver pieces. The Samaritan's action,
therefore, was not heroic, but he did everything that was necessary
to save the man.

[36]" *Which of these three seems to you to be a neighbor to the man
who fell among robbers?"* [37]*He replied: " The man who took pity
on him." Then Jesus said to him: " Go and do the same yourself."*

In Jesus' interpretation of the commandment of love, a person's neighbor is anyone who needs help. His nationality, religion, or party is of no importance. A person's neighbor is every human being. Where a person's need cries out for pity, the commandment of love cries out for action. It is action that Jesus demands: " Do the same yourself." Love for one's neighbor is an active love.

The best preparation for fulfilling the commandment to love one's neighbor is to have a heart which is open to men's needs. We must be ready to be moved to pity or, in plain biblical language, we must be " moved to the depths of our bowels " at the sight of human misery. When a man feels " bad " at the sight of misery, he is ready for love. " It is well for those who are merciful; they will obtain mercy " (Mt. 5:7).

LISTENING TO THE WORD (10:38–42)

³⁸While they were on their journey, he came to a place where a woman named Martha made him welcome in her house.

Jesus finds here what he had failed to find in the Samaritan village, somewhere to rest. We are not told where the village was or what it was called. According to St. John's account, it was Bethany (Jn. 11:1), a village near Jerusalem. St. Luke felt no need to mention this, even if he knew it. For him, Jerusalem was the goal of Jesus' journey; he would reach this only when the time for his death and ascension had come.

"A woman named Martha " made him welcome in her home. Jesus stayed in her house so that she might hear his word. Like Martha, other women, too, welcomed the messengers of the gospel and gave them shelter: "A God-fearing woman named Lydia, a dealer in purple from the town of Thyatira, heard them. The Lord opened her heart, so that she listened attentively to Paul's words.

When she and her household had been baptized, she begged him :
' If you regard me as a trustworthy person in the Lord's eyes, come
to my house and stay there,' and she pressed us " (Acts 16:14f.).

³⁹*And she had a sister called Mary who sat at the Lord's feet and
listened to his words.* ⁴⁰*Martha was drawn here and there by her
many tasks in laying the table. So she came to him and said:
"Lord, do you not mind that my sister should leave me all alone
to do the serving? Tell her to come and give a hand with me."*

Martha's sister Mary sat at Jesus' feet. She was like St. Paul at the
feet of Gamaliel, his teacher (Acts 22:3). Jesus was a teacher, while
Mary was his disciple. The Jewish scribes refused to explain the law
to women. But the teacher who was the Lord preached his message
to women as well (8:2). St. Luke describes the episode in terms
adopted from the usage of the early church; Jesus is the Lord, and
Mary listens to the word. The church is the assembly of those who
are always listening to the words of their glorified Lord (8:21).
During his stay, therefore, Jesus was honored in two ways. Mary
sat at the Lord's feet and listened resolutely to his word. " Martha
was drawn here and there," full of anxiety to get the table laid.
Jesus was honored by Martha's active love in serving him and by
Mary who listened to his word so carefully, by the active and con-
templative life, as the fathers of the church used to say.

Martha could not understand how Mary could listen to the word
without doing anything, when the table had to be laid for their
visitor. To her, serving at table was more important than serving
the word, which means listening to it, first and foremost. She did
not realize that Jesus wanted to give, not to receive, that he was sent
to proclaim salvation and that the best way to serve him was to
listen to his word and put it into practice. She spoke to him in a
slightly reproachful tone and wanted to take Mary away from
listening to the word to wait at table. She thought too much of her

own service and underestimated the importance of listening to Jesus' words; action seemed more important to her than listening.

⁴¹*But the Lord answered her: " Martha, Martha, you are anxious and disturbed about so many things,* ⁴²*but (only) one thing is necessary. Mary has chosen the good part which will not be taken from her."*

By addressing her twice, " Martha, Martha," Jesus showed the sympathy, care, and affection he felt for her. He acknowledged the efforts she was making, but the words he used to describe her activity showed what he thought of it. What she was doing was nothing more than an expression of restless anxiety which overlooked the most important thing of all: " Rather, seek the kingdom of God, and this, too, will be given to you " (12:31). God's word cannot bear fruit if those who hear it are held fast in the grip of restless anxiety (8:14).

(Only) one thing is necessary; Mary had chosen the good part. Jesus laid down the principle that listening to the word was the one thing necessary. He did not mean that Martha should only prepare one course or, at most, a few courses for the meal, so that she could come to listen to God's word sooner. She should not have prepared anything at all. Only one thing was necessary, to listen to the word Jesus proclaimed. The first place belongs to what is God's.

It is true that waiting on tables and all the other works of charity are important. As Christ tells us himself, they are really a service done to him (Mt. 25:40). However, they must not prevent a person from listening to the word, or make him think little of it. According to God's word, the apostles withdrew from waiting on the poor at table to be free to proclaim God's word, and left the service of the poor to deacons (Acts 6:1f.). The story of the good Samaritan finds its necessary complement in the story of Jesus' visit to Martha and Mary.

The New Prayer (11:1–13)

Nothing more is said about the journey to Jerusalem until 13:22. Various doctrinal discourses of Jesus are inserted into the story of the journey. Jesus brought a new message concerning the Father and the Holy Spirit; consequently, he also brought a new form of prayer (11:1–13). He proclaimed himself a new saviour, although both he and his teaching were very different from what those who were leaders in Israel had expected (11:14–54). The disciples of this Messiah have a character all their own which is discussed in a passage composed of various words spoken by Jesus (12:1–53). The new age Jesus inaugurated demands repentance on the part of all (12:54—13:21).

THE PRAYER OF JESUS' DISCIPLES (11:1–4)

¹It happened that, while he was praying in a certain place and had finished his prayer, one of his disciples said to him: " Lord, teach us to pray, as John, too, taught his disciples." ²And he said to them: " When you pray say: Father, may your name he held holy; may your kingdom come."

As a rule, Jesus prayed in solitude on a mountain side (6:12; 9:28, 29) away from his disciples (9:18). We are not told when or where he prayed on this occasion. Our attention was not to be distracted from the essential point, the teaching he gave about prayer.

The prayer Jesus taught them began with the address " Father," " *Abba* " This was the way Jesus himself spoke to God in his prayer (Mk. 14:36), and this is how his disciples, too, must address him (Gal. 4:6; Rom. 8:15). Jesus introduced his disciples into the relationship he himself enjoyed with God. The title *"Ab "* or *"Abi "* (" My Father ") was taken, not from conversational Aramaic, but from the ceremonial prayer language of the temple. The word throws a certain light on Jesus' unique relationship with God. This, too, was something characteristic of the time of salvation. " I thought to myself: How I want to place you among my sons and give you a wonderful country among the nations, a priceless inheritance. I thought: You will address me with the words ' My Father,' and never turn away from me " (Jer. 3 : 19).

" May your name be held holy." These words are a prayer, not a wish. God is called upon to make his name holy. The impersonal form of the petition emphasizes God's activity rather than the identity of the person who is praying. The petition is an expression of unbounded longing that God's name may be hallowed once and for all. God's name is God himself as he reveals himself; it is God in his saving activity, God for us. God sanctifies himself by revealing his power and showing that he is totally other. " Now will I make my great name honored, the name which was dishonored among the nations, because you dishonored it in their midst. Then the nations will see that I am the Lord, when I have shown myself holy for your benefit in their sight " (Ezek. 36 : 23). God affirms his holiness when he proves himself a Father by revealing his mercy, when he reveals himself to those who are of no account and makes them his children, and when he inaugurates his kingdom.

" May your kingdom come." The prayer that God's name might be held holy prepared the way for this petition. The prayer that God's kingdom may come is *the* petition of the " Our Father," just as Jesus' teaching concerning the kingdom formed the center of his preaching. God's kingdom is his supreme dominion. When God asserts his supreme authority, Satan is overthrown and the time of salvation begins. In Jesus, God's salvation had already appeared. " The welcome year of the Lord " was at hand (4 : 19). Jesus declared the disciples blessed because they had lived to see something which prophets and kings had looked forward to longingly (10 : 23f.). Despite this, he taught them to pray that God's kingdom might come. The period he had inaugurated was a time of salvation; yet it was only a beginning of what was still to come. What the kingdom of God involves can be seen in Jesus' life; his life was a concrete image of salvation at a particular moment in the course of salvation history. The glory which was revealed in him should make a Christian's prayer that God's kingdom may come all the more insistent. God's kingdom will come when he comes. The prayer for the kingdom is identical with the prayer that Jesus will come. " Our Lord, come—*Maranatha* " (1 Cor. 16:22).

[3]" *Give us, day by day, our daily bread;* [4]*and forgive us our sins; we, too, forgive those who are in our debt; and lead us not into temptation.*"

Jesus' disciples live in the period which lasts from the time of salvation marked by his life on earth until his second coming. In this interval they are still oppressed by the miseries of life, by sin, and by temptation. When the time of salvation is inaugurated definitively with Christ's second coming, all distress will be at an end. Ultimately, therefore, the petitions of " the second strophe " of the " Our Father " also express the prayer that God's kingdom may come.

" Give us, day by day, our daily bread." " Bread " here means everything we need for our daily life. We must pray for this bread because it is a gift from God. " In grace, love, and mercy, he [God] gives bread to every living thing, because his grace lasts forever . . . He gives food to all his creatures and cares for them, doing good to everyone and preparing nourishment for them. May all praise be yours, Lord; it is you who give us our food " (Jewish grace before meals). A true disciple prays for " our " bread, the bread which is so necessary both for himself and for the community. His prayer is not narrow or self-centered; it is offered with the universal concern characteristic of a child of the heavenly Father. Our " daily " bread is the bread we need each day. A Christian prays only for what he needs. " Give me neither poverty nor riches; only provide me with the food I need " (Prov. 30:8).

"Day by day"; a disciple must answer for his needs before the Father day by day and pray to him for his daily bread. He should pray without ceasing (18:1).

"Forgive us our sins." A disciple realizes that he is a sinner. Even when he has done everything, he is still only a worthless servant (17:10). He must acknowledge this, saying: God, be merciful to me a sinner (18:13). In the Bible, sin is depicted as an act of disobedience against God: "Against you only have I sinned" (Ps. 51:6). Consequently, only God can forgive it. The time of salvation Jesus proclaimed is a time of mercy and forgiveness; therefore, this prayer must be offered confidently. In St. Luke's Gospel especially, God's joy in forgiving sins appears as an incomparable and absolutely characteristic trait of Jesus' message concerning God's kingdom.

Forgive and you will be forgiven was part of the message Jesus preached (6:37). The man who forgives his brother can hope that God will forgive him. God's mercy at the judgment depends on our willingness to forgive our brother. Jesus' disciples are his true disciples only if they are filled with their Father's mercy. "Be merciful as your Father is merciful" (6:36). That is why when a disciple prays that his sins may be forgiven he adds: "We, too, forgive those who are in our debt." The man who is guilty of a crime against another incurs guilt, and this must be atoned for. He must make it good and offer restitution. He can do this by forgiving those who are in his debt.

"Lead us not into temptation." In the explanation of the parable of the sower, St. Luke speaks of those who believe for a time, but then fall away in the moment of temptation when tribulation and persecution arise over God's word (8:13). Temptation represents a danger to the faith, the danger of falling away. This prayer is inspired by a disciple's realization of his own weakness and the great power wielded by evil. The three petitions for deliverance from all human distress also involve an admission of this need. The man who acknowledges his distress before God has the assurance that God's supreme dominion will assert itself in him. It is well for those who are poor, who hunger, who mourn. The " Our Father " is the prayer of those in whom God's kingdom has dawned and makes its presence felt.

The whole of man's life is laid before God as a tragic existence: the present—" give us this day "; the past—" forgive us "; the future—" lead us not into temptation." It is God's rule which brings about the great transformation. God is our guarantee for this; he will give proof of his holiness and assert his greatness; as " *Abba*," he is God for us.

THE SHAMELESS FRIEND (11:5–8)

⁵*And he said to them : " If one of you has a friend to whom he goes in the middle of the night and says: ' Friend, lend me three loaves of bread, *⁶*because a friend of mine has turned in to me on a journey and I have nothing to offer him.' *⁷*And the other man who was inside answered and said: ' You should not put me to such trouble. The door is already locked and my children are in bed with me. I cannot get up and give it to you.' *⁸*I tell you: even if he will not get up and give him what he wants because he is his friend, if the other is shameless, he will get up and give him everything he needs."*

In Palestine, people liked to travel at night because it was cool. There were no such things as bakeries; the women baked the bread each morning before sunrise. Three loaves would be a meal for one person. In a small village, everyone would know who had bread to spare. It was a sacred duty to show hospitality to a guest. The man who was asked for a favor was annoyed. Although he was addressed as " friend," he did not use any similar title in reply. His house had only one room and the door was closed with a huge beam which served as a bolt. The " bed " was a mat spread out on the floor on which the children slept beside their parents. Opening the door would cause a lot of noise and bother; everybody would have to get up. It is not without reason that getting up is mentioned a number of times. " I cannot " really means " I do not want to."

" If one of you has . . .": how is it all going to end? Only like this; he will eventually give his friend what he wants. And Jesus tells us why: if not for the sake of friendship, at least because of the other's shameless importunity. Not out of love for his neighbor, but out of love for a night's sleep. That is what we human beings are like. And God? What is God like? If a disciple reflects on his own behavior, he will see how God will behave towards him. The friend eventually listened to his friend's request when he kept asking him stubbornly and shamelessly. In the same way, God hears those who pray to him " shamelessly " and with determination. As one of the scribes put it: "A man who is shameless will wear down even a wicked man; this will be far more true in the case of God who is so good." Persevering and confident prayer which refuses to give up even if it is not heard immediately is assured of an answer. God is good, infinitely more so than any human being. He is not content to give a man only what he prayed for; he gives him everything he needs. This was the way Jesus dealt with the Syro-Phoenician woman (Mt. 15:21ff.) and the blind man at Jericho (18:35ff.).

AN ASSURANCE OF BEING HEARD (11:9–13)

⁹"And I tell you: Ask and it will be given to you; seek and you shall find; knock and it will be opened to you. ¹⁰Every man who asks will receive, who seeks will find, and who knocks will have the door opened to him."

Jesus here assures us that God listens to our prayers. There is a correspondence between asking and receiving, between seeking and finding, between knocking and having the door opened. God is not deaf to man's needs; he does not hide from them. He is kind to men.

If a man prays, he asks, seeks, and knocks all at once. It is as paupers that we appear before God, as men who have strayed and are homeless. The man who realizes that he is lost, poor, and homeless, and feels this keenly, will find the way to God and to prayer. The only good which, according to Jesus' preaching, has power to satisfy all man's longing is the kingdom of God; this is the essence of all God's promises. The first condition for admittance into God's kingdom is that a man should acknowledge his own poverty. It is in prayer that the way to God's kingdom is opened.

[11]" If one of you is a father and your son asks for bread, will you give him a stone? Or if he asks for a fish, will you give him a snake instead of a fish? [12]Or if he asks you for an egg, will you give him a scorpion? [13]If you, then, who are evil, know how to give good gifts to your children, how much more will not the Father in heaven give the Holy Spirit to those who ask him?"

It is unthinkable that a father should fail to respond to his child's request by giving him gifts which are good. This is even more true of God. Men are evil, but God is good. If a human father is good to his child when he makes any request of him, surely God must be better still.

The good gift the Father gives to those who ask is the Holy Spirit, a gift which he gives from heaven. The Holy Spirit is a heavenly gift; it was through him that Jesus worked, and it is he who makes his disciples what they ought to be. He takes all their thoughts and actions under his control. Through him, they accomplish God's will. St. Matthew tells us that God gives good gifts, the gifts of salvation (Mt. 7:11), but according to St. Luke the gift he gives is the Holy Spirit. The disciples who live in the interval between the time of salvation Jesus inaugurated and his coming at the end of time receive the gift of the Holy Spirit. He is the saving gift which is characteristic of the era of the church. Prayer is necessary if we are to be able to live and work under his guidance.

The Messiah and His Opponents (11:14–54)

ONE WHO IS STRONGER (11:14–28)

[14]He drove out a devil which was dumb, and it happened that when the devil had gone out of him the dumb man spoke. The crowds were amazed. [15]But some of them said: " It is through Beelzebub, the chief of the devils, that he drives the devils out." [16]Others, however, wanted a sign from heaven from him, putting him to the test.

The fact of the cure was undeniable. How was it to be explained? The amazement felt by the people opened a way to faith, the faith that Jesus was the Messiah and that he acted in virtue of God's power. St. Luke does not say this explicitly, but the criticism which was raised was calculated to nip any such conclusions in the bud. According to this, Jesus acted, not in virtue of God's power, but by the power of the chief of the devils, who is called Beelzebub. The people must be turned against Jesus at all costs. Just as faith in the Messiah was beginning to take root, the objection was raised that he had not worked the sign which was expected, by which he must prove he was the Messiah. This was a sign from heaven, such as making the sun or the moon stand still, or some sign in the stars. Casting out devils and miracles of healing were not regarded as such signs. Jesus, therefore, was measured by human standards; God was told what he had to do, how he must convince human beings.

¹⁷But he knew their thoughts and said to them: " Any kingdom which is divided against itself is laid waste, one house falling on another. ¹⁸If, therefore, Satan is divided against himself, how can his kingdom last? You say that it is through Beelzebub that I cast out devils. ¹⁹But if it is through Beelzebub that I cast out devils, through whom do your own sons cast them out? It is for this reason that they will be your judges."

Jesus had the gift of reading people's minds, so that he knew what his critics were thinking. St. Luke obviously felt no compulsion to harmonize the different traditions which he puts together. He tells us first that the critics expressed their view openly, and then that Jesus knew their thoughts. St. Luke made use of the material he found in the tradition to affirm various important points, not to bring minor details into harmony.

Jesus refuted the criticism leveled at the way he cast out the demons, which was the essence of all the miracles of healing he worked over the sick. There was no question of magic or any kind of art which was practiced with the help of the devil. This was true of all the miracles he worked. The first reason Jesus gave for this was the result of a very simple consideration. The demons form a kingdom, the counterpart to God's kingdom. Surely the chief of the devils would not fight against his own kingdom. That would be civil war, and civil war destroys a kingdom, wiping out the population and ruining its cities.

The second reason Jesus cites is taken from the practice of exorcism among the Jews themselves. " Your sons," men who came from among the people, cast out demons. The Jewish exorcists used to try to cast out demons with the help of prayers, incantations, and formulas of adjuration which were attributed to Solomon. Therefore, there were other means of driving out devils without recourse to Beelzebub. Jesus defended the revelation he made with the help of reflections taken from ordinary human and religious experience.

[20]" But if I cast out demons by God's finger, the kingdom of God has arrived among you."

It was through God's power that Jesus cast the devils out. God's finger is a symbol of his might. The overthrow of Satan's rule through God's power which was active in Jesus showed that God's kingdom was at hand. It had already arrived, although it was not yet fully developed. The time of salvation had dawned and God's kingdom had triumphed over Satan's rule. When Jesus cast out demons, it was a sign of this.

[21]"As long as a strong man fully armed keeps watch over his palace, everything he has is in peace. [22]But when someone stronger than he comes upon him and overcomes him, he takes all his armor on which he relied away from him and divides the spoil. [23]The man who is not with me is against me, and the man who does not gather with me scatters."

The Messiah's activity is looked upon as a war; the battle is being fought out between him and Satan. Jesus then takes up one idea from the course of a war. There is a citadel guarded by a strong man who is fully equipped with a breastplate, helmet, shield, and spear. Everything is secure; but then a stronger man attacks the place and the strong man is overpowered. His armor is taken away from him and all his valuables are plundered and divided up. His security of tenure is no more. The basic idea of the parable is to be found in the contrast: peaceful possession—he divides the spoil. This was what was happening when the demons were cast out. Satan's kingdom was at peace; he had gained control of the human race and no one could overthrow him. Now that was all changed. The demons were being driven out and this showed that Satan was being forced to give up his prey, the human race. Therefore, he had been defeated.

²⁴" When the unclean spirit has gone out of a man, it wanders through waterless places seeking rest, and when it does not find it, it says: ' I will go back to my own house from which I came out.' ²⁵And when it comes, it finds it swept out and cleaned. ²⁶Then it goes and takes seven other spirits which are worse than itself with it and, when they have gone in, they live there, and the last state of that man is worse than the first."

When an evil spirit has been cast out, it behaves like a man who has been evicted from his home. In this passage, Jesus is not trying to give us an insight into Satan's psychology; neither is he putting forward the popular conception concerning the expulsion of demons, apart from the fact that he adopts the view that the demons' home was in the desert. The passage is really a sort of parable. The man who has been rescued from Satan's dominion must not regard himself as being immune from further attacks; he is not yet completely secure. The last state of a man who was converted may be worse than his original state, if he does not persevere in his resolution. The early church took this truth very seriously. The Epistle to the Hebrews warns against the dangers of falling away in language which can be easily misunderstood, but the author took this risk, to underline the frightful gravity of the matter: " It is impossible to bring to a fresh conversion those who have once been enlightened [baptized], who have tasted the heavenly gift, and partaken of the Holy Spirit, who have tasted God's priceless word and the powers of the world to come, and have then fallen away " (Heb. 6:4–6).

²⁷As he was saying this, it happened that someone raised her voice —a woman in the crowd—and said to him: " Blessed is the womb that bore you and the breasts you sucked." ²⁸But he replied: " Yes, indeed, blessed are those who hear God's word and keep it."

What can save a man from falling away? What can prevent him

from falling prey to Satan's rule once more? " Blessed is the womb that bore you." The praise bestowed on Jesus' mother redounded to the glory of her Son. A woman's happiness and glory consist in the sons she has borne and reared. The woman in the crowd had not been carried away by the criticism voiced against Jesus, like some of the others; she was overpowered by his majesty. He defeated Satan's power and brought salvation! The glory won for himself by the Son redounded to his mother's credit.

THE SIGN (11:29–36)

Jesus rejects the demand for a sign (11:29–30) and issues an appeal for repentance (11:31–32). He emphasizes the necessity of the enlightenment which comes through faith (11:33–36). Jesus is not announced by a sign from heaven; on the contrary, he himself is the sign which presupposes an interior enlightenment if it is to be recognized.

²⁹*The crowds were growing and he began to speak: " This age is a wicked age. It looks for a sign and no sign will be given it, except the sign of Jonah. ³⁰As Jonah was a sign for the Ninivites, so the Son of man will be a sign for this age."*

In this passage, Jesus takes a stand on the demand for a sign. The crowds about him had grown in numbers. The basic reason for the demand for a sign was lack of obedience to God's word as Jesus preached it. Those who demanded a sign were not content with the powerful actions he had performed to the amazement of the people. First of all, they would have to be converted, undergo a change of heart. Only a man who was ready to listen to Jesus' word and welcome it would be capable of recognizing the signs God worked through Jesus as signs that in Jesus the time of salvation had dawned. When Jesus explained in the presence of John's disciples that the cures he worked were a sign of the time of salvation, he added a note of warning: " It is well for the man who is not scandalized in me " (7:22f.). In Nazareth he had refused to perform the signs they demanded because the people of his own town did not believe (4:23ff.). When the crowds demanded a sign, he was forced to tell them: " This age is a wicked age; it refuses to believe."

God would later give this unbelieving age a sign, the sign of Jonah. Jonah was swallowed by the whale and emerged only three days later. It was as such, as a man who had been restored to life, that God gave him to the people of Niniveh, as a sign that they should repent. The Son of man was a sign for this evil and unbelieving age, just as Jonah had been for the Ninivites. He rose from the dead and he will come again to pronounce judgment. When he appears in his power and glory, no one will be able to deny that God has given him all power. Then, however, he will no longer be a sign leading to faith and salvation; he will be a sign to condemn those who refused to believe. This was the sign with which Jesus threatened his enemies, when he appeared before the Sanhedrin: " That is what I am [the Messiah, the Son of the blessed God]. And you will see the Son of man sitting on the right hand of power and coming on the clouds of heaven " (Mk. 14:62). The Son of man is the sign which will appear in heaven, and at the sight of it all the tribes of the earth will mourn (Mt. 24:30).

[31]" *The queen of the south will rise up at the judgment with the people of this age and condemn them. She came from the ends of the earth to hear Solomon's wisdom and, see, there is One here who is greater than Solomon.* [32]*The people of Niniveh will rise up at the judgment with the people of this age and condemn them. They repented when Jonah preached to them and, see, there is One here who is greater than Jonah.*"

Jesus' contemporaries shut their hearts against God's wisdom and his appeal for repentance. That was why the only sign given them was one which would condemn them at the last judgment: the Son of man who comes as a judge. Jesus had acted in virtue of God's power; in his own person, he was a sign which should have led them to believe, but they refused to believe in him. The pagans, the queen of the south and the people of Niniveh, will be there to accuse Jesus' contemporaries, his own fellow countrymen, when they appear with them at the judgment. The Queen of Sheba sought out Solomon's wisdom and welcomed it gladly (1 Kings 10:1); the Ninivites took Jonah's appeal for repentance to heart (Jon. 3:5). By rejecting Jesus and demanding a sign, Israel sinned before God.

[33] " *No one who lights a lamp puts it in an obscure corner or under a bushel measure; he puts it on a lampstand, so that those who come in can see the light shining."*

Jesus is the sign God gave the world. He is the light of the world (Jn. 8:12). God did not hide this light in obscurity; he revealed it publicly so that it would give light to all men.

[34] " *Your eye is your body's light. If your eye is simple, your whole body, too, is lit up; but if it is bad, your body, too, is in the dark.* [35] *Take care, therefore, that the light which is in you is not darkness."*

A man's body is here thought of as a house. His eyes are the windows which let light into the house, so that his whole body is lit up. If his eye is diseased, if it sees double and is not simple, everything is in darkness. Whether the light is recognized for what it is or not, depends on a man's own makeup. Jesus can be recognized as the final teacher of wisdom and preacher of penance only if a man's interior, his heart, is simple and totally consecrated to God.

"Take care that the light which is in you is not darkness." Man was created for God's truth. He has within him a light which is the power to recognize God's revelation for what it is. A man must exercise care if this light is not to become darkness. A man does not receive the light simply because Jesus had appeared as the one who brings light; he himself must be receptive for the light.

[36]" *If, therefore, your whole body is lit up, so that it has not the least darkness, it will be all light, as when a light illuminates you with a dazzling beam."*

If a man places no obstacle in his heart to the light which God gives him in Jesus, so that his whole body is lit up, Jesus will illuminate him like a lightning flash; he will be completely penetrated with the fullness of his revelation.

THE TRUE TEACHER OF THE LAW (11:37–54)

The scribes and Pharisees had great influence over the people. They regarded themselves as the true successors of the prophets and teachers of wisdom. However, it was Jesus who really fulfilled this role, not they. They represented various prescriptions as being God's will which were, in fact, nothing of the kind. This was true of the question of ritual impurity (11:37–41). As a prophet, Jesus pronounces three warning woes concerning the Pharisees (11:42–44) and three concerning the scribes (11: 45–52). The conspiracy formed by the Pharisees and scribes against Jesus showed how much they lacked God's wisdom and all feeling for his will (11:53f.). Expressions similar to those quoted by St. Luke are found in St. Matthew's gospel. Both evangelists drew on a common tradition. St. Matthew presents the discourse as a sentence of judgment and condemnation; in St. Luke the break is not yet complete or definitive; Jesus' words are represented as an insistent appeal for repentance. St. Matthew places the discourse at the close of Jesus' public life; St. Luke represents it as a conversation which occurred during a meal.

[37]*While he was speaking, a Pharisee invited him to take his early meal with him, so he went and reclined at the table.* [38]*The Pharisee*

saw it and wondered why he had not washed before the early meal.
³⁹But the Lord said to him: " You Pharisees, you clean the outside
of a cup or dish, while everything within you is full of robbery and
wickedness. ⁴⁰Fools! Was it not he who created the outside that also
created what is inside? ⁴¹And now, give everything that is inside as
alms and see, everything becomes clean for you."

While he was on his journey, Jesus was invited to a meal. The early
meal was the midday meal which was a Roman custom. In St.
Luke's gospel, important doctrines are often presented in the form
of table talk. To the Pharisees ritual cleanliness was very important.
A person had to wash his hands before taking a meal (Mk. 7:2).
The vessels used in eating or drinking were cleaned with scrupu-
lous care. To the Pharisee's surprise Jesus ignored the regulations
about washing one's hands.

Who is clean in God's eyes? The Pharisees believed that a man
was pure in God's eyes when he observed the rules of ritual purity
by cleaning the outside of a cup or dish. However, God is interested especially in moral cleanliness, about which the Pharisees
thought too little. " Everything within you is full of robbery and
wickedness." A man is clean in God's eyes when his conscience has
been purified of all injustice and immoral behavior. God demands a
conscience that is clean.

The Pharisees were like fools, like men who were not truly wise,
so that they neglected God and refused to recognize him. God is
the creator, not merely of what is outside, the things which appear,
but also of what is within, of men's hearts and consciences. Whether
something is good or bad depends primarily on these. Therefore, it
is a mistake and a false interpretation of the correct attitude towards
God to attribute so much importance to cleaning dishes, instead of
attending to the moral cleanliness of one's own heart.

Purity of heart is acquired by giving alms, by that love which
finds its expression in action. Give away as alms what is contained

in the cups and dishes; " then everything will be clean for you "—words that anticipate St. Augustine's daring phrase: " Love, and then do what you like." Love fulfills the whole law.

[42]" *But woe to you Pharisees. You pay tithes on mint and rue and every kind of garden herb, but you overlook justice and the love of God. Yet it is necessary to practice these, without neglecting the others.* [43]*Woe to you Pharisees. You love the first places in the synagogues and being saluted in the marketplaces.* [44]*Woe to you. You are like tombs which are unrecognizable, so that the people who walk over them are unaware of it."*

In lapidary phrases, Jesus here reproaches the Pharisees on three counts based on his experience of them. He exhorts them and pronounces his woes against them. They observed the law scrupulously in small things, but transgressed it in essential points. They were ambitious. Externally they pretended to be irreproachable, but interiorly they were far from the true spirit of the law. These reproaches were obviously intended to apply to the Pharisees in general, although it is possible that individual members of the group had managed to avoid such conduct.

Jesus wanted the law to be observed perfectly, even in its smallest details. It is " necessary to practice these." The way he wanted it observed presupposed three things. What was most important in the law must also be observed as the most important thing in real life. This, of course, is the commandment of love (10:27); justice towards one's fellow men and love for God. These are the two great commandments, the two great claims, which form the goal of all the rest. Ambition can never be the reason for fulfilling the law, but only the will of the Father in heaven. " Take care that you do not display your virtue before men to be seen by them. If you do, you will receive no reward from your Father who is in heaven " (Mt. 6:1).

⁴⁵*One of the lawyers answered and said to him : " Master, when you say this, you are bringing us into disgrace too." ⁴⁶But he replied : " Woe to you, too, you lawyers. You load people with burdens which are unbearable. You will not touch these burdens yourselves even with a single finger. ⁴⁷Woe to you. You erect monumental tombs to the prophets whom your own fathers put to death. ⁴⁸You are witnesses, therefore, and you approve what your fathers did. They murdered the prophets and you raise monuments to them. ⁴⁹That is why God's wisdom tells you : ' I will send prophets and apostles to them, and they will murder and persecute some of them,' ⁵⁰so that the blood of all the prophets which was shed from the beginning of the world will be laid at the door of this age, ⁵¹from the blood of Abel to the blood of Zechariah who was executed between the altar and the holy house. Yes, I tell you, this age will have to answer for it all. ⁵²Woe to you lawyers. You have taken away the key of knowledge. You have not entered yourselves and you have stood in the way of those who wanted to enter."*

The Pharisees were the docile pupils of the teachers of the law; they had implicit faith in them. They put the lawyers' teaching into practice in their own lives. The reproaches Jesus made against the Pharisees, therefore, reflected on the lawyers. The lawyers put themselves on the same plane as the prophets; they demanded that people should listen to them, just as they listened to the prophets, to Moses, or to the law. " They are seated in Moses' chair " (Mt. 23:2). The lawyer in this passage addressed Jesus as " Teacher." At the same time, he attacked him for bringing lawyers into disrepute, by speaking blasphemously in criticizing them. For him, the inviolable sanctity of the law made it unthinkable that Jesus should attack him.

Three woes were pronounced against the lawyers, just as three had been pronounced against the Pharisees. God gave the law for man's benefit and salvation; by their teaching and interpretation, they made it an intolerable burden. They hedged it round about, but they themselves knew how to avoid its obligations with the help of subtle distinctions. They raised monuments to the prophets who had been murdered by their own ancestors for the sake of God's word. These were intended as an indication that they wanted to have nothing to do with such crimes, yet they killed Jesus, the greatest of all the teachers and prophets. They claimed the exclusive right to interpret scripture and expound God's will. This would give them a monopoly of the knowledge of God and of the way to eternal life. But they rejected Jesus and prevented others from recognizing him and attaining knowledge and eternal life through his message and his ministry.

Israel's history ended with the destruction of Jerusalem. This catastrophe was interpreted by the early church as a punishment for their violent rejection of God's word. This age will have to answer for the blood of all the prophets. The history of the world is the history of God's word among men. The root of the lawyers' crime lay in the fact that they had set up their own wisdom, not God's word, as the center of everything.

Jesus' Disciples and the World (12:1-53)

Jesus is the one who is stronger; he is the sign, the prophet who proclaims God's will. He gathers disciples about him who will meet with the same fate as that which awaits him in Jerusalem. St. Luke in this section uses various sayings recorded in tradition, to illustrate the instruction Jesus gave his disciples. Jesus demanded that his disciples should profess their faith in him fearlessly (12:1-12); they must be detached from earthly possessions and from over-anxious care for their lives (12:13-34). They must keep watch and remain steadfast in their loyalty to their Lord who is coming; his coming confronts them with an ineluctable choice (12:35-53).

St. Luke divides the discourse into three parts by means of brief incidental remarks. God's word must penetrate Jesus' disciples to the depths of their being (12:1–3). They must not be afraid to profess their faith before men, because God will take care of them (12:4–7). Jesus promises the greatest blessings to those who profess their faith in him courageously (12:8–12).

¹Meanwhile, ten thousand people had gathered so that they were walking on top of one another, and Jesus began to speak to his disciples first of all: " Beware of the leaven of the Pharisees; it is all hypocrisy. ²There is nothing that is hidden which will not be revealed, nothing veiled which will not be made known. ³For this reason, everything you have said in darkness will be heard in the light: what you have whispered into people's ears in darkened rooms will be proclaimed on the housetops."

The number of people who were interested in Jesus and his word increased. On this occasion, a crowd of ten thousand had gathered. Before addressing the masses (12:54), Jesus spoke to his disciples first. His disciples were intended to mediate between him and the people.

Leaven was regarded as a hidden force which was pernicious both in itself and in its effects. It was something like the " power of evil ". In the Pharisees, this force was hypocrisy; outwardly they pretended to be something other than they were inwardly. Jesus' disciples must beware of such pretence. They must be interiorly what they teach and proclaim exteriorly. Indeed, what use would it be to pretend? " What is hidden will be revealed; what is veiled will be made known." A man's secret disposition forces its way into the open. The first thing Jesus demands of his disciples is that they should be changed inwardly; this is fundamental.

If God's word has succeeded in transforming a disciple interiorly,

232

his personal conviction and attitude will force its way into the open. What was said to a small group in secret will force its way into the light, into the full glare of publicity. Even if their field of activity appeared small and strictly limited, Jesus' disciples were not to be worried because their influence did not reach the world at large. If, in times of persecution, they were reduced to preaching their message in whispers at night or in darkened rooms, they were to rest assured that God's word was powerful enough to force its way into the light; no force in the world could restrain it. God's word is a force which is charged with power.

⁴"I say to you, my friends, do not be afraid of those who kill the body and after that they have nothing more that they can do besides this. ⁵I will show you whom you must fear. Fear him who, after death, has the power to cast into hell. Yes, I tell you, you must fear him. ⁶Are not five sparrows sold for twopence? Yet, not a single one of them is forgotten in God's sight. ⁷Even the hairs of your head have all been counted. Do not be afraid ! You are worth more than a flock of sparrows."

Jesus' disciples were his friends. He had bestowed his love on them and initiated them into the secret of his message; later, they would also share his fate. " You are my friends if you carry out the commission I am giving you. I do not call you servants any more; a servant does not know what his master is doing. I have called you friends, because I have revealed everything I heard from my Father to you " (Jn. 15:14f.). Jesus is about to tell his disciples a number of important truths. That is why he reminds them first of all that they are his friends. He was on his way to Jerusalem where he would be taken up. His disciples, too, would have enemies who would threaten them with death.

To take away their fear of death, Jesus had recourse to a straightforward piece of reasoning. Those are not to be feared who can kill the body, but have no means of influencing a person's life in the world to come. God is to be feared; he has power to cast into hell. Jesus counters fear with fear.

The fear of God, however, is not the last word Jesus has to say to strengthen his disciples in the face of death. God will take care of his disciples and never forget them. He cares even for those who are the least and most insignificant, for the sparrows in the air and the hairs of a disciple's head. He has the interests of all at heart. If he cares for such trivial things, he will be much more ready to care for Jesus' disciples. Confidence in God's loving providence enables a man to endure the greatest difficulties. These, too, have their place in the plan of God's providence.

[8]" *But I tell you, everyone who acknowledges me before men will be acknowledged by the Son of man before God's angels.* [9]*But if a man denies me before men, he also will be disowned before God's angels.* [10]*Anyone who says a word against the Son of man will be forgiven; but the man who blasphemes against the Holy Spirit will not be forgiven.* [11]*When they haul you before the synagogues and before magistrates and those who wield authority, do not be worried how or with what words you will defend yourself, or about what you should say.* [12]*In that hour, the Holy Spirit will teach you what you need to say.*"

God, the Son of man, and Jesus are intimately bound together. " Everyone who acknowledges me before men will be acknowledged by the Son of man." Jesus seems to make a distinction between himself and the Son of man who is to come. The best way to do justice to these words would be to take them as implying that Jesus realized that he had been appointed by God to cooperate at the judgment as the Son of man. Moreover, God and the Son of man are also closely connected. Everyone on whose behalf the Son of man appears before God at the judgment will be saved; everyone he disowns will be condemned by God. God, therefore, has given the Son of man authority over men in his presence, an authority which is decisive. God, the Son of man, Jesus, how are they all inter-related?

His saving activity is so much part of Jesus that, although St. Luke says: " The Son of man will acknowledge him before God's angels," he does not say that the Son of man will disown the man who did not acknowledge Jesus. Instead, he speaks impersonally: " He, too, will be disowned." The judicial sentence of condemnation is not attributed directly to Jesus, because Jesus is first and foremost a saviour.

" Anyone who says a word against the Son of man will be forgiven." Jesus lived as a man among men; he was the Son of man in his lowly state. The man who judges him by the light of reason alone and sees him as nothing more than a man may not be conscious of the crime he is committing in reviling Jesus, the Son of man. God will forgive him. As he went to his death, Jesus prayed: " Father, forgive them. They do not know what they are doing " (23:34).

On the other hand, " the man who blasphemes against the Holy Spirit will not be forgiven." A disciple who has once acknowledged Jesus as the (glorified) Son of man blasphemes the Spirit if he denies Jesus or falls away from him. It was under the influence of the Holy Spirit that he acknowledged Jesus as the Son of man to whom God gave all power. The man who has been endowed with the Spirit in this way and then says a word against Jesus abuses the Holy Spirit. This sin will not be forgiven. Forgiveness of sin and salvation can be attained only by faith in Christ.

But Jesus also had a word of encouragement concerning the Holy Spirit. If a disciple is hauled before a Jewish or pagan court because of his faith, it will be for the Holy Spirit to provide for his defense. He will not say anything wrong against Jesus; on the contrary, he will lead evidence which will display Christ's glory to the full. Jesus promised his disciples the support of the Holy Spirit in their hour of trial. He would teach them what they needed to say.

FREEDOM FROM ATTACHMENT TO MATERIAL THINGS (12: 13–21)

Even when following Jesus, a man remains a human being. As such, he is exposed to anxiety concerning earthly possessions. This is something which is deeply rooted in man. Jesus' disciples, therefore, must have the right attitude towards wealth. Jesus refused to arbitrate in a dispute concerning an inheritance (12: 13–14) and issued a warning against greed (12: 15). By means of a parable, he showed where true security is to be found (12: 16–21).

> ¹³*One of the crowd said to him: " Master, tell my brother to share the inheritance with me." ¹⁴But he replied: " Man, who made me a judge or an arbitrator between you? "*

The Jewish law of inheritance was based on the mosaic law. This presupposed an agricultural society and provided that the eldest son should inherit the land and two thirds of the movable property (Deut. 21 : 17). In the case which was brought before Jesus, the elder brother seems to have refused to part with anything. Because the law of inheritance was governed by the mosaic law, the scribes were always glad to be approached for advice and a decision. The man from the crowd addressed Jesus as a doctor of the law. He approached him for a decision in the matter of his inheritance in the hope that he would influence his unjust brother by his authority.

Jesus' reply made it clear that he refused to intervene in the troubled affairs of this world. His authority was not to be used to decide in favor of this or that particular social order or system. His mission came from his Father's will, as did his consciousness of what he was called to do. He had explained what his mission was in Nazareth at the beginning of his ministry. Even before this, he had laid it down once and for all and affirmed it repeatedly in the temptations in the desert. He was sent to proclaim the good news of salvation to the poor, to call sinners (5:32), to save those who were lost (19:10), to give his life as a ransom for many (Mt. 10:45), and to give divine life to the world (Gen. 10:10).

¹⁵*But he said to them: " Take care and keep yourselves from all greed. It is not in having too much that a man's life consists, or in what belongs to him."*

Jesus condemns the urge to multiply one's wealth as a danger the disciples must beware of. Greed shows that a man has been deluded into thinking he can secure his life by his wealth or by having more than he needs. Life is a gift from God; it is not the product of earthly possessions or of a superfluity of riches and wealth. It is God, not man, who disposes of life.

¹⁶*Then he addressed a parable to them, saying: "A rich man's land had yielded a good harvest. ¹⁷And he thought to himself and said: ' What will I do? I have nowhere to store my crops.' ¹⁸And he said: ' This is what I will do. I will tear down my barns and build bigger ones. There I will gather all my corn and my other goods. ¹⁹And I will say to my soul: Soul, you have plenty of goods stored up there for many years. Make yourself comfortable, eat, drink, and be happy.' ²⁰But God said to him: ' Fool! This night they will claim your soul from you. ²¹And what you have put aside, to whom will it belong?' So it is with a man who amasses treasures for himself, but is not rich where God is concerned."*

All purely human planning suffers from a delusion. A man's life is not in his own hands to be disposed of as he wishes. He cannot limit his discussion of it to himself alone; God must play a part in any such discussion. He must also take other men into consideration, but often he is as indifferent to them as he is to God. A man is a fool if he thinks that he can make his life secure by his own efforts or by his wealth. Anyone who refuses to take God into consideration, so that he denies him in practice, is a fool (Ps. 14:1). Death makes it clear that our lives cannot be made secure by wealth or material possessions. "They will claim your soul from you," the angel of death, Satan who executes a commission given him by God. This very night! And the rich man has looked forward to many years.

Freedom from Anxious Care (12:22–34)

²²Then he spoke to his disciples : " Therefore, I tell you, do not worry anxiously about your life, what you are to eat, or for your body, what you are to wear. ²³Your life is greater than food, your body than clothing. ²⁴Remember the ravens. They do not sow or reap; they have no storerooms or barns, and yet God feeds them. Surely you are very different from the birds. ²⁵Which of you can add even a brief space to the length of his life, for all his anxious worrying? ²⁶If, then, you have no power even to do the least thing, why do you worry so agonizingly over everything else? ²⁷Remember the lilies and how they grow. They do not work or spin; yet, I tell you, not even Solomon in all his glory was dressed like one of these. ²⁸If, then, God so clothes the grass in the fields which is here today and will be thrown into the oven tomorrow, surely he will be much more ready to clothe you, for all your little faith. ²⁹You must not even seek what you are to eat or drink. You must not worry yourselves. ³⁰This is what the pagans in the world seek. Your Father knows that you need this. ³¹Rather, seek his kingdom and this will be given to you as well."

It is only in God and not by means of his own wealth that a man can keep his life safe. The wonderful happiness and freedom this principle brings are expressed in a didactic poem which is made up of three strophes. The first and second strophe are intended to free us from anxious care; the third attempts to channel man's avaricious self-seeking towards its proper goal. Into this basic framework various motives are introduced which should save us from anxious care and put an end to our restless yearning. Jesus speaks here as a poet; he mentions ravens and the beautiful anemones. His eye was " simple " and sound (see 11 : 34); it saw God in the birds and the flowers, and his loving providence in everything. The last strophe does not speak of God any more, but of the Father who knows our needs.

Jesus is determined to give God and his kingdom precedence over everything else; he wishes to free man from the weight of anxiety which presses a person down, when he thinks that he can and must make his earthly life secure by his own efforts. Jesus' disciples who live by the gospel are well aware that they were not promised a life of luxury and ease simply because they seek God's kingdom. Even the saints had to endure affliction, hunger, and distress (2 Cor. 11 : 23ff.). No matter what God disposes concerning a disciple, he does it as his Father who is determined to give him the greatest of all his gifts, his kingdom, which contains the fullness of his blessings.

[32]*" Fear not, little flock. It has pleased your Father to give you the kingdom."*

Jesus' disciples form a little flock. The people of God in the last stage of time is compared to a flock. Despite their limited numbers, their insignificance, powerlessness, and poverty, God will give them his kingdom, a power and a dominion which surpass all other kingdoms. This little flock is the holy people the Most High has chosen (Dan. 7 : 27). They live in God's love; God is their Father. By God's design, the unique and deepest reason for which is his own good pleasure, this little flock is destined for great things.

Jesus had said that his disciples' only care should be God's kingdom, but theirs must not be an anxious care. " Fear not." The Father's eternal love assures the disciples that they will receive the kingdom. " What can separate me from the love of God which is in Christ Jesus? " (Rom. 8:39). It is in the Father's good pleasure that a man's life is made secure; peace to the men who are the objects of God's good pleasure.

[33]" *Sell your belongings and give alms. Make yourselves purses which do not grow old, a treasure in heaven which does not depreciate, where no thief can come near it or any moth destroy it.* [34]*Where your treasure is there your heart will be too."*

The question as to how treasure could be amassed where God is concerned (12:21) was left open. Sell your belongings and give alms with the proceeds; that is how a treasure is amassed in heaven. A treasure like this is never lost. No one can ever say about it: " What you have prepared, to whom will it belong now? "

When a man has risked a lot for something, he will cling to it with his whole heart. A man who has lived his life for God will cling to God; a man who has given up a lot for the kingdom of heaven will never lose sight of it. If a man's treasure and all his wealth are in heaven, he himself will be there, too, with all his heart and all his longing. If a man lays up treasure in heaven by giving alms, God's kingdom will become the center of his whole life.

VIGILANCE AND FIDELITY (12:35-53)

Jesus' disciple looks forward to his Lord's coming. By the time St. Luke wrote his gospel, Christians no longer expected Jesus to come in the immediate future; instead, they reckoned with a longer space of time. The age of the church runs from the time Jesus accomplished his saving activity until his coming in glory. The Christians who live in the age of the church look back to Jesus' life on earth, while at the same time looking forward to his coming. The basic eschatological attitude of a Christian who expects Christ to come in the immediate future must be shared also by those who live in the age of the church; no one knows when the Lord will come. St. Luke mentions some aspects of this attitude. A Christian must be vigilant (12:35-40). Those in charge of the church are exhorted to be particularly faithful (12:41-48). Jesus' first coming was a time of decision; in the same way, a Christian must look upon his life as an opportunity to decide for God's will (12:49-53).

35" Your loins must be girded and your lamps burning. 36You must be like men waiting for their lord on his return from the wedding so that, when he comes and knocks, they can open to him immediately. 37It is well for those servants whom the Lord when he comes finds watching. I tell you truly : he will gird himself and make them recline at table, and then he will come and wait on them. 38And if he comes in the second or in the third watch of the night and finds them like this, it is well for them. 39But you must know this : if the master of the house knew at what hour the thief was coming, he would not have allowed his house to be burrowed into. 40You, too, must be ready, because you do not know when the Son of man is coming."

The disciples must be awake and ready when Jesus comes, because no one knows when it will be. They have an example of such readiness in the servant who is waiting for his master to come back at night time from a wedding. The moment his master knocks, the servant must be at the door to open it and let him in, leading him into the house. Therefore he stands ready, with his long outer garment tucked up, as it had to be for walking, working, or fighting; his loins are girded and he carries a burning torch in his hand.

Jesus greets his disciple who is ready with the word " salvation." The blessings which await the servant who is faithful and keeps a constant watch without tiring are framed by two beatitudes. His Lord will "wait on him at table" (22:27). The exact opposite of what we should expect! The servant is treated like a lord and the Lord acts as his servant. God grants those who keep watch a share in his glory. The glory of God's kingdom is often compared to a banquet which God prepares for those whom he welcomes into his kingdom. He honors his guests by waiting on them; he gives them a share in his glory.

A third group of two sayings exhorts us to be constantly prepared. The burglar in this case burrows an entrance under the wall of the house which was set on the ground without any foundation. If the owner of the house knew when the thief was coming, he would have stopped him digging. If Christ's disciple knew exactly when the Lord was coming, he would make sure to be ready to meet him. We know for certain that the Lord is coming, but we do not know when. What follows from that?

⁴¹*But Peter said: "Lord, do you address this parable to us or to everybody?" ⁴²And the Lord said: "Who is a faithful and prudent steward whom his master will place over his servants, to give them their fixed amount of food at the right time? ⁴³It is well for the servant whom his master finds doing this when he comes. ⁴⁴I tell you truly, he will put him over all his possessions. ⁴⁵But if that servant says in his heart: ' My master is taking his time about coming,' and begins to beat the men and the maids, eating and drinking himself drunk, ⁴⁶his master will come on a day when he is not expecting it, at a time he does not know, and cut him to pieces. He will assign him his lot among the unbelieving. ⁴⁷However, the servant who knew his master's will and did not make ready, or do his will, will receive many blows, ⁴⁸whereas he who did not know and yet did something which deserved punishment will receive only a few. Much will be demanded of the man to whom much was given; more will be demanded of the man who was entrusted with more."*

The attitude demanded of the apostles is explained in a parable. The master of a house is staying away from home. For the time of his absence, he entrusts the due and proper care of the household to an overseer. Such an office demands loyalty and prudence: loyalty, because the overseer is only an administrator, not an owner, so that he must act in accordance with the owner's wishes; prudence, because he must never forget that his master will come without warning and demand an account of his administration. If the overseer acts conscientiously, his master will make him administrator of all his goods. But if he acts unjustly and maliciously, ill-treating the members of the household and abusing his position selfishly to live a life of gluttony, he will be punished severely. He will be cut to pieces with a sword, following a Persian custom.

The explanation of the parable, as St. Luke interprets it, is already implied in his description of the image. The servant is a steward. The apostles are put in charge of the Lord's house; they have the key (11:52). " We must be regarded as Christ's servants and stewards of God's mystery " (1 Cor. 4:1). It is expected of a steward that " he will be loyal " (1 Cor. 4:2). The apostles will be loyal and prudent if they remember that the Lord is coming, if they are prepared to meet him at any moment, and never forget that they must give an account of their stewardship before him.

For a steward, the obvious temptation will be to think: " The Lord is taking his time "; he will not come yet. His selfish desires and his caprice prompt him to act unfaithfully. St. Luke seems to attribute greater significance to the word about the Lord's coming being delayed than it had in the original version of the parable. It is possible that when St. Luke was writing, loyalty, watchfulness, and prudence were being neglected by many church leaders. Jesus had not come immediately; when he is coming is uncertain. Jesus' coming is connected with the judgment, when everyone will have to give an account of his stewardship. When compared with the certainty that he is coming and the realization of what this coming involves, knowing when exactly he is coming seems less important. The evangelist is not interested in describing what will happen at the end of time, but he is interested in the fact that these events will take place. The leaders of the various local churches must not allow themselves to be led into temptation, because the parousia is delayed.

"Do you address this parable to us, or to everybody?" This was the question Peter asked; he thought the apostles were in no more danger, that they were sure of sharing in the promises. He had heard Jesus' word about the little flock to which it had pleased God to give his kingdom. An apostle, too, must prove himself by his loyalty and prudence if he is to have a share in the kingdom; the possibility of incurring punishment exists for him, too. The sentence depends on the degree of guilt on a person's consciousness of his obligation and his responsibility. The apostles were more richly endowed with knowledge than anyone else; therefore, more was demanded of them. Their punishment would be all the more severe if they were at fault. The man who did not know the Lord's will, but did something which deserved to be punished, will be punished less severely. He was never initiated into the Lord's thoughts and his plans; therefore, his sentence of punishment will be less severe. Yet he, too, will be punished, even if only a little, because there was much he knew which he should have done, but did not do. Everything a man receives from God is given to him in trust, so that he can work with it.

 49" I have come to cast fire on the earth and what do I wish other than that it should be kindled already. 50But I have to receive a baptism, and how oppressed I am until it is accomplished! 51Do you think I am here to bring peace on earth? No, I tell you, I am here rather to bring dissension. 52From now on, five people in the same house will be divided; they will be divided three against two and two against three. 53The father against the son and the son against

244

the father; the mother against the daughter and the daughter against the mother; the mother-in-law against her daughter-in-law and the daughter-in-law against the mother-in-law.''

Jesus introduced the time of salvation. But what signs were there of it? The time of salvation was announced as a time of peace; the Messiah was a peacemaker. In reality, what had happened? There was uproar and whole families were drawn into disputes.

The Messiah had been announced as a peacemaker; this was what was expected of him. He was the prince of peace; his birth was to bring peace to men on earth. " Peace " means well-being, order, unity. Before the age of peace and salvation dawns, however, there will be a period of strife, dissension, and disputing, which will affect even those areas where peace should be most firmly established. The prophet Micah had spoken of this period of distress and strife which would precede the time of salvation : " The son despises his father; the daughter is opposed to her mother, the daughter-in-law to her mother-in-law. The members of the same household are at enmity with one another. But I am looking out for the Lord, I am waiting for God who is my help. My God hears me " (Mic. 7 : 6f.). These divisions were becoming apparent at this time. Families were divided over Jesus; men were forced to take a stand in relation to him (2 : 34). These divisions and dissensions were a sign that the events which mark the last period of time had begun, those events which demand that every man should make a choice.

An Appeal for Repentance (12:54—13:21)

Jesus speaks to the crowds once more, and no longer to the disciples alone. If even his disciples were in danger of failing to recognize the significance of the age they lived in (12:52), this must have been far more true of the crowds. The signs which accompanied Jesus' time needed to be properly interpreted (12:54–59). The events of his life called for repentance from everybody (13:1–9). His time was a time of salvation, an age which began in a small and hidden way, but would be all-encompassing in the future (13:10–21).

THE SIGNS OF THE TIME (12:54–59)

⁵⁴He used say to the crowds: " When you see a cloud rising towards the west, you say immediately: ' There is rain coming,' and so it happens. ⁵⁵And when you notice the south wind blowing, you say: ' It is going to be hot,' and so it is. ⁵⁶Hypocrites! You know how to read the face of earth and heaven, but you cannot interpret this hour. How is that?"

The people enjoyed a penetrating gift of observation when it came to interpreting the weather or anything else that took place on the surface of the earth or in the firmament. They were able to draw the right conclusion concerning the significance of the different events. Yet this critical faculty failed them when the events concerning Jesus and their own salvation were in question. They did not even take the trouble to examine the significance of the age in which they lived. Men are hypocrites; the people knew how these signs were to be interpreted; they only pretended that they did not understand them. They did not want to interpret them as indicating that this was a time of decision appointed by God, because they did not want to make a decision. They refused to be converted; they were determined to continue their old way of life. Their will hampered their judgment.

⁵⁷" But why do you not judge what is right by yourselves? ⁵⁸As you are on your way to the magistrate with your opponent, make an effort while you are still on the way to be quit of his claim. Otherwise, he will haul you before the judge and the judge will hand you over to the bailiff and the bailiff will put you in prison. ⁵⁹I tell you, you will not come out of there until you have paid the last farthing."

Jesus then told them a parable concerning the courts with the intention of encouraging them to interpret the age they lived in properly and do what was necessary. St. Luke was writing for pagans and he was thinking of Roman legal procedure. This form of procedure was well known for its inexorable rigor. From the magistrate, the person charged was brought before the judge; from the judge he was brought to the bailiff, who led him away to prison. There could be no going out of there until everything had been paid, down to the smallest amount. The only right thing to do in such circumstances was to be quit of the claim before coming to court.

With Jesus' coming, the moment of decision which is characteristic of the last stage of time had dawned. The last stage of time is a time of judgment. Once judgment has begun, everything will go its inexorable way according to strict justice. No one is free from guilt in God's eyes. What must be done, therefore? We must use what time there is still left before the judgment. By repentance and true conversion, we must free ourselves from the relentless course of judgment while there is still time.

CONTEMPORARY EVENTS AS A CALL TO REPENTANCE (13:1–9)

¹There were some people there at that time who spoke to him about the Galileans whose blood Pilate had mixed with their sacrifices. ²And he answered them saying: " Do you think these Galileans were greater sinners than all other Galileans, because they met with this fate? ³No, I tell you, if you do not repent you will all be similarly destroyed."

As Jesus was speaking about the significance of the present time as a time of decision appointed by God, there were some—probably

Galileans—who told him that Pilate, the Roman procurator, had massacred a number of Galileans while they were offering sacrifice in the courtyard of the temple. There is no extra-biblical account of this incident. However, in the history of Pilate's administration, such an event was not impossible. The Galileans were always ready for a fight, especially the party of the Zealots; they wanted to bring about a political revolution by force. Pilate was a harsh and cruel ruler. The crime was all the more horrible because the blood of those offering the sacrifice was " mixed " with the victims' blood. This brutal act of repression must have taken place at the Paschal feast. The people were shocked that the Romans should lay their hands even on what was consecrated to God.

It is obvious that the people told Jesus about this incident because they thought he, too, would inevitably be shocked and perhaps do something about it. They wondered why God had allowed them to be killed while they were offering sacrifice. They thought the explanation might be that these Galileans were sinners who were punished for their wickedness in this way. The Jews used to say : " There can be no punishment without guilt." Great disasters presuppose great sins. Jesus interpreted the event about which he had been told in the light of his preaching concerning the significance of the present age. In this passage, he does not deny that there is a connection between sin and punishment. It is wrong, however, to conclude from this incident that the Galileans concerned were any worse than the rest of the people of Galilee. All men are sinners; all are fit subjects for God's sentence of condemnation. Therefore, all men must repent, if they are to escape the impending sentence of condemnation.

[4]" *Or that eighteen on whom the tower fell at Siloam and killed them—do you think that they were more guilty than all the others who live in Jerusalem?* [5]*No, I tell you, if you do not repent, you will all be similarly destroyed."*

There is no mention of this accident in extra-biblical writings either. The southern wall of the city of Jerusalem went as far as the well at Siloam. It is probable that there was a tower built into the wall there. It has been suggested that this may have collapsed during the construction of an aqueduct. The disaster was still fresh in people's minds. In this incident, the catastrophe was not due to any direct human intervention. It seemed even more fitting, therefore, to suppose that God had intervened to punish these men. Jesus did not deny that the accident was a punishment. But what had happened constituted a warning for everybody and an appeal for repentance. The eighteen inhabitants of Jerusalem involved in the accident were not worse sinners than the rest of the population.

⁶But Jesus told them this parable: "A man had planted a fig tree in his vineyard, and he came looking for fruit on it but found nothing. ⁷Then he told the vinedresser: ' See, I have been coming to look for fruit on this fig tree for three years and I have never found anything. Cut it down. Why should it be exhausting the soil?' ⁸But he replied saying: ' Master, leave it for this year, until I have time to dig around it and manure it. ⁹Perhaps it will bear fruit then. If not, you can still cut it down in time to come'."

In Palestine, people like to plant trees in the vineyards. Their care, like that of the vines, is left to the vinedresser who is employed by the owner of the vineyard. Vineyards were the best place and were preferred especially for fig trees. Therefore, the owner was perfectly justified when he expected his fig tree to bear fruit. Yet for three years he looked for it in vain. His patience was at an end. The tree must be cut down; it was a useless drain on the soil. However, the gardener wanted to give it one last chance; he wanted to treat this privileged tree in a privileged way. If this last, patient effort was in vain, the sterile tree could be chopped down.

This parable, too, was meant as an interpretation of the time in which Jesus lived. This was the last gracious respite God the Father offered. The image Jesus chose evokes God's activity in salvation history. Israel had already been compared to a vineyard by the prophets. " The house of Israel is the vineyard of the Lord of hosts; the men of Judah are his own sowing " (Is. 5:7). Salvation history has already attained its goal. The last stage of time has dawned and judgment is imminent. This is the last chance of conversion; Jesus' ministry is a last prayer to God, to show patience still; a final laborious effort aimed at saving the world. Jesus' time gave men a last chance to decide, an opportunity made available by his love alone. His ministry was a plea on Israel's behalf; the unwearying love which accompanied it was intended to lead Israel to conversion.

The Dawn of the Time of Salvation (13:10–21)

¹⁰He was teaching in one of the synagogues on the sabbath. ¹¹And there was a woman there who had a spirit of illness for eighteen years. She was bowed and could not stand straight. ¹²But Jesus saw her and called her to him, saying: " Woman, you are freed of your illness." ¹³And he laid his hands on her and immediately she was made straight and she gave glory to God. ¹⁴The synagogue superintendent was annoyed that Jesus should heal on the sabbath and he answered, saying to the people: " There are six days on which work can be done. Come and be healed on them, and not on the sabbath." But the Lord answered him with the words: ¹⁵" Hypocrite! Will not any one of you loosen his ox or his ass from the stall on the sabbath and take it away to let it have a drink? ¹⁶But this woman here who is Abraham's daughter, whom Satan has held bound for eighteen years, can she not be loosened from these bonds on the sabbath day?" ¹⁷And when he said this all those who were hostile to him were put to shame and all the people rejoiced at the wonderful things he did.

The cure of the crippled woman was a sign that the time of salvation had begun. In this woman, the significance of Jesus' time is outlined briefly but profoundly. Jesus was here confronted with a case of profound misery. He regarded her compassionately and called her to him. He addressed his word to her and laid his hand on her. This is a brief outline of what Jesus had always done. Salvation began to make its presence felt in this woman; she was loosed from Satan's bonds and from her illness; she was raised up and was free to glorify God. The program outlined by Jesus on his first appearance in the synagogue was still being followed: " To proclaim deliverance for those in bonds and sight for the blind " (4 : 18). Salvation had come.

The superintendent of the synagogue did not recognize the signs of the times. He was one of those hypocrites who could read the signs on earth or in the heavens correctly enough, but he shut his heart against the coming of salvation. His interpretation of the law, his stubborn attachment to human traditions, his lack of understanding of Jesus' love and pity for a suffering human being, made it impossible for him to grasp the significance of the age in which he lived. The inevitable fate of those who oppose Jesus is to be put to shame, before the people and still more before God.

[18]*He said therefore: " What is God's kingdom like, to what must I compare it?* [19]*It is like a mustard seed which a man has taken and sown in his garden. It grew into a big tree and the birds of heaven made their home in its branches."* [20]*Once more he said: " To what must I compare God's kingdom?* [21]*It is like yeast which a woman took and put into three measures of meal, until the whole lot was leavened."*

The introductory formula: " God's kingdom is like a mustard seed, . . . like yeast," means: with God's kingdom, things are the same as with . . . What is compared is the contrast in both instances between the small beginning and the impressive final result. Mustard seed is the smallest seed used for sowing in the whole world (Mk. 4:31); it is no bigger than the head of a pin. Yet if it is sown in a garden and takes root, it becomes a tree, big enough for the birds to build their nests in its branches. On the shores of the sea of Galilee, mustard shrubs reach a height of from seven and a half to nine feet. It was the same with yeast. The women used to bake the bread for the family every morning, after mixing the yeast with the dough the evening before. A little yeast, a handful at most, was enough for a large quantity of dough. Overnight, the mixture was leavened by the yeast; the tiny, obscure beginning is contrasted with the magnitude of the end result.

God's kingdom dawned with Jesus' ministry. Jesus inaugurated and proclaimed it; by his word, he passed it on to his disciples and they, too, proclaimed it. The miracles Jesus performed showed that it had come; his miracles of healing and casting out devils were so many signs heralding the dawn of God's kingdom. However, it did not come in such a way that each and every one was forced to say: God's kingdom is here. Only those who shared God's wisdom could see what had happened. The only way to such knowledge is by faith. God's kingdom was still a mystery; only the disciples, not the people at large, had been initiated into it. Jesus' disciples must still pray that God's kingdom may come (11:2). The disciples who had a part in it were still only a little flock (12:32). However, as with the mustard seed and the yeast, the small beginning involves an assurance that God's kingdom will come in all its glory and majesty. It will grow from a small beginning. So far, it included only a few persons, but one day it would encompass all creation.

By his preaching and his ministry, Jesus inaugurated God's kingdom; his time was a time of salvation, even if it was an insignificant looking beginning. God's kingdom will one day achieve its full development. These parables refer not merely to the beginning and the end, but also to the period between. The mustard seed grows

252

and becomes a big tree; the yeast is hidden in the dough until the whole lot is leavened; it is not inactive. God's kingdom does not cease to be effective in the time between Jesus' ascension into heaven and his coming in glory. God's kingdom has come, and yet it is still to come; it was visible in Jesus' ministry, and yet it is still on the way; it is real, and yet it is still realizing itself.

It is certain that Jesus' activity indicated that God's kingdom had come; it is certain also that it has not yet reached its full development. But no clear statement is made about the time between the beginning and the end; Jesus was thinking primarily only of the beginning and the end. God's kingdom is growing; no power can halt its progress.